ORGANIZATIONAL COMMUNICATION

ORGANIZATIONAL COMMUNICATION

foundations for human resource development

R. WAYNE PACE
Brigham Young University

PRENTICE-HALL, INC. *Englewood Cliffs, New Jersey 07632*

Library of Congress Cataloging in Publication Data

Pace, R. Wayne.
  Organizational communication, foundations for human
resource development.

  Includes bibliographies and index.
  1. Communication in organizations. I. Title.
HM131.P22 1983   302.3′5   82-16539
ISBN 0-13-641324-2

Editorial/production supervision by Marion Osterberg
Cover design by Marvin Warshaw
Manufacturing buyer: Ron Chapman

Printed in the United States of America

10 9 8 7 6 5 4 3 2 1

ISBN 0-13-641324-2

Prentice-Hall International, Inc., *London*
Prentice-Hall of Australia Pty. Limited, *Sydney*
Editora Prentice-Hall do Brasil, Ltda., *Rio de Janeiro*
Prentice-Hall Canada Inc., *Toronto*
Prentice-Hall of India Private Limited, *New Delhi*
Prentice-Hall of Japan, Inc., *Tokyo*
Prentice-Hall of Southeast Asia Pte. Ltd., *Singapore*
Whitehall Books Limited, *Wellington, New Zealand*

CONTENTS

3 √·

Organizations: Behavioral and Systems Theories   19

4 √.

The Organizational Communication System   30

PART TWO
ISSUES IN ORGANIZATIONAL COMMUNICATION

5 √

The Directions of Information Flow   39
what is communicated, to whom,
and how in organizational communication

6

Organizational Communication Cost Analysis   60

7

Managerial and Leadership Styles   70

8 ⁄

Motivation and Communication   85
why some people communicate better

9 ⁄

Organizational Communication Relationships   94

10

Interpersonal Styles in Organizational Communication   109

15

Organizational Communication Policies   183

PART THREE
HRD ROLES AND ORGANIZATIONAL COMMUNICATION

16

Analysis in Organizational Communication   199
the analytical role in human resource development

17

Strategies of Organizational Communication   225
the strategic role in human resource development

COVER FIGURE

The cover figure symbolizes the central feature of organizational communica-
ion: a person in a position. C. E. Redfield alluded to this conception in his book
Communication in Management when he explained that ". . . we find in any formal organization a phenomenon which can be designated as positional communication. The entire organization, as it appears on an organization chart, can be
referred to as a positional communication network." Redfield articulated an idea
that many people believed when he observed that "people in positions are required
to communicate in accordance with their positional roles to a certain extent, and in
connection with some matters they do so to a surprisingly great extent."[1]

W. Charles Redding reiterated this view in his classic chapter on the Organizational Communicator in *Business and Industrial Communication* when he stated
that "this chapter will take the position that a member of any organization is, in
large measure, the kind of communicator that the organization compels him to be."
He summarized the point by noting: "The organizational member is *not* free to
behave as he wishes—unless, that is, he is willing to accept punishment in some
form. If the organizational manager is to communicate effectively, he cannot avoid
being bound by certain expectations that are the result of the role he is perceived
as occupying."[2]

The cover figure, used throughout the book to indicate important information, is an attempt to symbolize positional communication and remind us that we
are all, to some extent, organizational communicators.

---

[1]Charles E. Redfield, *Communication in Management* (Chicago: The University of
Chicago Press, 1953), p. 11.

[2]W. Charles Redding, *Business and Industrial Communication: A Sourcebook* (New
York: Harper & Row, Pub., 1964), p. 29.

PREFACE

To write a book is to be, in some sense, a futurist. Writing requires some assumptions about what the future holds, what life is going to be like, and what one's colleagues and, as yet unenrolled, students are going to want to know. This is an effort to prepare a statement about organizational communication that gathers from the past and points toward the future.

This book gained its footing in countless discussions with friends and colleagues around the country, in preparation for classes in organizational communication in at least five different colleges and universities, in listening to convention papers and workshop presentations, in reading and teaching, in hours of contemplation and mental analysis, in years of engaging in training and development activities, and in working with student interns in human resource development.

This book is an introductory statement of the concepts and issues in organizational communication. The chapters are written and developed with simple models and basic ideas. This allows the instructor to fill in some of the framework with personal knowledge and unique interpretations. The richness of concepts and the detail of technical information can be added where appropriate. The book is divided into three parts: systems, issues, and roles.

This book represents an attempt to introduce the study of organizational communication as preparation for a career in human resource development. The study of organizational communication is a natural base for work in the general personnel function of an organization. In addition, this book provides support for Barnard's observation that "the first function of the executive is to develop and maintain a system of communication."[1] This book tries to show how the study of organizational communication can contribute to more professional performance by executives, managers, supervisors, or other organizational communicators. Thus this

[1] Chester I. Barnard, *The Function of the Executive* (Cambridge, Mass.: Harvard University Press, 1938), p. 225.

book introduces organizational communication as a foundation upon which prospective line managers and staff as well as human resource development specialists can build their more specialized careers. Line and staff employees are both equally dedicated to making the organization effective. The study of organizational communication provides a foundation for both groups of prospective employees. Beyond this introduction, advanced courses in organizational behavior and communication refine a person's career in human resource development.

Students who understand something about communication in organizations are uniquely prepared to participate with other organization members in devising ways to develop human potential throughout the organization. Communication concepts are central to understanding behavior of all types in organizations. Few concepts stand in such a fundamental position as communication for understanding and improving individual, group, and system functioning.

This book is planned as a text for undergraduate courses in organizational communication. The content, style, and treatment are designed to ensure a positive response from students at the undergraduate level. The format and layout of the book are uniquely adapted to the introductory course.

I take full responsibility for the presentation and interpretation of ideas, for errors, and for unusual pedagogical suggestions. Nevertheless, I am deeply appreciative of the assistance and guidance in both my early days studying industrial/organizational communication under W. Charles Redding and my later years learning from colleagues and students of organizational communication at Parsons College, California State University at Fresno, the University of Montana, the University of New Mexico, and Brigham Young University. I am especially indebted to my colleague, coauthor, and leader, Brent D. Peterson, for insight and inspiration and as a resourceful member of Organizational Associates, our consulting partnership.

I wish to acknowledge the enormous contribution to communication in our little organization of eight called a family that my partner, Gae Tueller Pace, has so beautifully provided on a regular basis but especially while a book has been in process.

I thank my son, Greg, for preparing sketches of figures and tables when he was already too busy with his work as an art student.

I wish to salute the American Society for Training and Development (ASTD), an organization of professionals in human resource development who know the importance of communication in their work.

I wish to thank Sally Jenson for her steady typing hands and lovely disposition during the preparation of this manuscript.

I wish to thank the reviewers, editors, and other members of the publisher's organization who made these ideas into a book.

R. Wayne Pace

ORGANIZATIONAL COMMUNICATION

1

THE FIELD
OF
HUMAN RESOURCE
DEVELOPMENT

Human resource development (HRD) is the career area within an organization that focuses on changing and improving the capacities of individual human beings to contribute to the success of the organization.

⟨Communication has been recognized as the means by which both people and ✓ the organization survive.⟩When human beings lack the ability to cope with life, the source of the problem is often a lack of appropriate information. Incomplete and unorganized information places a heavy strain on the ability of people to make sense out of their existence. Their performance of a job depends on having the necessary information; having the skills to do a job depends on the quality of communication during the skills acquisition period.

Since organizations consist of people, the information-processing problems of individuals are transported to the larger unit or organization through its employees. When confronted with the unique and often unusual problems that come from the organization as a social system, individuals may find their personal problems compounded.

Because people are probably the most critical resource of an organization, the development of those human resources may have an impressive and enduring influence on the organization. Since communication is the most central of all human processes and plays the most important role in the total process of working with, managing, and developing the capacities of an organization, the study of organizational communication is a natural foundation for careers in human resource development.

COMMUNICATION IN ORGANIZATIONS

The study of communication in organizations brings together a unique variety of topics and provides a pragmatic perspective for understanding their impact on human beings. A communication orientation seeks to discover how and why mes-

1

sages affect people's understanding and how and why messages affect relationships among people. A communication approach is different from the approaches of other disciplines in that communication "makes the nature and role of messages in life and society its central organizing concern" (Gerbner, 1968, p. 18). Miller (1980) argues that "communication is our chief vehicle for exercising *control* over our environments" (p. 15). Katz and Kahn (1966) point out that the study of communication encompasses nearly all of the critical topics that are basic to understanding human behavior in general and human functioning in organizations in particular: "Communication is thus a social process of the broadest relevance in the functioning of any group, organization, or society. It is possible to subsume under it such forms of social interaction as the exertion of influence, cooperation, social contagion or imitation, and leadership" (p. 224).

Meier (1962), in fact, noted that cities evolved primarily for the facilitation of human communication. Berlo (1960) asserted that "social systems are produced through communication" (p. 147). Katz and Kahn (1966) also argue that "communication—the exchange of information and the transmission of meaning—is the very essence of a social system or an organization" (p. 223). Hawes (1974), on the other hand, has been very convincing in his position that "a social collectivity is patterned communicative behavior; communicative behavior does not occur *within* a network of relationships but is that network" (p. 500).

Changes and improvements in the capacities of human beings to do their work more efficiently, in how people process information for themselves, in how they relate to one another, in how they present information, and in how they make their needs and preferences known *are changes and improvements in communication*. Civilized, cooperative, organized activity occurs only through communication. Developments in a person's capacity to handle communication are developments in a person's capacity to cooperate with others, to solve problems, to engage in organized activities, and to acquire the skills and attitudes necessary to prepare for advancement along career lines. An understanding of individual, group and institutional communication may be the most crucial understanding for success in a human resource development career.

The study of organizational communication provides the background for understanding the functioning of human beings in organizations. With specific courses in the activities performed by human resource development specialists, organizational communication is an ideal preparation for careers in human resource development.

DEFINITION OF HRD

Human resource development refers to a set of activities that prepare employees to perform their current jobs more effectively, to assume different positions in the organization, or to move into jobs, positions, and careers that are as yet unidentified and undefined. The implication, if not the explicit statement, of this definition is that development may occur in a variety of forms, under a variety of conditions, with a variety of subjects, and for a variety of general and specific objectives.

Human resource development involves helping every employee to realize and use his or her full potential in contributing to personal and organizational effectiveness. Of great concern is the effective utilization of human resources available in this country and in the world, with the ultimate goal of creating a good life for everyone. Systematic HRD lies at the heart of success in all areas of organized life.

Although we shall use the term *employee* frequently throughout this book, the intent is to include individuals who are members of organizations of all types—business, industry, education, government, labor, religious, service, recreation, community, and, especially, volunteer whether paid or unpaid, whether member or leader, whether operator or executive. Although there is ususally an impelling order of progress in an organization, ranging from new member through top leadership, concerns about development are somewhat comparable at all levels. Nevertheless, the specific activities may differ according to the person's position in the organization.

Nadler (1979), for example, identified three areas of activity in human resource development: (1) *Training*, which includes learning activities that enable the employee to perform his or her present job (or a directly related one) better; training occurs in three areas—skills, attitudes, and knowledge. (2) *Education*, which includes learning activities that enable the employee to move into new positions in an existing or planned organization; the primary purpose of education is to prepare a person for upward mobility within the organization. (3) *Development*, which includes learning activities that enable the employee to acquire conceptual and problem-solving skills, attitudes, and knowledge so as to produce a viable and flexible work force for moving into an uncertain future; development provides employees who can activate and guide organizational change and renewal; development also establishes a foundation for the release of the human resource potential of the organization.

HRD ASSUMPTIONS

Human resource development is based on a number of important assumptions: (1) that human beings are important in their own right as resources to achieve organizational goals; (2) that human beings have the right to be satisfied with the way in which they contribute to the organization; (3) that changing conditions, environments, markets, and resource demands necessitate the continual preparation of human beings to assume different positions; (4) that human beings do not come to the organization with all of the knowledge and skills they need to fulfill any and every demand placed upon them; (5) that a pool of developing workers, supervisors, and managers constitute a body of individuals who can help meet future human resource needs; (6) that development constitutes more than technical training, but involves an understanding of human behavior, how people respond and relate to one another, how human beings contribute to organizational productivity as well as to their own well-being; and (7) that the quality of work life is a legitimate and valuable concern of human beings in all areas of development.

A CAREER IN HUMAN RESOURCE DEVELOPMENT

Through the study of organizational communication and behavior, you can prepare for a career in human resource development. It is certainly not essential to enter such a career just because you have taken a class or two in this subject, but careers are available for individuals who have the interests and skills. The title of positions in human resource development are not currently standardized, but there are sufficient similarities to enable us to list some of the key job titles:

Training specialist

Employee development specialist

Management education specialist

~ Employee relations specialist

Industrial relations specialist

Organization development specialist

Education and development specialist

Training and development specialist

~Personnel development specialist

~ Employee communication specialist

~Organizational communication specialist

~Human resource development specialist

Although we have used the generalized title of *specialist* to designate all of these positions, it should be apparent that there is an hierarchical order within the departments when more than one employee is involved. Some employees may have the title of *director, manager,* or *vice president* of each of the functions identified, whereas other employees may be *assistants* or *specialists.* The entry-level position is usually that of *specialist.*

It is only fair to point out, however, that human resource development is widely considered to be one of the many functions of *personnel.* Recruitment, selection, placement, compensation, evaluation, and development are often part of a *personnel department,* although organizational development and employee and organizational communication may be located in other departments or be departments of their own. Patterns are not stable and depend upon historical circumstances within the organization. Nevertheless, since human resource development is often part of personnel, preparation of HRD should include courses and experiences in personnel management, personnel psychology, industrial sociology, organizational behavior, organizational development, industrial relations, and business management. Courses in a variety of communication areas and skills are also fundamental to human resource development.

ACTIVITIES OF AN HRD SPECIALIST

In what kinds of activities does an HRD specialist engage? This is a common question asked by students interested in organizational communication and human resource development. To aid training and development professionals in managing their own development programs, the American Society for Training and Development (ASTD) commissioned a nationwide study of the activities performed by T & D specialists. The results fell into nine activity areas and serve as a fair set of guidelines for the preparation of future HRD specialists. We shall provide a brief summary of each of the nine activity areas for your review (White, 1979).

Area 1: Analyzing needs and evaluating results. Skills in this area include conducting task analysis, needs assessment, and problem analysis to establish development priorities. HRD specialists need to be able to design questionnaires, conduct interviews, and analyze job requirements. This area also necessitates keeping abreast of Equal Employment Opportunity—Affirmative Action as well as Occupational Safety and Health Administration regulations. Occasionally it is appropriate to know how to administer achievement tests, aptitude tests, and personal skills inventories.

Area 2: Designing and developing training programs and materials. HRD specialists should know how to establish behavioral and learning objectives; determine program content; develop workbooks, exercises, and cases; and determine the appropriate sequence of materials, including program length, number of participants, and choice of techniques. A specialist in HRD ought to be able to develop or select exercises and self-assessment tools, such as checklists, manuals, and structured experiences. It is also desirable, in this area of expertise, to be able to prepare scripts and instructions for films and videotapes, prepare artwork, copy slides, and create overhead projections or transparencies.

Area 3: Delivering training and development programs or services. In this area the HRD specialist should be able to conduct training sessions, using behavior modeling, role playing, simulation and gaming, laboratory and sensitivity training, discussion, organization development, and lecture techniques. A person in HRD should be able to use films, videotapes, and even closed-circuit television and operate all types of audiovisual equipment. The HRD specialist is usually responsible for establishing and maintaining a library of career development information.

Area 4: Advising and counseling. The HRD specialist uses coaching and counseling techniques to aid individuals with their career development plans and to work with managers and supervisors on training and development needs. The HRD specialist assists others in implementing their training and development programs.

Area 5: Managing training activities. HRD specialists organize and staff the HRD function or department in the organization. They must be able to arrange program logistics such as facilities, lodging, and meals; to prepare budgets and make plans for programs and projects; to obtain external instructors and resource people; to hire outside consultants; to supervise the work of others; to maintain information on costs and benefits of development activities; and to evaluate internal and external instructors and resource people. HRD specialists may need to administer tuition reimbursement programs, arrange for university courses, and contract with outside vendors for programs and supplies.

Area 6: Maintaining organization relationships. Living in a complex organization necessitates skill in establishing and maintaining good working relationships with others, but in HRD every member of the organization is a potential client with special problems. The HRD specialist determines employee awareness of the availability of HRD programs; prepares and disseminates program announcements; makes formal presentations of plans for training and development programs and projects to management; explains recommendations so as to gain acceptance for them; writes reports, proposals, speeches, articles, memos, announcements, and manuals; and communicates with government and educational communities.

Area 7: Doing research to advance the training field. The HRD specialist experiments with new training and development techniques, interprets data and statistics on training and development, and presents data on progress in the field.

Area 8: Developing professional skills and expertise. HRD specialists keep abreast of training and development activities in other organizations, attend seminars and conferences for personal development purposes, and keep informed on new training and development concepts, theories, techniques, and approaches through membership in professional organizations such as ASTD and scholarly organizations such as the International Communication Association, the American Business Communication Association, and the Speech Communication Association.

Area 9: Developing basic skills and knowledge. Every HRD specialist must have the ability to communicate effectively orally and in writing. He or she needs the ability to gather and analyze data, to solve problems, and to use group process skills. Finally, the HRD specialist should have knowledge of training resources, of the subject matter being taught, and of learning theory as it relates to adults.

Nadler (1979) summarizes the roles of the human resource development specialist as follows:

> Learning Specialist—instructor, curriculum builder, and methods and materials developer;
>
> Administrator—personnel developer, supervisor of ongoing programs, maintainer of community relations, and arranger of facilities and finance;
>
> Consultant—advocate, expert, stimulator, and change agent.

Hopefully you are able to get some sense of the potential and excitement of a career in human resource development. The breadth of skills needed is enormous but not impossible to attain. On the other hand, the skills have wide applications in all kinds of organizations in every community. HRD specialists contribute enormously to the organization in which they are employed, but they also have a great deal to give to the community in which they live.

Fest (1979), a professor of organizational communication, suggests that the challenge of human resource development is to "help workers become contributing human beings, and human beings to become committed workers" (p. 86). He suggests that the cause is just and important, and that "human resource development is emerging from an incidental, peripheral and uncertain status to one that is central and essential. We need trained professionals to conceive, manage and conduct the development programs within the total organizational framework and in consonance with both individual and organizational needs and goals" (p. 83).

COMPENSATION IN HRD

Recently both the *Training and Development Journal* (July 1980) and *Training Magazine* (July 1980) ran short analyses of the salaries of HRD specialists. Cook (1980) concluded from an examination of the types of HRD jobs being offered through the ASTD Position Referral Service that there has been an "increased corporate awareness in the importance of the HRD function and, as a result, an increase in the number of available HRD positions" (p. 5). The trends were clearly toward HRD openings with attractive salaries, good benefits, and high-level positioning on the corporate ladder.

Training concluded that "top organizational-development (OD) executives command salaries as high as or higher than those for any other position in the personnel/industrial-related/training field" (p. 14). Although such factors as a company's size and geographical location and an individual's experience and education affect compensation and benefits, a national survey (Abbott, Langer & Associates, Box 275, Park Forest, Illinois 60466) indicates that top OD executives were comparable in salary with compensation and benefits executives.

SUMMARY

Human resource development is an exciting and action-packed career field based on theories of organizational communication and concerned with preparing employees to perform their current jobs more effectively, to assume different jobs, and to move into jobs that are as yet undefined. Seven important assumptions about people and organizations which underlie HRD were described. Titles of positions in human resource development were listed and nine activity areas of HRD specialists were defined. A brief discussion of compensation in HRD suggested that salaries are competitive and comparable with those of positions in such fields as personnel.

The opportunity and challenge is yours. Through the study of organizational communication, you should discover the foundations of human resource development and get a glimpse of the potential of this field for you.

REFERENCES

BERLO, DAVID K., *The Process of Communication.* New York: Holt, Rinehart & Winston, 1960.

COOK, MICHAEL H., "HRD People—'You're Worth Your Weight in Gold!' " *Training and Development Journal,* 34 (July 1980), 4–5.

Editorial (unsigned), "Salary Research Gives Benchmark for Measuring Your Career Growth," *Training Magazine,* 17 (July 1980), 14.

FEST, THORRELL B., "HRD within Organizational Settings: Contexts and Relationships," *Training and Development Journal,* 33 (March 1979), 80–86.

GERBNER, GEORGE, "A Theory of Communication and Its Implications for Teaching," in *Teaching: Vantage Points for Study,* Ronald T. Hyman, ed. Philadelphia: Lippincott, 1968.

HAWES, LEONARD C., "Social Collectivities as Communication: Perspectives on Organizational Behavior," *Quarterly Journal of Speech,* 60 (December 1974), 500.

KATZ, DANIEL, and ROBERT L. KAHN, *The Social Psychology of Organizations.* New York: John Wiley, 1966.

MEIER, RICHARD L., *A Communications Theory of Urban Growth.* Cambridge, Mass.: M.I.T. Press, 1962.

MILLER, GERALD R., "Introduction to Communication," *Human Communication: Principles, Contexts, and Skills.* New York: St. Martin's Press, 1980.

NADLER, LEONARD, *Developing Human Resources* (2nd ed.). Austin, Tex.: Learning Concepts, 1979.

WHITE, TOD, "Increasing Your Effectiveness as a Training and Development Professional," *Training and Development Journal,* 33 (May 1979), 3-12.

2

ORGANIZATIONS: CLASSICAL THEORIES

The work of Blau and Scott (1962) serves as the foundation upon which we shall base our concept of organization. They distinguish between the general structure of *social organization* and the more specific structure called *formal organization*, about which we shall be concerned.

SOCIAL ORGANIZATION

The term *social organization* refers to the patterns of social interaction (the frequency and duration of contacts between persons; the tendency to initiate contacts; the direction of influence between persons; the degree of cooperation; feelings of attraction, respect, and hostility; and status differences) and the observed regularities in the social behavior of people that are due to their social circumstances rather than to their physiological or psychological characteristics as individuals.

To have pattern or regularity in social interaction implies that there are some linkages between people that transform them from a collection of individuals into a group or from an aggregate of groups into a larger social system. For example, a busload of people going to work at different locations in a city does not really constitute a social organization, but a busload of booster club members on their way to a football game does represent a social organization. The boosters are connected by some shared beliefs that result in a structure that is more than the sum of the individuals composing the group. The patterns of interaction among boosters may result in status differences. For example, highly integrated group members are different from isolates, leaders differ from followers, those who are highly respected are different from those who are not highly regarded. Social status differences develop a hierarchy in the social structure.

9

Relations also develop between groups, producing a different aspect of social status. The status of the group in the larger social system becomes part of the status of its members. For example, the status of the booster club tends to influence the status of those who belong to it; likewise, membership in an ethnic group, such as the American Indian, also affects their status.

The networks of contacts and the shared beliefs of a group are usually referred to as its *structure* and its *culture.* Contacts serve to organize human conduct in an organization. As a person conforms to the expectations of group members, that conformity influences relations with others and in turn affects his or her social status; a person's status then begins to affect behavior so that it is consistent with social norms and will improve the person's chances of achieving important goals, resulting in socially organized interaction.

Berlo (1960) suggests that communication is related to social organization in three ways:

First, social systems are produced through communication. Uniformities of behavior, and pressures to conform to norms, are produced through communication among group members.

Second, once a social system has developed, it determines the communication of its members. Social systems affect how, to and from whom, and with what effects communication occurs among members of the system. One's social status in the system, for example, increases the likelihood of talking to people of comparable status and decreases the probability of communicating with people of much higher or much lower status than ours. In addition, the system determines the frequency of messages by restricting the kinds and numbers of people with whom occupants of a particular position can communicate. Finally, the system may affect how members treat their messages. A style develops that is characteristic of members of the social organization. A civic club, a government agency, or a large corporation develop ways of doing things, writing about activities, and talking about their work that are imposed on members of the system. People who communicate with one another over time tend to develop similar behavior patterns. As individuals are immersed in the system, their unique behaviors adapt to the demands of the system, resulting in behavior similar to those of other members of the system.

Third, knowledge about a social system can help us make accurate predictions about people without knowing much more than the roles they occupy in the system. A *role* refers to both a set of behaviors and a given position in a social system. We can, for example, talk about the role of *manager.* A manager is a role in a social system we call a *formal organization.* The term *manager* refers both to a set of behaviors that are performed in the company and to a position in the company. For every role there is a set of behaviors and a position. If we know what behaviors go with a role, we can make predictions about the person who occupies the position. There are, within a range, certain behaviors that go with the role of chief executive officer, supervisor, secretary, union steward, salesperson, clerk, accountant, public relations specialist, or training specialist. When we meet a person who occupies a given role-position, we can predict that he or she will do certain things because of the position. As Berlo summarizes, "Even if we do not know a person as an individual, even if we have had no prior communication with him to determine his attitudes, his knowledges, his communication skills, we still can make fairly accurate predictions from a knowledge of his position in one or more social systems" (p. 150).

FORMAL ORGANIZATION

In contrast to social organization that emerges whenever people associate with one another, there are organizations that are created deliberately for certain purposes. If the accomplishment of a particular objective requires some sort of collective effort, an organization is designed to coordinate the activities of many individuals and to furnish incentives for others to aid them. Businesses, for example, are formed to produce materials that can be sold, unions are organized to increase their bargaining power with employers, government agencies are created to regulate commerce. In these cases the goals to be achieved, the rules to be followed, and the status structure are consciously designed to anticipate and guide interaction and activities of members. The term *formal organization* is used to refer to these kinds of systems.

We shall look at some distinctive characteristics of formal organizations—popularly called *bureaucracies*—in an effort to understand important features of formal systems. The somewhat simplistic analysis that follows is intended to highlight and focus attention on aspects of formal organizations that may have implications for a preliminary understanding of organization communication. To clarify the characteristics of a formal organization, we shall present ideas derived from the writings of Max Weber (1947), pronounced Mox Veber, as analyzed and summarized by numerous scholars in the field. The enumeration of characteristics is consistent with those of other analysts, but this list is unique to our view.

To hold an appropriate perspective on Weber's analysis of bureaucratic or formal organizations, we need to realize that he developed his theory of organizations as an *ideal type*. That is, he did not describe organizations as they actually functioned nor did he provide a summary of the usual characteristics of bureaucracies; rather, he identified characteristics that are distinctive of the ideal formal organization. Weber attempted to portray a perfectly bureaucratized organization. He said, in effect, that bureaucracies are those organizations that exhibit the following combination of characteristics. For example, Weber's theory of bureaucracy suggests that efficiency is related to a hierarchical pattern of authority. This may or may not be true. Nevertheless, if a study of a number of organizations were to discover that hierarchical authority was *not* related to efficiency in those organizations, that finding would not be a basis for rejecting Weber's claims; it would only show that the organizations studied were not fully bureaucratized.

CHARACTERISTICS OF A WEBERIAN BUREAUCRACY

Most modern organizations, as well as some ancient ones, are organized consistent with Weber's theory of formal organizations. Although Weber was writing as early as 1910, his theory serves admirably well for comprehending key aspects of organizations, and communicative interaction that occurs in that context, even today.

Nevertheless, Weber's theory has been criticized and refined, leading to more so-phisticated concepts of organizational functioning. Perrow's (1973) description of the rise and fall of bureaucratic theory suggests, however, the continuing interest in Weber's ideas:

> At first, with his celebration of the efficiency of bureaucracy, he was received with only reluctant respect, and even with hostility. All writers were against bureaucracy. But it turned out, surprisingly, that managers were not. When asked, they acknowledged that they preferred clear lines of communication, clear specifications of authority and responsibility, and clear knowledge of whom they were responsible to. . . . Gradually, studies began to show that bureaucratic organizations could change faster than nonbureaucratic ones, and that morale could be higher where there was clear evidence of bureau-cracy. (p. 6)

What are the characteristics of an ideally bureaucratized organization? Analy-ses of Weber's work suggest the following ten features:

1. An organization consists of stipulated relationships among *positions*. The basic building blocks of any formal organization are positions. Organizational posi-tions are almost always designated by titles, such as supervisor, machinist, lieuten-ant, sergeant, lecturer, senior analyst, trainer.

2. The broad purpose or plan of the organization is subdivided into tasks; or-ganization tasks are distributed among the various positions as *official duties*. The definitions of duties and responsibilities are inherent in the position. Job descrip-tions are, of course, one method of meeting this characteristic. A clear division of labor among positions is implied by this feature which makes possible a high degree of specialization and expertness among employees.

3. *Authority* to perform the duties is vested in the position. That is, the only time that a person is authorized to perform the duties of the position is when he or she legitimately occupies the position. Weber referred to this as *legal* authority. Authority is legitimized by a belief in the supremacy of the law. In such a system, obedience is owed to a set of principles, not to a person. This feature includes the requirement to follow directives originating from an office that is superior to one's own, regardless of who occupies the higher office. The government, a factory, the army, a welfare agency, churches, university, and a grocery store are examples of organizations based on legal authority.

4. The lines of authority and the positions are arranged in a *hierarchical order*. The hierarchy takes on the general shape of a pyramid, with each official being responsible to his or her superior for subordinates' decisions, as well as for his or her own. The scope of authority of superiors over subordinates is clearly circum-scribed. The concepts of *upward* and *downward* communication express this con-cept of authority, with information moving down from the position of broadest authority to the position of narrowest authority.

5. A formally established system of general but definite *rules and regulations* governs the actions and functions of positions in the organization. Much of the effort of administrators in the organization goes into applying the general regula-tions to particular cases. The hypothetical case of having the Internal Revenue Ser-vice determine your taxes is a good example. If you were to go to an IRS office

to argue for a reduced tax load, the decision would most likely be made on the basis of a regulation specifying the rules for making such a decision. The official would then apply the regulation to your case and explain how much tax you owe. Regulations help ensure uniformity of operations and provide for continuity regardless of changes of personnel.

6. _Procedures_ in the organization are formal and impersonal—that is, the rules and regulations are applicable to everyone who falls within the category. Officials are expected to assume an impersonal orientation in their contacts with clients and other officials. They are to disregard all personal considerations and to maintain emotional detachment. Impersonal procedures are designed to prevent the feelings of officials from distorting their rational judgment in carrying out their duties.

7. An attitude of and procedures for enforcing a system of _discipline_ is part of the organization. For individuals to work efficiently, they must have the necessary skills and apply them rationally and energetically; however, if members of the organization were to make even rational decisions independently, their work would not be coordinated, making the efficiency of the organization suffer. Individuals who do not accept the authority of those above them, who fail to carry out the duties assigned to their positions, and who apply regulations with capriciousness are not pursuing organizational objectives consistent with the philosophy of efficiency; thus, the organization needs a program of discipline to help ensure cooperation and efficiency.

8. Members of the organization are to maintain _separate private and organizational lives._ Families of organization members, for example, are not to make contact with employees during working hours. Some organizations take great pains to accommodate the personal lives of employees in order to allow them to devote their complete attention to their jobs. Many corporations buy the homes of employees, care for their families in country club surroundings, and discourage using the telephone for private calls to maintain the separation of private and organizational affairs.

9. Employees are selected for employment in the organization on the basis of _technical qualifications_, rather than on political, family, or other connections. Officials are appointed to positions rather than elected by a group of constituents, *Hmm ...* making them dependent on superiors in the organization. The administration of civil service examinations by the U.S. government is one way of trying to select employees on the basis of technical competence. Recent decisions to require employers to select employees on the basis of bona fide occupational qualifications (BFOQs) is perfectly consistent with this characteristic of Weber's ideal bureaucracy.

10. Although employment in the bureaucracy is based on technical competence, advancements are made according to seniority as well as achievement. After a trial period, officials gain tenure of positions and are protected against arbitrary dismissal. Employment in the organization constitutes a lifelong career, providing _security in the position._

These characteristics lead toward rational decision making and administrative efficiency. Experts with much experience are best qualified to make technical decisions. Disciplined performance governed by abstract rules, regulations, or policies and coordinated by hierarchical authority fosters a rational and consistent pursuit of organizational goals.

POSITIONAL COMMUNICATION
AND INFORMAL CONTACTS

The characteristics of a formal organization lead to a phenomenon which we call *positional communication* (Redfield, 1953). Relationships are established between positions, not people. The entire organization consists of a network of positions. Those who occupy the positions are required to communicate in ways consistent with the positions. Nevertheless, positional communication is upset in practice because not all activities and interactions conform strictly to the positional chart. The relationship between Position A and Position C does not exist separately from the relationship between Andrew and Zebe. The official organization chart can never completely determine the conduct and social relations of organization members. Yet, although it is impossible to completely insulate a position from the occupier's personality, organizational productivity depends most of the time on positional communication. This does not deny or discount the tremendous impact of informal relations on communication. In every formal organization there is likely to develop informal groups. However, since informal relations arise in response to the opportunities created by the environment, the formal organization constitutes the immediate environment of the groups within it and influences greatly the number and functioning of informal relations.

Although Weber's analysis of organization theory appears to describe many current operating organizations, a number of other philosophies and theories have contributed to an understanding of organizational functioning and, especially, organizational communication. Two lines of theory, in addition to communication theory, have provided useful insights: these are management theories and organization theories. Sometimes writers make little distinction between a theory of managing and a theory of organizing because they are often very much alike, but occasionally they differ. We shall briefly report on a classical theory of management that is compatible with Weber's formal theory of organization.

TAYLOR'S SCIENTIFIC MANAGEMENT

Weber's theory of bureaucracy focused primarily on organizing; it is considered to be the most important statement on formal organization, but it may be true that all theories of organization are basically theories of managing. Frederick W. Taylor (1856–1917) lived about the same time as Weber and also wrote about organizations; however, Taylor published *Principles of Scientific Management* whereas Weber's work was translated as *The Theory of Social and Economic Organization.* Both books dealt with issues of business enterprise from similar philosophies. Scott (1961) states that the classical doctrine of organizations and management can be traced directly back to Taylor's interest in functional supervision. Taken together, Weber and Taylor represent theories of organization and management that deal almost exclusively with the anatomy of formal organization and are referred to as classical theories. Taylor's approach to management is built around four key elements: division of labor, scalar and functional processes, structure, and span of control. Following Sofer's (1972) analysis closely, we shall briefly review the meaning of these four pillars.

Division of Labor

Division of labor refers to how the tasks, duties, and work of the organization are distributed. In bureaucratic terms the duties of the company are systematically assigned to positions in a descending order of specialization. Taylor suggested that workers should be relieved of the task of planning and of all clerical activities. If practicable, the work of every person in the organization should be confined to the execution of a single function, which is the notion of division of labor. Although not entirely serious, Parkinson (1957) formulated a number of principles that help explain how people in the organization manipulate this element. Parkinson studied the British Navy and concluded that

Work expands to fill the time available for its completion.

He called the statement *Parkinson's Law.* His observations led him to realize that in organizations the task to be executed swells in importance and complexity in direct ratio to the amount of time to be spent on the task. Thus, he argued, the amount of work and the number of workers are not related. He illustrates how any small task can expand to fill the time available by describing a person who has all day to prepare a memo. An hour will be spent locating some paper, another in hunting for a pencil, a half an hour in search of the names and addresses, an hour and a quarter composing the memo, twenty minutes deciding whether to distribute it by hand or send through the mails. The total effort will occupy a busy person for three minutes in total but will leave this person exhausted after a full day of doubt, anxiety, and toil.

Of course, managers, workers, and administrators begin to age and feel reduced energy with such exhausting days. According to Parkinson, the manager has three choices: resign, share the work with a colleague, or ask for assistance in the form of two subordinates. Only the third alternative is ever used. The corollary to Parkinson's Law is that

An official wants to multiply subordinates, not rivals.

The inevitable consequence is called the *Rising Pyramid,* the second great pillar of classical management theory.

Scalar and Functional Processes

Scalar and functional processes deal with the vertical and horizontal growth of the organization. The *scalar process* refers to growth of the chain of command or the vertical dimension of the organization. By acquiring two assistants the manager has increased the size of the organization vertically, creating changes in the delegation of authority and responsibility, unity of direction, and obligations to report.

The division of work into more specialized duties and the restructuring of the more specific parts into compatible units are matters related to *functional processes* and the horizontal expansion of the organization. Both scalar and functional changes lead to the third pillar of classical management theory.

Structure

Structure has to do with logical relationships among functions in the organization. Classical theories concentrate on the two basic structures called *line* and *staff.* The line structure involves the authority channels of the organization as they relate to accomplishing the major goals of the organization. For example, in a valve manufacturing company, the line structure follows the order of positions responsible for getting the valves manufactured; the line authority consists of the president, the vice president of manufacturing, the managers, supervisors, and operatives who produce the valves. In the military the line authority involves those who have command functions, such as the company commander, the first sergeant, the squad leaders, and patrol leaders. The *staff structure* represents those positions that provide support for or help the line positions do their work better by offering advice, assistance, or service. Typical staff functions include purchasing and receiving, traffic control, business research, production planning, public relations, and training and development.

LINE

The primary value of differentiating between line and staff is in the area of decision making. The term *line* simply means that the final authority rests with positions in that structure. At the university, for example, the line structure for teaching and curricular decisions includes faculty members, department chairpersons, deans, and the academic vice president. The arrangement is hierarchical or pyramidal, since there are more faculty members than there are department chairs, more chairs than deans, and more deans than academic vice presidents. The library of a university is a staff function in support of teaching (and research, of course); however, the library has its own line structure, beginning with the director of the library and moving through functional heads such as circulation, acquisitions, and reference, down to specialty librarians in such areas as the social sciences, education, business, and physical sciences. Secretaries, clerks, and researchers represent staff positions.

STAFF

Staff personnel have traditionally provided advice and service in support of the line. The line has authority to command. The staff advises and persuades on behalf of its recommendations but has no authority to order the line manager to follow the suggestions. When a staff specialist's recommendations are accepted by his or her line superior, they are issued on the line manager's authority, not the staff specialist's. In this way the full authority of the line manager remains intact, and subordinates receive orders only from their line superior, thus maintaining a unity of command.

The role of staff as strictly advisory has changed radically over the years. Staff members are now often assigned limited line or command authority rather than general authority over an organizational unit. For example, the personnel department or the training and development department, even though a staff function, may prescribe the methods for on-the-job training of all new employees, regardless of their line assignment.

Tall and Flat Structures

Organization structures may take many forms, but at the extremes are two main types: the *tall* or *vertical* and the *flat* or *horizontal.* The tallness or flatness of an organization is determined almost solely by the differences in numbers of levels of authority and variations in the span of control at each level. Tall structures have many levels of authority with managers exercising a narrow span of control. Tall organizations are often characterized by close supervision, team spirit, competition through personal relationships, gradual increases in responsibility, constant insecurity about status, emphasis on the techniques of management, and an abundance of rules and regulations. Flat organizations, on the other hand, seem to be characterized by and encourage individualistic and entrepreneurial activities. Flat structures have only a modest amount of direct supervision and fewer rules and regulations. Personnel assume wider responsibility at lower levels in flat structures, and the manager has less contact with them. The manager has to judge subordinates by less personal, objective standards of performance, and subordinates openly compete with one another in terms of their actual work rather than on the basis of their personal relations with the boss. Flat structures seem to be more appropriate for loosely supervised and technically simple, although individually more challenging, activities such as sales, service, political, and religious organizations. With its greater scope of individual freedom, flat structures more often tend to produce attitudes of enthusium and result in higher morale among employees.

Span-of-Control

Span of control refers to the number of subordinates a superior has under his or her supervision. Although it has frequently been stated that five or six subordinates is about all a manager can supervise, in practice the span of management varies widely. For example, in a retail chain that has only four levels of authority between the company president and first-line store supervisors, a manager may have 20 or 30 supervisors reporting to him or her. In contrast, in a manufacturing operation, with seven levels of authority, a manager may have only five to ten subordinates reporting to her or him. Some companies have as many as 12 levels of authority between the president and the first-line supervisors; in such situations the span of control may run below five.

SUMMARY

This chapter distinguished between two types of organizations: social and formal. Although the regularities in social behavior that produce social organizations make it possible to predict somewhat accurately how people will behave, formal organizations are specifically designed to produce efficiency and predictability in work settings. Ten characteristics of a formal, bureaucratic organization derived from the writings of Max Weber were discussed. Some principles of scientific management consistent with the ideas of Frederick Taylor were also identified. The works of Weber and Taylor represent the classical view of organization and management.

REFERENCES

BERLO, DAVID K., *The Process of Communication.* New York: Holt, Rinehart & Winston, 1960.

BLAU, PETER M., and W. RICHARD SCOTT, *Formal Organizations.* New York: Harper & Row, Pub., 1962.

PARKINSON, C. NORTHCOTE, *Parkinson's Law.* New York: Ballantine, 1957.

PERROW, CHARLES, "The Short and Glorious History of Organizational Theory," *Organizational Dynamics,* 2 (Summer 1973), 2–15.

REDFIELD, CHARLES E., *Communication in Management.* Chicago: The University of Chicago Press, 1953.

SCOTT, WILLIAM, G., "Organization Theory: An Overview and an Appraisal," *Journal of the Academy of Management,* 4 (April 1961), 7–26.

SOFER, CYRIL, *Organizations in Theory and Practice.* New York: Basic Books, 1972.

TAYLOR, FREDERICK, W., *Principles of Scientific Management.* New York: Harper & Row Pub., 1911.

WEBER, MAX, *The Theory of Social and Economic Organization,* trans. A.M. Henderson and Talcott Parsons; Talcott Parsons, ed. Glencoe, Ill.: The Free Press and Falcon's Wing Press, 1947.

3

ORGANIZATIONS:
BEHAVIORAL
AND
SYSTEMS THEORIES

This chapter will explore the transition from classical theories of organization and management to the modern behavioral and systems theories. Like eras in the history of people, aspects of earlier traditions form the foundation for contemporary and futuristic thinking about people and things. The older conceptions continue to exercise important influences on how we conceive of organizations, but refinements in our models begin to bring about curious and often practical changes in our formulations about organizations.

BEHAVIORAL THEORIES

Chester Barnard's Authority-Communication Theory

Perrow (1973) indicates that concerns had been expressed from the beginning about the implications of the classical theory of organization and the scientific doctrine of management. " 'Bureaucracy' has always been a dirty word, and the job design efforts of Frederick Taylor were even the subject of a congressional investigation" (p. 10). However, it was not until Barnard (1938) published his *The Functions of the Executive* that a new line of thought emerged. He proposed that organizations are people systems, not mechanically engineered structures. A good, clear mechanical structure was not enough. Natural groups within the bureaucratic structure affected what happened, upward communication was important, authority came from below rather than from above, and leaders needed to function as a cohesive force.

Barnard's definition of formal organization—a system of consciously coordinated activities of two or more persons—highlighted the concepts of *system* and *persons*. People, not positions, make up a formal organization. His stress on the cooperative aspects of the organization reflected the importance placed on the human element. Barnard stated that the existence of an organization (as a cooperative system) depended on the ability of human beings to communicate and on their willingness to serve and work toward a common goal. Thus, he concluded that

The first function of the executive is to develop and maintain a system of communication.

Barnard also maintained that authority was a function of willingness to go along. He cited four conditions that must be met before a person will accept a message as authoritative:

1. The person can and does understand the message.
2. The person believes, at the time of the decision, that the message is not inconsistent with the purpose of the organization.
3. The person believes, at the time of the decision to go along, that the message is compatible with his or her personal interest as a whole.
4. The person is able mentally and physically to comply with the message.

This set of premises became known as the *acceptance theory of authority*— that is, authority originating at the top of an organization is, in effect, nominal authority. It becomes real only when it is accepted. However, Barnard recognized that many messages cannot be deliberately analyzed, judged, and accepted or rejected; rather, most types of directives, orders, and persuasive messages fall within a person's *zone of indifference.*

To visualize the idea of a zone of indifference, think of a horizontal line having a scale with zero percent as the center point and 100 at both ends. The wider the person's zone, the farther it extends in both directions towards the ends. A 100 percent willingness to go along shows the zone extending in both directions to the 100 percent marks. A complete rejection of the message (directive, order, request) shows a zone in which the marks are both touching zero.

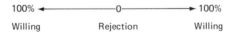

| 100% | ◀—————————0—————————▶ | 100% |
| Willing | Rejection | Willing |

Many messages in an organization are designed to widen the zone of indifference of employees. The width of a subordinate's zone tends to be different for each order; in one instance the subordinate may be warmly receptive and very willing to accept a request, for another the subordinate may be reluctant although not adamant about rejecting it, whereas in a third the subordinate may completely reject the request.

An instance of total authority communication rejection occurred during the Russo-Japanese War (1904–1905). The Russian ship *Potemkin,* according to the report, was conducting purposeless maneuvers in the Black Sea. The usual grudges held by sailors against officers were multiplied by a policy of harsh discipline. Knowing that the Russo-Japanese War was being badly mismanaged, agitators attempted to incite mutiny but made little progress on the Potemkin. However, one day the crew saw some maggoty meat hanging in the galley. In order to assure them that the meat was edible, the ship's doctor had to be called. At dinner the crew was served borscht made with the spoiling meat. As an act of rebellion the crew ate only bread and water, leaving the sickening soup untouched. This enraged the captain who verbally attacked the crew in an effort to get them to eat. His effort failed, so the next officer in command stepped into the tense situation, called the armed guard, and ordered all sailors willing to eat to step forward. Of all the hundreds of crew members, all but 30 did. The officer ordered the stubborn crew members to be covered with a tarpaulin in preparation for having them shot. As the sailors huddled under the covering, the order to fire was given. The guards hesitated. At that moment other sailors rushed forward urging the guards to turn their rifles on the officers rather than their shipmates. While the senior officer shrieked commands and other officers stood aghast, the guards fired upon them. Most of the officers, including the captain, were shot and thrown overboard. Thus the formal authority was totally ineffective because it was rejected by both the crew and the armed guards (Moorehead, 1958).

Barnard equated authority and effective communication. The rejection of a communication was tantamount to rejection of the communicator's authority. By accepting a message or directive from another, a person grants authority to the formulator of the message and therefore adopts the position of a subordinate. Thus, Tannenbaum (1950) argued, the "sphere of authority possessed by a superior is defined for him by the sphere of acceptance" of his subordinates. The decision *not* to accept the authority and messages of a superior because the advantages may not be sufficient may result in some disadvantages, such as disciplinary action, monetary loss, or social disapproval. In some organizations the fear of such coercive acts may produce a willingness to accept a message even when the disadvantages alone do not.

Beyond a close relationship between authority and communication, Barnard viewed communication techniques (both written and oral) as essential to attaining the organization's goals and as the source of problems in the organization. "Communication techniques," he said, "shape the form and the internal economy of the organization. The absence of a suitable technique of communication would eliminate the possibility of adopting some purpose as a basis of organization" (p. 90). Thus it was largely Barnard who made communication a meaningful part of organization and management theory. He seemed thoroughly convinced that communication was the major shaping force of the organization.

Elton Mayo's Human Relations Theory

A year following Barnard's publication of *Functions,* Roethlisberger and Dickson (1939) issued their massive report on a large-scale investigation of productivity and social relations at the Hawthorne plant of the Western Electric Company. Referred to as *Management and the Worker,* it quickly became known as the *Hawthorne Studies.* The studies were conceived and directed by Elton Mayo with the assistance of Fritz Roethlisberger, professors at Harvard University. Miller and Form (1951) refer to the Hawthorne Studies as the "first great scientific experiment in industry." A journal reviewer called it "the most outstanding study of industrial relations that has been published anywhere, anytime" (Miller & Form, p. 50). However,

Whitehead, the statistician working on the studies, found "not a single correlation of enough statistical significance to be recognized by any competent statistician as having any meaning" (Miller & Form, p. 49).

What, then, was discovered that lead to such disparate, but at times laudatory, reactions to Mayo's work? The most pertinent results occurred during experiments on illumination. At first the researchers assumed that the higher the lighting, the higher the worker output. Thus they decided to establish an experimental room with variable light conditions and a control room with constant light conditions. Two groups of workers were chosen to do their work in two different areas. Over a period of time illumination in the experimental room was increased to blinding intensity and then decreased to practically an absence of light. The results went like this: As the amount of illumination increased, so did worker efficiency in the experimental room; however, the efficiency of workers in the control room also increased. As lighting was diminished in the test room, efficiencies of both the test and the control groups increased slowly but steadily. When the illumination reached three foot-candles in the test room, operators protested, saying that they were hardly able to see what they were doing; at that point the production rate decreased. Up to that time the assemblers maintained their efficiency in spite of the handicap.

The results of the illumination experiments intrigued the researchers as well as management. So from 1927 to 1929, a superior team of researchers measured the effects of a wide variety of working conditions on employee production. The results were again consistent with the illumination experiments—regardless of the working conditions, production increased. The researchers came to the conclusion that these unusual and even amazing results occurred because the six individuals in the experimental room became a team, with group relations being more important and powerful in determining morale and productivity than any of the working conditions— good or bad. The researchers concluded that the operators had no clear idea why they were able to produce more in the test room, but there was the feeling that "better output is in some way related to the distinctly pleasanter, freer, and happier working conditions" (Miller & Form, p. 48).

Two impelling conclusions have evolved out of the Hawthorne Studies, often referred to jointly as the *Hawthorne Effect:*

*The very act of paying attention to people
may change their attitudes and behavior.*

*High morale and productivity are promoted
if employees have opportunities for interaction with each other.*

Mayo, later in life (1945), wrote what has become a summation of the interests communication specialists bring to the analysis of organizations:

I believe that social study should begin with careful observation of what may be described as communication: that is, the capacity of an individual to communicate his feelings and ideas to another, the capacity of groups to communicate effectively and intimately with each other. That is, beyond all reasonable doubt, the outstanding defect that civilization is facing today. (p. 21)

Taken together, the work of Barnard and Mayo represents a behavioral approach to organizations. Mayo is often attributed with initiating the *human relations movement*. In fact, Perrow (1973) asserts that, building on the insights of Barnard and Mayo, the human relations movement came into its own following World War II. Sofer (1973) pointed out that Mayo and his colleagues created a scientific demonstration showing that "a group had a life of its own, complete with customs, norms, and effective social controls on its members" (p. 80). Guilbot (1968) observed that "after the Hawthorne studies it had to be granted that an informal structure of social relations did exist behind the formal organizational structure and that numerous phenomena could not be explained on any other grounds" (pp. 232-233). One great contribution of the early behavioral theorists was the reorientation of thinking about organizations and management from that of purely structure and task to considerations of people and morale.

One pointed criticism of the human relations movement is its overwhelming preoccupation with people and their relationships and its disregard of the total resources of an organization and its members. A concern about responding to both personal and organizational needs has been a significant consequence of the groundwork laid by early behavioral theorists. An important distinction is made currently between developing good human relations and developing the human resources of an organization. Organizational communication seeks to provide the background for developing the quality of human resources in an organization, rather than just developing the quality of human relations, as important as they may appear.

Bakke and Argyris' Fusion Theory

Sensing the enormity of the problem associated with satisfying both the divergent interests of individuals and the essential demands of the bureaucratic structure, Bakke (1950) proposed a *fusion process*. He reasoned that the organization, to some degree, molds the individual, while at the same time the individual also influences the organization. The result is an organization that is *personalized* by the individual employee and individuals who are *socialized* by the organization. Hence every employee takes on characteristics of the organization, and every position appears to be uniquely like the individuals who occupy them. After fusion (a.f.), every employee looks more like the organization, and every position in the organization is modified to the special interest of the individual.

Argyris (1957), a colleague of Bakke's at Yale University, expanded and refined Bakke's work. He argued that there is a basic incongruity or incompatibility between the needs of mature employees and the requirements of the formal organization. The organization has goals to accomplish that clash with the goals of individual employees. Employees experience frustration as a consequence of the incongruence; some may leave, some may adapt, and some may stay and lower their work standards, becoming apathetic and uninterested. Through this conflict others learn not to expect satisfaction from the job. Many people have learned from personal experience that adjusting to the demands of a formal organization is not easy and should not be expected to occur automatically.

Likert's Linking Pin Theory

Rensis Likert of the University of Michigan is credited with developing what is popularly known as the *linking pin model* of organization structure. The linking pin concept is one of overlapping groups. Each supervisor is a member of two groups: the leader of a lower unit and member of an upper unit. The supervisor functions as a linking pin, tying the work group to another group at the next level. The linking pin structure provides a group-to-group, in contrast to a person-to-person, relationship. Rather than fostering a downward orientation, a linking pin organization encourages an upward orientation; communication, supervisory influence, and goal attainment are all directed upward in the organization. As Figure 3.1 implies, group processes play an important role in making the linking pin organization function efficiently. All groups must be equally effective, also, since the organization can be no stronger than its weakest group.

Luthans (1973) argued that the linking pin concept tends to emphasize and facilitate what is supposed to occur in the bureaucratic, classical structure. The superior-subordinate, hierarchical pattern, however, often results in a downward focus, while inhibiting upward and lateral communication. The slowness of group action, which is part of the linking pin organization, must be balanced with the positive advantages of participation—contributions to planning, more open communication, and member commitments—that accrue from the linking pin structure.

FIGURE 3.1
Linking Pin Model of Organization

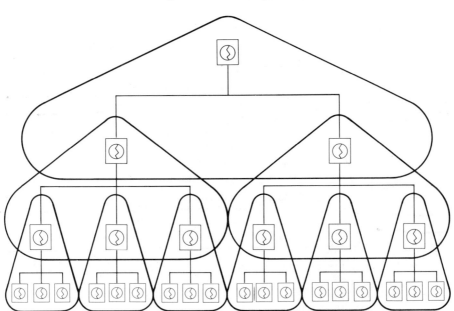

FIGURE 3.2
The Parts of an Organizational System

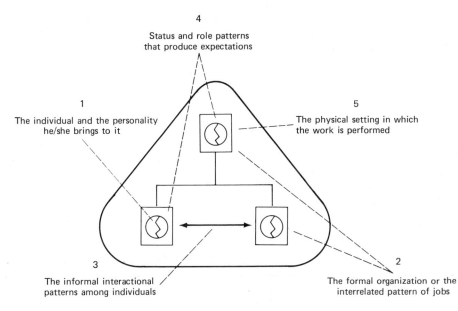

4

Status and role patterns
that produce expectations

1

The individual and the personality
he/she brings to it

5

The physical setting in which
the work is performed

3

The informal interactional
patterns among individuals

2

The formal organization or the
interrelated pattern of jobs

SYSTEMS THEORIES

Scott (1961) argues that "the only meaningful way to study organization . . . is as a system" (p. 15). He suggests that the basic parts of an organizational system are the individual and the personality which he or she brings to the system; the formal structure, which we have discussed at length earlier; the informal pattern of inter-actions; status and role patterns that create expectations; and the physical environment of work (Figure 3.2). These parts are woven into a configuration called an *organizational system.* All of the parts are interrelated and interact with each other. Each part is linked to all of the other parts. Although there are other theories about how the parts are connected, the primary linking process is communication.

Katz and Kahn's Social Systems Theory

Classical and behavioral theories often refer to communication primarily in terms of forms of communication activity, rather than as a linking process. Communication as a linking process takes on special meaning if we accept Katz and Kahn's (1966) telling point that social structures differ from mechanical and biological structures. Physical and biological entities such as automobiles and animals have anatomical structures that can be identified even when they are not functioning. When a biological organism ceases to function, the physical body can still be examined in a postmortem analysis.

When a social system ceases to function, it no longer has an identifiable structure. The reason is that social systems are structures of events or happenings rather than physical parts and have no structure apart from their functioning. The communication network of an organization, for example, has little resemblance to the circulatory or nervous system of biological organisms, although we tend to compare the two quite often. Because the analogies seem impelling, we are frequently deterred from grasping the essential differences between social systems and biological systems.

Social systems consist, on the whole, of people. They are imperfect, but the constancy of relationships can be very high. In fact, organizations can have a very high turnover but still exist and function effectively. The *relationships among the people*, not the people themselves, allow an organization to persist far longer than the biological people who fill positions in the organization. Formal organizations have procedures by which the parts (people) can be readily replaced so they can continue to function into an unspecified future. Biological organisms have forces that wear out their parts which often cannot be replaced.

Katz and Kahn explain that most of our interactions with others are communicative acts (verbal and nonverbal, spoken and silent). "Communication—the exchange of information and the transmission of meaning—is the very essence of a social system or an organization" (p. 223). They assert that it is possible to subsume under the concept of communication such forms of social interaction as "exertion of influence, cooperation, social contagion or imitation, and leadership" (p. 224). As you shall see, we take a perspective consistent with this view and consider communication as the primary linking process in organizations with a number of corollary processes emerging out of the communicating that occurs in organizations. We refer to those special forms of communication as organizational communication skills and activities.

Systems theory recognizes that an organized state requires the introduction of constraints and restrictions to reduce random communication to channels that are appropriate for accomplishment of organizational goals. Organizational development, for example, may require the creation of new communication channels. Katz and Kahn claim that the "very nature of a social system . . . implies a selectivity of channels and communicative acts—a mandate to avoid some and to utilize others" (p. 226).

In summary, Scott (1961) points out that "organizations are comprised of parts which communicate with each other, receive messages from the outside world, and store information. Taken together, these communication functions of the parts comprise a configuration representing the total system" (p. 18). It might be said that, from a systems point of view, communication is the organization. Hawes (1974), in fact, has expressed this very point: "A social collectivity is patterned communicative behavior; communicative behavior does not occur *within* a network of relationships but is that network" (p. 500). For our purposes in an introductory book on organizational communication, we can assume the existence of organizations and proceed to explain and hopefully understand something about their functioning, the manner in which the people interrelate, and some of the impelling issues that affect the way in which the people and the organization develop. We shall treat some of these basic issues in the next part of this book.

Ad-hocracy and the Buck Rogers Theory

Some of our most improbable visions of space exploration have come from the fantasies of the creators of the fictional and famous figure, Buck Rogers. Taking the lead from Buck, futuristic authors such as Alvin Toffler (1970) have written about *future shock* and the inevitable consequences of rapid change on all aspects of our lives. Formal organizations have been touched in these analyses. Toffler dedicates an entire chapter to "Organizations: The Coming Ad-hocracy." Bennis (1966) predicts "The Coming Death of Bureaucracy." Luthans (1973) observes that "many practicing managers are becoming disenchanted with traditional ways of organizing" (p. 168). The predictions indicate that we are moving into a post-bureaucratic era of organizational theory based on the futuristic concept of rapidly changing organizational structures. Toffler describes it this way: "What we see here is nothing less than the creation of a disposable division—the organizational equivalent of paper dresses or throw-away tissues" (p. 133).

According to Bennis (1966), the social structure of the *new* bureaucracy will be, in a word, *temporary*. The organization will consist largely of *task forces* that are created in response to a particular problem. The manager, in an organization of continuously changing structure, becomes a coordinator, a connector, a linker of various project groups. Skills in human interaction and communication will be of great value, since some of the major tasks will be relaying information and mediating understanding and differences between groups. Bennis argues that people will "have to learn to develop quick and intense relationships on the job, and learn to bear the loss of more enduring work relationships" (p. 35).

Toffler summarizes the characteristics of the new bureaucracy, called an *ad-hocracy,* as fast-moving, rich with information, highly active, constantly changing, filled with transient units and extremely mobile individuals. In the ad-hocracy, it is the work itself, the problem to be solved, the task to be done that attracts the commitment of employees, rather than the organization. Even professional loyalties become short term, because specialists derive their rewards from the intrinsic satisfaction of doing a difficult task well. They are loyal to their standards, not their superiors; to their problems, not their jobs. The ad-hocrats employ their skills and talents in solving problems within the temporary groups and environment of the organization, but only as long as the problems interest them.

Toffler notes that the titles of positions in some ad-hocracies are prefaced by the term *associate.* The term suggests an equality typical of the new organization —that is, *associate* connotes one who works with, rather than is subordinate to, others in the organization. Its use reflects a shift from vertical hierarchies to more lateral communication patterns. In my own consulting and training company, we adopted the title *Organizational Associates* to convey the meaning that colleagues are coequals in the attack on organizational problems. Our professional staff of associates is highly task oriented, deriving satisfaction from the anticipation of dealing with problems wherever they occur.

Toffler offers some words of caution that may lead us to the next part of this book. He guardedly observes that the "Ad-hocracy increases the adaptability of organizations; but it strains the adaptability of people" (p. 150). Each change of relationship in the organization brings with it some costs in personal adjustment, meaningful relations, and satisfaction. Social tension, psychological strain, and individual coping are all aggravated by the rapid change, temporary work circum-

27

stances, and lack of organizational commitment. The constant changes in organizational relationships place a heavy adaptive burden on people. Scrambling, we are propelled by our work into the Buck Rogers organization of the future.

For some the future may be arriving too soon. For most of us the future is now. For example, in 1965 Stewart provided guidelines for "Making Project Management Work." Project organization is the nearest equivalent we currently have to ad-hocracy. Even today the literature on organization theory is replete with descriptions of *matrix* organizational patterns, *intermix* project organization, *aggregate* project organization, *individual and staff* project organization, and *free-form* organization. The most common contemporary Buck Rogers theory of organization is the matrix organization. It is a project organization superimposed on the more traditional functional organization. The functional department heads have line authority over projects by collaboration between the appropriate functional and project managers. Many conclude, consistent with Toffler's speculations, that matrix organization has reduced corporate loyalty and identification with the organization. Nevertheless, Luthans (1973) pointed out "that many modern organizations which are facing tremendous structural and technical complexity have no choice but to move to such an arrangement" (p. 177).

Matrix, project, and ad-hocratic organizations are the communication organizations of the present and future. The study of communication is, in such circumstances, the study of organization. Management in matrix ad-hocracies is simply the practice of organizational communication. Present organization practices confirm early theoretical predictions; the first function of an executive is, indeed, to create and maintain a system of communication. The communication system is the organization. Organizational communication is the Buck Rogers theory of organization.

SUMMARY

In this chapter, we analyzed behavioral and systems theories of organization. Behavioral theories included Barnard's authority-communication theory which made the first function of an executive that of developing and maintaining a system of communication; Mayo's human relations theory which made informal group relations more important and powerful in determining morale and productivity than working conditions; Bakke and Argyris' fusion theory which proposed an incompatibility between employee needs and organization needs which is minimized by personalizing the organization and socializing the individual and results in the fusion of employee and organization; and Likert's linking pin theory which conceives of the organization as a number of interconnected groups in which each supervisor is a leader of a lower unit and a member of a higher unit and serves as the linking pin connecting the groups. Katz and Kahn's social systems theory which focuses on relationships among people and conceives of an organization as parts which communicate with each other, receive messages, and store information, and Toffler's and Bennis' futuristic ad-hocracy which functions with temporary relationships, disposable divisions, associates, and matrix patterns were offered as current views of organizations.

REFERENCES

ARGYRIS, CHRIS, *Personality and Organization.* New York: Harper & Brothers, 1957.

BAKKE, E. WIGHT, *Bonds of Organization.* New York: Harper & Row, Pub., 1950.

BARNARD, CHESTER I., *The Functions of the Executive.* Cambridge, Mass.: Harvard University Press, 1938.

BENNIS, WARREN G., "The Coming Death of Bureaucracy," *Think Magazine* (November–December 1966), pp. 30–35.

GUILBOT, O. BENOIT, "The Sociology of Work," *International Encyclopedia of the Social Sciences,* Vol. 7, pp. 232–233. New York: Macmillan, 1968.

HAWES, LEONARD C., "Social Collectivities as Communication: Perspective on Organizational Behavior," *Quarterly Journal of Speech,* 60 (December 1974), 500.

KATZ, DANIEL, and ROBERT L. KAHN, *The Social Psychology of Organizations.* New York: John Wiley, 1966.

LIKERT, RENSIS, *New Patterns of Management.* New York: McGraw-Hill, 1961.

LUTHANS, FRED, *Organizational Behavior.* New York: McGraw-Hill, 1973.

MAYO, ELTON, *The Social Problems of an Industrial Civilization.* Cambridge, Mass.: Harvard University Press, 1945.

MIDDLETON, C. J., "How to Set Up a Project Organization," *Harvard Business Review* (March–April 1967), p. 73.

MILLER, DELBERT C., and WILLIAM H. FORM, *Industrial Sociology.* New York: Harper & Row, Pub., 1951.

MOOREHEAD, ALAN, "The Russian Revolution, Part II: Relentless Rise of the Conspiracy," *Life,* 44 (January 20, 1958), 60–70, 75–82.

PERROW, CHARLES, "The Short and Glorious History of Organizational Theory," *Organizational Dynamics,* 2 (Summer 1973), 2–15.

ROETHLISBERGER, FRITZ, J., and WILLIAM, J. DICKSON, *Management and the Worker.* Cambridge, Mass.: Harvard University Press, 1939.

SCOTT, WILLIAM G., "Organization Theory: An Overview and Appraisal," *Journal of the Academy of Management* (April 1961), pp. 15, 18.

SOFER, CYRIL, *Organization in Theory and Practice.* New York: Basic Books, 1973.

STEWART, JOHN, M., "Making Project Management Work," *Business Horizons* (Fall 1965), pp. 57–59.

TANNENBAUM, ROBERT, "Managerial Decision Making," *The Journal of Business,* 23 (1950), 22–39.

TOFFLER, ALVIN, *Future Shock.* New York: Random House, 1970.

4

THE
ORGANIZATIONAL
COMMUNICATION
SYSTEM

The term *organizational communication* refers technically to communicating that occurs within the network of positions that comprise the organization. Organizational communication as a concept, however, is sufficiently broad that it includes transactions with people in other organizations in the external environment as well as with individuals in the organization. Our treatment of the subject, nevertheless, will deal more directly with internal communication than external communication, although the two may be part of the total communication program of an organization.

A COMMUNICATION UNIT

A system has been defined by de Sola Pool (1960) as "any continuing entity capable of two or more states " (p. 3). In a communication system the *states* are connections between people. In an organizational communication system the states are connections between *people in positions.* The basic unit of organizational communication is a person in a position. Figure 4.1 symbolizes that important relationship by portraying a person as the circle located inside the square position. As Bakke (1950) and Argyris (1957) explained, the person is socialized by the position, creating a circle that conforms more closely to the shape of the position; at the same time, the position is personalized, producing a figure that conforms more closely to the shape of the person.

DEFINITION OF COMMUNICATION

Communication refers to a multitude of different experiences. Dance and Larson (1976) listed 126 different published definitions of communication. It is neither practical nor feasible for us to review all of those definitions here. The question

FIGURE 4.1
A Communication Unit

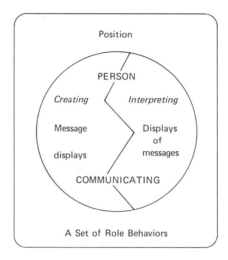

that we shall pursue for a moment, however, is: What acts distinguish communication behavior from other forms of behavior in organizations? The answer is both simple and complex. For example, is hammering a nail a form of communication behavior? Is jogging communication? Is filing letters in a cabinet a type of communication? Is looking out the window on the 25th floor of an office building an example of communication? Is writing a memo a form of communication? The answer to these questions depends on the precision with which you think about the activities that constitute communication behavior.

The simple answer is that none of the preceding behaviors are actually communication. The complex answer is that, in a sense, all of them are part of the communication process. If we look at what happens when a person engages in communicating, two general types of actions take place:

1. *Creating messages* or, more precisely, displays
2. *Interpreting messages* or displays

Figure 4.1 portrays these two processes by dividing the person with an uneven line.

Message-Display

To *display* means that you bring something to the attention of another or others. *The Random House Dictionary of the English Language* (1967) states that "to display is literally to spread something out so that it may be most completely and favorably seen." Thus to display is "to put something in plain view and usually in a favorable position for particular observation." Hammering a nail or filing a letter or writing a memo, by themselves, may not constitute forms of communication.

31

However, they would be considered communication behaviors *if* they made something else visible or put something into plain view or brought something to the attention of another person. For a display to be a form of communicative behavior, it must represent or stand for or symbolize something else. When you create a message-display, you engage in one aspect of communication—that aspect is calling attention to something. For example, when you get dressed in the morning, you create a display of yourself. You put yourself, or at least what you feel you think about yourself, in plain view. We think you are putting yourself in a favorable position for particular observation. Your clothing, jewelry, and facial covering (make-up or beard) represent yourself to others—they are your display.

There is an axiom of communication that says

A person cannot not communicate

(Smith & Williamson, 1977, p. 61). Technically that means that a person cannot avoid being a message-display. What you show or put in plain view does represent you. You are a walking message-display. The same can be said of your office (Goldhaber, 1979). The office is a message-display. A campus, no matter how it looks, is a message-display for those who visit. Of course, a memo is also a message-display, since the memo represents the ideas being expressed. A speech is a message-display. A drawing, a newspaper, a flower arrangement, and a layout are all message-displays, provided they are designed to stand for something else, such as an idea or image or another object.

Message Interpretation

The second type of behavior that occurs when a person engages in communication is called interpreting message-displays (Redding, 1972). To *interpret* means to set forth, to bring out, or make sense of something. According to the *Random House Dictionary,* to interpret means to construe or understand something in a particular way. Communication can be distinguished from all other human and organizational behaviors because it involves the mental process of making sense out of people, objects, and events, which we called message-displays. The only message that really counts in communicating is the one that results from the interpretative processes (Redding & Sanborn, 1964). You may consciously or intentionally create a display of words, sounds, artifacts, and actions to portray a meaning you have, but the only meaning that has an effect on people is the meaning they assign. What you had in mind makes little difference; how the other person interprets what you did and said is what affects his or her feelings and actions.   *their perceptions*

INFORMATION AS MESSAGE-DISPLAYS

It is not uncommon for authors to define communication as the *transfer* (Luthans, 1973) or *exchange* (Kahn & Katz, 1966) of information. In this context, for example, *information* refers to the words (in written messages) and the sounds (in spoken messages) in our displays. Luthans (1973), however, included within his definition of information such things as sensory stimuli; languages of all types, including FORTRAN, statistics, and accounting; and nonverbal behavior. Ference (1970) referred to a "five-year forecast of industry sales" as information but defined information as "any input to a person in a communication system" (p. 83). Frequently throughout this book, reference will be made to information, in such contexts as "the flow of information" and "information processing." *Information* is a term used to designate what we have called message-displays and is frequently used to refer to profit-and-loss figures, performance evaluations, personal opinions expressed in letters and memos, technical reports, and operating data.

THE FALLACY OF MEANING TRANSFER

Although we seem to recognize that sending a person a letter, memo, or report, or even talking to him or her face to face, consists only of creating and delivering a display to the other person, we often fail to realize that the delivery of information is different from making sense out of the information. Frequently we behave as if the delivery of information or message-displays is actually the transfer of meaning from one person to another. We think that saying something—such as "pick up the binder and meet me at the administration building"—should mean exactly the same thing for both people involved. At least when you show up with a ball of string and I was expecting a ring binder, I am surprised that *you* made a mistake. Since I *told* you what to do, you should have done it. I said the words just right, and you should have gotten the meaning. In a statement like that, meaning sounds like something you throw at another person. It's their fault if they fumble it.

The realities of communication suggest that people interpret displays and create meanings. Meanings are *not* contained in the displays or events or words (Lee & Lee, 1967). The fallacy of meaning transfer is expressed in this great principle of communication:

$$\left(\textit{Meanings are in people, not words.}\right)$$

Postman and Weingartner (1969) recognized the operation of this fallacy in our schools when they observed that some teachers believe "that they are in the 'information dissemination' business. . . . The signs that their business is failing are abundant, but they keep at it all the more diligently" (p. 13). The real business of people involved in communicating, including teachers, is helping people create meanings, helping people understand displays. When they assume that meanings are in the displays, they are perpetuating one of the great fallacies of communication.

What is the significance of understanding this meaning-transfer fallacy for a manager, section head, or supervisor? What should an organizational communicator do differently if he or she understands this fallacy? The answer is that the supervisor will

Listen to the person, not just to his or her words.

The plaintive appeal to "Listen to what I mean, not what I say" is often heard after something has gone wrong. Remember, there are few, if any, instructions that cannot be misinterpreted by somebody. For example, the simple explanation of the airline attendant when handing out chewing gum that "It's for the ears" seemed clear until a passenger complained that gum was all right, but wouldn't something less sticky work better?

In summary, in organizational communication, the basic unit is a person communicating in a position. An organizational communication system consists of connections between communication units. People in the positions communicate by creating message-displays or information and by interpreting message-displays. A major fallacy of organizational communication is the assumption that meanings exist in information or message-displays and that meanings can be transferred from one person to another. In reality, information and displays can only be presented or delivered to people; the recipients must make sense out of the displays. Thus we say:

A person cannot not display.

Meanings are in people, not words.

Listen to what a person means, not what he or she says.

Messages may be displayed in verbal (involving language) or nonverbal (nonlanguage) forms and by oral, written or pictorial means. Table 4.1 shows the most common categories of displays.

For a message-display of information to be meaningful, someone must interpret it as standing for something else—that is, the display serves a symbolic function. Any aspect of people and things may be given meaning by someone. Goldhaber (1979) suggests that meaning can be assigned to all of the following: the body and its appearance, especially the mouth and eyes, gestures, touching, posture, and general bodily shape; the volume, tone, rate, pauses, and nonfluencies of vocal expression; the environment, including spaces between people and the territorial cues they offer; time factors such as tardiness and promptness; building and room designs; clothing—dress for success; the display of material things such as artwork; parking spaces; and the number of staff members.

Both verbal and nonverbal message-displays are central to the functioning of an organizational communication system. In fact, the contact people have with one another and the interpretations they assign to the behavior, objects, and events, both present and absent from the immediate environment, constitute the crux of the organizational communication system.

TABLE 4.1
Examples of Types of Messages

	VERBAL	NONVERBAL
Oral	Interview	Speaking softly
Written	Report	Diagram or layout
Pictorial	Description of a scene	Sketch of a scene

DEFINITION OF ORGANIZATIONAL COMMUNICATION

⟨S⟩ *Organizational communication* may be defined as the display and interpretation of messages among communication units who are part of a particular organization. An organization is comprised of communication units in hierarchical relations to each other and functioning in an environment. Figure 4.2 portrays the concept of an organizational communication system. The dotted lines represent the idea that relations are stipulated rather than natural; they also suggest that the structure of an organization is flexible and may change in response to internal, as well as external, environmental forces. Relations among positions, nevertheless, change officially only by declaration of organizational officials.

⟨S⟩ Organizational communication occurs whenever at least one person who occupies a position in an organization interprets some display. Because our focus is on communication among members of an organization, the analysis of organizational

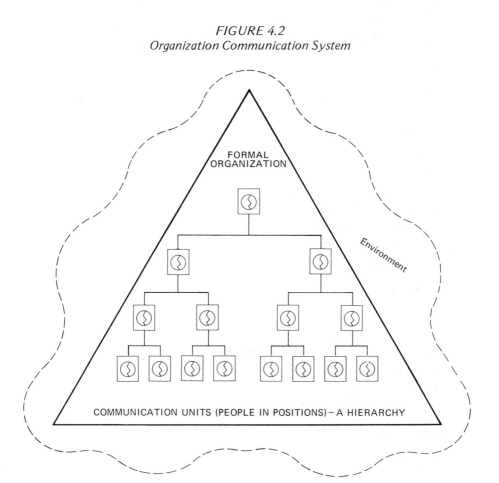

FIGURE 4.2
Organization Communication System

communication involves looking at many transactions occurring simultaneously. The system involves displaying and interpreting messages among dozens or even hundreds of individuals at the same time who have different types of relationships connecting them; whose thinking, decisions, and behaviors are governed by policies, regulations, and "rules"; who have different styles of communicating, managing, and leading; who are motivated by different contingencies; who are at different stages of development in various groups; who perceive different communication climates; who have different levels of satisfaction and information adequacy; who prefer and use different types, forms, and methods of communicating in different networks; who have varying levels of message fidelity; and who require the expenditure of different levels of materials and energy to communicate effectively. The interplay among all of those factors, and possibly many more, is what we call the *organizational communication system.*

No system of organizational communication may function as smoothly and logically as portrayed in this book. In fact, Weick (1969) postulates that "the activities of organizing are directed toward the establishment of a workable level of certainty" (p. 40). He suggests that the process of organizing simply serves to narrow the range of possibilities to a level that is regarded as sufficient for those involved to take action. Thus people in positions communicate with one another in an effort to reduce the number of things that might occur, to produce some degree of predictability in the activities of the organization.

Weick also suggests that "organizations continue to exist only to the degree that they are able to maintain a balance between flexibility and stability" (p. 39). He reasons that the attainment of stability must be at the expense of a degree of flexibility. Flexibility is important in order to adapt to changes in the environment, which if not done leaves the organization outmoded. Too much flexibility, however, makes it difficult to maintain a sense of identity and even continuity. Flexibility allows for the discovery of more efficient ways of doing things; however, stability provides for handling problems in established and routine ways, which are efficient. What the organization must do is constantly seek to locate the best balance between stability and flexibility.

Nevertheless, in any system there are forces that divert, modify, undo, simplify, and make things less orderly. Few processes occur in the same way each time; thus for something to take place in a similar way each time, "its components must be reinstated, reaffirmed, and reaccomplished" time after time (Weick, p. 36). The tendencies toward confusion, uncertainty, and/or unorganization must constantly be countered with efforts to create circumstances that approximate what happened earlier. Nothing can ever unfold exactly the same way twice; it can only approximate the past.

Finally, Weick (1969) suggests that "goal-governed behavior" is not very evident in organizations. The idea that people create goals and organize to accomplish them is not all that clear in organizations. In fact, much of the activity in an organization does not seem to be directed toward the goals of the organization. What seems to happen is a type of "retroactive" summation of activities. Orderliness develops when organization members look back on what has taken place and state goals as summaries of past actions. Goals in this view are postdecisions that make sense out of what happened in the past. Behaviors in the organization are made to appear sensible after they have occurred. As Weick states: "It is difficult for a person to be rational if he does not know precisely what it is that he must be rational about" (p. 38). A person can make sense out of things and actions better after they have occurred rather than before.

The actual functioning of an organization probably follows the premises set down by Weick. That is, there are probably fewer explicit goals established in advance and considerably more postdecision goals that allow organization members to rationalize what happened. Also, the forces operating to divert and undo most orderly movement toward some objectives are fairly strong and require a great deal of repositioning and reaccomplishing of things to keep a degree of stability. At the same time the discovery of better ways of doing things builds into the system a degree of uncertainty and flexibility. All in all the organization functions as a result of the constant efforts and activities of its members to make sense out of what they are doing. The process of working in an organization under those conditions is less orderly than what may appear on the surface.

Pacanowsky (1978) revealed something important about organizations when he observed that "organized activity is an instance where people make their actions make sense to one another—a process that is greatly facilitated by communication" (p. 9). If the activity is structured by a set of rules or policies, such as formal organizations are, it is easier for participants to hold similar concepts of the situation or activity. Nevertheless, a person's behavior is a function of "the individual's monitoring of the situation" so that actions can be "tuned and modified based on messages and signals that the individual receives from others" (p. 9).

Pacanowsky also suggests that the more people do things together the more similar their meanings tend to become. As they do things separately, the greater is the likelihood that their meaning will be less similar. Thus the more the organization's tasks are divided and subdivided to take advantage of efficiencies in the division of labor, the greater the likelihood that communication will be less efficient because of the differences in meanings. On the other hand, as people do work that is similar or overlapping, their task efficiency decreases, but their communication efficiency increases. He concludes that "efficiencies in communication and coordination can be achieved only by giving up some of the efficiencies in the division of labor" (p. 10).

We may conclude from this that the very act of seeking task efficiency reduces our communication efficiency. The organizational communication system must balance the tendencies toward specialization and task efficiency, toward incoherence and uncertainty produced by forces that divert and make things less orderly, toward too much flexibility, and toward irrelevant retroactive goal setting and rationalization, with those forces and tendencies that lead toward communication efficiency; toward stability, coherence, and lack of change; toward predetermined and inflexible goal setting; and toward fewer alternatives.

SUMMARY

Organizational communication is both the product of and the producer of action; human action is both the product of and the producer of meaning. An understanding of organizational communication is an understanding of both the organizing process and the products that issue from an organization. The structure, rules, expectations, and meanings govern some of the communication activities that take place in an organization; at the same time the communication activities produce, create, and affect the organization. Hence organizational communication is at the heart of the organization; it both affects and is affected by the organization.

The interplay of these forces and activities bring forth what we shall call the *issues* of organizational communication. An issue is a point in question, a point at which a matter is ready for decision. We shall look at some of those points in the next part of this book.

REFERENCES

ARGYRIS, CHRIS, *Personality and Organization*. New York: Harper & Row, Pub., 1957.

BAKKE, E. WIGHT, *Bonds of Organization*. New York: Harper & Row, Pub., 1950.

DANCE, FRANK, E. X., and CARL E. LARSON, *The Functions of Human Communication: A Theoretical Approach*. New York: Holt, Rinehart & Winston, 1976.

DE SOLA POOL, ITHIEL, "Communication Systems," *Handbook of Communication*, eds. Ithiel de Sola Pool and Wilbur Schramm. Skokie, Ill.: Rand McNally, 1973.

FERENCE, T. P., "Organizational Communication Systems and the Decision Process," *Management Science*, 17 (1970), 83–96.

GOLDHABER, GERALD M., *Organizational Communication* (2nd ed.). Dubuque, Iowa: Wm. C. Brown, 1979.

JACKSON, JAY M., "The Organization and Its Communications Problem, *Advanced Management* (February 1959), pp. 17–20.

KATZ, DANIEL, and ROBERT L. KAHN, *The Social Psychology of Organizations*. New York: John Wiley, 1966.

LEE, IRVING J., and LAURA L. LEE, *Handling Barriers in Communication*. New York: Harper & Row, Pub., 1957.

LUTHANS, FRED, *Organizational Behavior*. New York: McGraw-Hill, 1973.

PACANOWSKY, MICHAEL E., "Toward a Communication Theory of Organization." Unpublished paper presented at the annual meetings of the International Communication Association, Chicago, 1978.

POSTMAN, NEIL, and CHARLES WEINGARTNER, *Teaching as a Subversive Activity*. New York: Delacorte Press, 1969.

REDDING, W. CHARLES, *Communication within the Organization: An Interpretive Review of Theory and Research*. New York: Industrial Communication Council, 1972.

REDDING, W. CHARLES, and GEORGE A. SANBORN, *Business and Industrial Communication: A Source Book*. New York: Harper & Row, Pub., 1964.

SMITH, DENNIS R., and L. KEITH WILLIAMSON, *Interpersonal Communication: Roles, Rules, Strategies, and Games*. Dubuque, Iowa: Wm. C. Brown, 1977.

STEIN, JESS, ed., *The Random House Dictionary of the English Language*. New York: Random House, 1966.

THAYER, LEE, *Administrative Communication*. Homewood, Ill.: Richard D. Irwin, 1961.

WEICK, KARL E., *The Social Psychology of Organizing*. Reading, Mass.: Addison-Wesley, 1969.

5

THE
DIRECTIONS
OF
INFORMATION FLOW

what is communicated, to whom,
and how in organizational communication

The direction of something is the line along which it proceeds with regard to a terminating point. In organizational communication we talk about information that proceeds formally from a person of higher authority to one of lower authority —downward communication; information that proceeds from a position of lower authority to one of higher authority—upward communication; information that moves along people and positions of approximately the same level of authority— horizontal communication; or information that moves among people and positions that are neither superior nor subordinate to one another and that are in different functional departments—cross-channel communication. We also refer to information that flows informally along the "grapevine." We shall examine each of these types of directional communication more closely. Figure 5.1 portrays the four formal directions of information flow in an organization. We shall discuss those first.

DOWNWARD COMMUNICATION

Downward communication in an organization means that information flows from positions of higher authority to those of lower authority. We usually think of information moving from management to employees; however, in organizations most of the links are in the management group (Davis, 1967). Figure 5.2 shows how the communication structure of a university has six management levels and only one operative level.

You can see how the emphasis in organizational communication can often move toward managerial communication in which the primary concerns are with downward communication, getting information through the management group and *to* the operative group. There are two important concerns that we shall discuss: (1) what kinds of information are disseminated from management levels to employees and (2) how the information is provided.

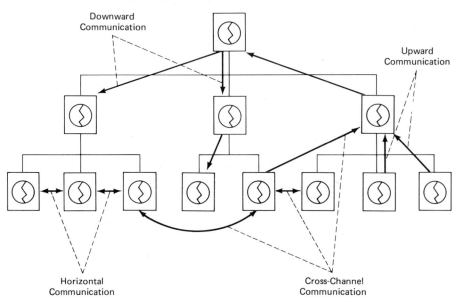

FIGURE 5.1
Four Directions of Organizational Communication

Downward Communication

Upward Communication

Horizontal Communication

Cross-Channel Communication

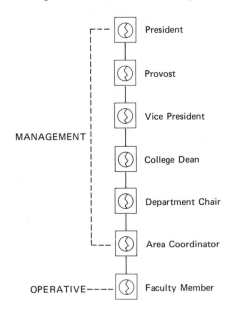

FIGURE 5.2
Organization Chart Showing Six Levels
of Management and One Level of Operative

President

Provost

Vice President

College Dean

Department Chair

MANAGEMENT

Area Coordinator

OPERATIVE — Faculty Member

Kinds of Information Communicated down the Line

Five types of information are usually communicated from superiors to subordinates (Kahn & Katz, 1966): (1) information about how to do a job, (2) information about the rationale for doing jobs, (3) information about organizational policies and practices, (4) information about an employee's performance, and (5) information to develop a sense of mission.

How to do a job. This type of information concerns what employees are expected to do and how they are to do it. Job instructions in the form of orders, directives, explanations, operations manuals, and job descriptions are some of the more common ways of providing this kind of information.

Rationale for doing jobs. This type of information is designed to let employees know how their jobs are related to other tasks and positions in the organization and why they are doing a particular job. In a broader sense this type of information helps employees to recognize how their jobs aid the organization to accomplish its objectives.

Organizational policies and practices. In addition to information about specific job duties and how they fit into the total organization, employees are informed about hours of work, salaries, retirement programs, health benefits, vacation and sick leave, incentive programs, and penalties and punishments. Faculty members, for example, are obligated to attend general university faculty meetings, commencement exercises, and occasionally special convocations and forums. The university also has policies governing grading practices, office hours, research activities, and consulting that must be communicated to employees.

Employee performance. Information about how well things are going is important to the efficient and effective functioning of a system. Information for employees about how well they are doing in their jobs is also extremely important in maintaining a successfully operating organization. Employees frequently complain, however, that they do not know how their supervisors view their performances. Performance appraisal interviews, management-by-objectives, merit reviews, wage and salary administration, performance evaluation or rating programs are all ways of assessing the adequacy of employee job performance. However, the single most difficult task for most supervisors is communicating information about how their subordinates are doing. Informing hard-working employees that their job performance has inadequacies strikes fear in the hearts of even the most fearless supervisors. Negative information tends to reduce motivation and may potentially affect performance negatively, resulting in less effective work than before the appraisal. On the other hand, the performance of some workers is pretty much determined by the system, making individual evaluations of performance meaningless. Assembly-line workers, for example, are often unable to do their jobs more efficiently than the entire line permits.

Mission of the organization. Loyalty to the organization, its products, services, and contributions to society is an important ingredient in organizational strength. One company reported coming to the conclusion that the good it was doing for employees and the country would not be understood unless (1) "its deeds would, in fact, measure up to sound economic analysis; (2) unless it could somehow help its employees understand the rudiments of business economics; and (3) unless

its employees had some sound basis for evaluating the fairness of the countless decisions the company had to make if it was to continue to operate in the balanced best
interests of its employees, its customers, its share owners, its suppliers and distribution associates, and the rest of the public" (Merrihue, 1960, pp. 46–47). Identification with the mission of the organization is the consequence of communicating
information about the broad goals and objectives of the organization and the contributions the organization is making not only to employees but also to society in
general.

Employees at all levels in the organization feel a need to be informed. Top
management lives in an information world. The quality and quantity of information
must be high in order to make meaningful and accurate decisions. Top management
must have information from all units in the organization, and it must get information out to all units. The flow of information from top management down to
operatives is a continuous and difficult activity. The selection of ways to provide
information involves not only the expenditure of direct monetary resources but
also psychic and emotional resources.

How information is provided down the line. The methods by which information is communicated down the line may be grouped into four classes: (1) oral,
(2) written, (3) pictorial, (4) oral-written-pictorial combinations. Before listing a
variety of oral, written and pictorial methods of downward communication, two
issues deserve consideration: (1) what methods seem to be viewed by managers
as most effective in getting the word out and (2) what methods seem to be used
most frequently.

Level (1972) surveyed supervisors and asked them to rate the effectiveness
of different combinations of methods for different types of communication situations (Table 5.1). The four methods were (1) written only, (2) oral only, (3) written followed by oral, and (4) oral followed by written. The oral-followed-by-written
method was rated *most effective* in six of the ten situations and was never rated as
inappropriate for any situation. Situations requiring immediate action but with
some follow-up later, those of a general nature with documentation desired, and
those involving positive interpersonal relations seemed best handled by the oral-
followed-by-written method.

The oral-only method was ranked *most effective* in situations involving reprimands and settling disputes but *least effective* in six other situations, although four
of the six situations were also ranked most effective for the combination oral-
followed-by-written method. This implies that the oral method is desirable but
not by itself.

The written-only method was ranked most effective when information for
future action was needed, when the information was general, and when no personal
contact was necessary. The written-followed-by-oral method was not ranked most
effective or least effective for any situation.

Dahle (1954) studied the actual effectiveness of five methods of transmitting
information from management to employees (downward) in business and industrial
settings. The results of his study are summarized in Table 5.2 and indicate that
using oral and written methods to present information was most effective.

In contrast to the research on effectiveness of different methods of transmitting information to employees, studies of the frequency with which certain
methods are used suggest an upside-down relationship. Peters' (1949, p. 42) early
report indicated that "posters and bulletin boards" were used by 96 percent of the

TABLE 5.1
Most Effective versus Least Effective Methods
for Communicating with Employees in Ten Different Situations (Level, 1972)

SITUATION	MOST EFFECTIVE	LEAST EFFECTIVE
1. Communicating information requiring immediate employee action	Oral followed by written	Written only
2. Communicating information requiring future employee action	Written only	Oral only
3. Communicating information of a general nature	Written only	Oral only
4. Communicating a company directive or order	Oral followed by written	Oral only
5. Communicating information on an important company policy change	Oral followed by written	Oral only
6. Communicating with your immediate supervisor about work progress	Oral followed by written	Oral only
7. Promoting a safety campaign	Oral followed by written	Oral only
8. Commending an employee for noteworthy work	Oral followed by written	Written only
9. Reprimanding an employee for work deficiency	Oral only	Written only
10. Settling a dispute among employees about a work problem	Oral only	Written only

Reprinted by permission of Dale A. Level and the American Business Communication Association, publisher of *The Journal of Business Communication.*

TABLE 5.2
Relative Effectiveness of Five Methods of Transmitting Information
from Management to Employees in Business and Industrial Settings (Dahle, 1954)

RANK ORDER	MOST EFFECTIVE
1	Presenting information in both oral and written forms (*oral and written*)
2	Presenting information to a group orally, using no written materials or visual aids (*oral only*)
3	Presenting information to each member of the group in written form, with no supplementary oral or visual explanation (*written only*)
4	Posting the information on a bulletin board (*bulletin board only*)
5	Making no presentation of the information in either oral or written form (*grapevine only*)

LEAST EFFECTIVE

companies in his survey, whereas only 32 percent used small group meetings. Level and Dahle both discovered that oral and oral accompanied or followed by written methods were most effective. Bulletin boards and written only were both less effective. Although contemporary organizations are usually more sensitive to these issues, there is a strong tendency to use methods that are less costly on the surface and that appear to provide some degree of effectiveness.

Criteria for Selecting Methods

Six criteria are often used for selecting methods of communicating information to employees (Level & Galle, 1980), although a comprehensive theory has not been fully stated (Melcher & Beller, 1967).

1. *Availability.* Those methods that are currently available in the organization will tend to be used. After an inventory of available methods, the organization can decide what methods could be added for an overall more effective program.

2. *Cost.* The method judged to be least costly will tend to be selected for routine and nonurgent information dissemination. When nonroutine and urgent dissemination is necessary or desirable, more costly but faster methods will probably be used.

3. *Impact.* The method that seems to provide the greatest impact or impression will frequently be chosen over a method that lacks flair or is fairly standard.

4. *Relevance.* The method that seems most relevant to the purpose to be achieved will be chosen more often. A short, informative purpose may be accomplished with a conversation followed by a memo. If the communication of complex details is the purpose, a written technical report may be the method chosen.

5. *Response.* The method selected will be influenced by whether a specific response to the information is desired or necessary. In a training setting it may be desirable to use a method that allows and encourages trainees to react and ask questions. In such a case a face-to-face meeting would probably be the method chosen.

6. *Skills.* The methods that seem to fit the abilities of the sender to actually use and the abilities of the receiver to comprehend will tend to be used over those that seem beyond the skills of the communicator or that seem beyond the capabilities of the employee to understand. A glossy brochure will probably not be used if the communicator does not feel capable of producing it; if the employees' level of education is limited, a complex manual of instructions would probably not be a good method to use.

A SHORT INVENTORY OF COMMUNICATION METHODS

Methods of communicating in organizations are described in detail in other books and articles (Brown & Reid, 1979; Hunt, 1980; Level & Galle, 1980; Peters, 1949; Reuss & Silvis, 1981; Rosenblatt, Cheatham, & Watt, 1977; Sigband & Bateman,

1979). We shall simply provide an inventory of methods that may trigger some alternative ideas when considering what communication methods to use.

Oral Methods

Employee meetings
   Large group, mass, or informational
   Small discussion groups or task
   Social meetings
Collective bargaining
Grievance interviews
Labor-management committees (outside of collective bargaining)
Public address systems
Counseling interviews
Company chaplains
Radio programs
Phonograph recordings
The grapevine
Telephone
Intercom system
Paging system
Closed-circuit television
Speeches and oral reports
Conferences
Teleconferences
Briefings
Lectures and training workshops
Videotape presentations
Daily interpersonal contacts
Recognition and special award activities
Supervisor's home visits
Family night
Luncheons with selected employees
Unstructured visits to the shop and office
Audio tape recordings

Written Methods

Letters
Memos and reports
Facsimile reproductions
Teletype
Telegrams
Electronic longhand
Newspapers
Magazines
Handbooks

Manuals
Bulletins
Inserts and enclosures
House organ?
Daily news digest
Individualized benefits reports
Annual financial report
Magapapers
Progress reports
Directory of employees
Anniversary books
Booklets
Job descriptions
Policy manuals
Announcement flyers
Postcards to employees
Paycheck stub messages
Research and development brochures
Industry books
Tour booklets

Pictorial Methods

Ad reprints
Calenders
Sample product kits
Billboards
Corporate art exhibits
Films
Slide presentations
Puzzles and quizzes
Picture books
Photographs
Exhibits and displays
Graphics
Logo and trademarks
Charts and graphs
Posters
Cartoons and comic strips
Visits to the plant

The design, development, creation, display, and use of various methods has become highly specialized. At many universities and colleges, programs in design, advertising, marketing, journalism, public relations, film, video, and instructional media are dedicated to making the methods of communication more exciting and effective. The ability to recognize and select appropriate methods for enhancing human resource development is important for individuals in organizational communication interested in careers in HRD. Individually and in combination, these methods help get information down the line.

UPWARD COMMUNICATION

Upward communication in an organization means that information flows from lower levels (subordinates) to higher levels (supervisors). All employees in an organization, except possibly those at the top level, may communicate upward—that is, any subordinate may have good reason to either request information from or give information to someone with more authority than he or she has. A request or comment directed toward an individual with broader, higher, or more extensive authority is the essence of upward communication.

Values of Upward Communication

Upward communication is important for a number of reasons. We shall list a few functions, values, and arguments for up-the-line communication.

1. The upward flow of information supplies valuable information for decision making by those who direct the organization and supervise the activities of others (Sharma, 1979).
2. Upward communication lets supervisors know when their subordinates are ready for information from them and how well subordinates accept what they have been told (Planty & Machaver, 1952).
3. Upward communication allows, even encourages, gripes and grievances to surface and lets supervisors know what is bothering those who are closer to the actual operations (Conboy, 1976).
4. Upward communication cultivates appreciation and loyalty to the organization by giving employees an opportunity to ask questions and contribute ideas and suggestions about the operation of the organization (Planty & Machaver, 1952).
5. Upward communication permits supervisors to determine whether subordinates got the meaning that was intended from the downward flow of information (Planty & Machaver, 1952).
6. Upward communication helps employees cope with their work problems and strengthen their involvement in their jobs and with the organization (Harriman, 1974).

What Should Be Communicated up the Line?

Most analyses and research on upward communication suggest that supervisors and managers ought to get information from subordinates that

1. Tells what the subordinates are doing—their work, achievements, progress, and plans for the future.

2. Describes unsolved work problems on which subordinates may need or would like some type of assistance.
3. Offers suggestions or ideas for improvements within their unit or the organization as a whole.
4. Reveals how subordinates think and feel about their jobs, their coworkers, and the organization.

Figure 5.3 summarizes some of the information that supervisors and managers ought to learn about subordinates through upward communication.

FIGURE 5.3
What Supervisors Should Learn through Upward Communication
(Planty & Machaver, 1952)

What Employees Feel about Their Jobs

1. How satisfied are employees with their pay in relation to other jobs in the organization, similar jobs in the industry and community?
2. Are working hours and shift rotations felt to be reasonable?
3. Is the work load fairly distributed?
4. Are the tools, equipment, and office furniture of good quality and adequate?
5. Are the formal standards for personal appearance well known and accepted?
6. Do subordinates believe that supervisors observe the rules and regulations that they are expected to follow?
7. Do subordinates feel that all possible candidates for promotion from within are given full and honest consideration?
8. Do employees feel that people are laid off or discharged unreasonably?
9. Do employees feel that the company is willing to discuss policies, plans, and actions that affect their jobs?
10. Do employees feel that supervisors are interested in helping with personal or family problems that may affect attitudes at work?

What Employees Feel about Coworkers

1. Do employees feel that their coworkers, supervisors, subordinates, department, and company are efficient?
2. Do employees feel that supervisors have favorites?
3. Do employees feel that they are adequately supervised?
4. Do subordinates feel that they are being trained and developed to advance in the organization.
5. Do employees feel that supervisors and managers resist new ideas of subordinates without evaluating their worth?
6. Are grievances handled promptly and fairly?
7. Do employees feel that supervisors and managers understand their needs and desires?
8. How do subordinates get along with their coworkers?

FIGURE 5.3 (cont.).

What Employees Feel about the Organization

1. Does the organization's actions live up to its promises and expressed policies as an employer?
2. Is the organization financially strong?
3. Are organization managers able to maintain its competitive position?
4. What is the organization's reputation in the community?
5. What do employees' families think of the employees' jobs and opportunities in the organization?
6. Do employees feel they know far enough in advance about serious changes so they can adjust to them?
7. Do employees feel that equal pay is given for equal work?
8. Do employees know and accept personnel practices regarding illness, leave of absence, vacation, leave, and so forth?
9. Do employees believe that the health, insurance, and retirement programs are fair and adequate?
10. Do employees feel that the recreational and educational or training facilities are adequate and available?
11. Do employees understand the annual report?
12. Do employees consider lunch and snack food prices to be fair and the food to be of high quality?

Why Is It Difficult to Get Information up the Line?

Merrihue (1960) observed that "it would have been wiser to have first bulldozed and paved an uphill street from employees to top management, but that is a much more complex and time-consuming task and most of us are not quite sure that we, as yet, know how to do it" (p. 195). Harriman (1974) reported that "we surveyed hundreds of companies in the United States and Canada. . . . We encountered no experts, studies or programs on upward communications" (pp. 148-149). They may be right. Upward communication may be too complex and too time-consuming and have too few organization managers who know how to get information up the line.

The difficulty of getting information up the line was alluded to by Davis (1967) when he noted that a manager's "status and prestige at the plant are different from the workers'. He probably talks differently and dresses differently. He can freely call a worker to his desk or walk to his work station, but the worker is not equally free to call in his manager. The worker usually lacks ability to express himself as clearly as the manager, who is better trained and has more practice in communication skills. Neither can the worker have a specialist prepare his communication, but this service is usually available to the manager. Just as the worker lacks technical assistance, he also usually lacks the use of certain media, such as plant magazines, public-address systems, and meetings. The worker is further impeded because he is talking to a man with whose work and responsibilities he is not familiar" (p. 344).

Sharma (1979) lists four reasons why upward communication seems so difficult:

1. *The tendency for employees to conceal their thoughts.* Studies have shown, for example, that employees feel that they will get into trouble if they speak up to their supervisors and that the best way to move up in the organization is to agree with your superiors.
2. *The feeling that supervisors and managers are not interested in employee problems.* Employees report quite frequently that their managers are not concerned about their problems. Managers may not respond to employee problems and may even stifle some upward communication because it might make them look bad to their superiors.
3. *A lack of rewards for employee upward communication.* Frequently supervisors and managers fail to provide either intangible or tangible rewards for maintaining open upward communication channels.
4. *The feeling that supervisors and managers are inaccessible and unresponsive to what employees say.* Either supervisors are too busy to listen or the subordinate cannot find them. If the supervisor is located, he or she is unresponsive to what the subordinate says.

The combination of these four feelings and beliefs creates a powerful deterrent to the expression of ideas, opinions, and information by subordinates, especially if the process and procedures by which upward communication is to occur are unwieldly and cumbersome.

How Can Information Get up the Line?

Jackson (1959) noted that the forces that direct communication in an organization are, on the whole, motivational. Employees tend to communicate in order to accomplish some goal, to satisfy some personal need, or to try to improve their immediate circumstances. He suggests that any program of organizational communication must be based on a climate of trust. When trust exists, employees are more likely to communicate ideas and feelings more freely, and supervisors are more likely to interpret what employees mean more accurately.

The importance of creating and maintaining a climate of trust cannot be stated too frequently. Upward communication just will not occur when supervisors feel that they must guard against employees talking to the manager above them. Rogers and Agarwala-Rogers (1976) describe an effort by a large Eastern bank to stimulate upward communication with a "sound-off" program. Employees were encouraged to take their complaints and suggestions to the personnel department or to managers above their supervisors if they did not receive satisfaction from their immediate supervisors. It was discovered that supervisors felt that any contact between their subordinates and the supervisor's boss was threatening and improper. Employees did not think it was improper, but they did feel that it was dangerous. As one employee said, "You bypass the supervisor once and go to Personnel, the first thing they do is get the supervisor on the phone and tell him everything.

Next, you're in trouble" (p. 98). Wendlinger (1973) discovered a similar situation in a large West Coast bank. He reported "that there was no way to confidently express an opinion or solve a problem when normal channels had broken down. Some employees feared the possibility of reprisals as a result of bypassing their supervisors with such ideas or proposals, and others were concerned that management—seemingly remote in a rapidly growing organization—was not really interested in their attitudes and opinions" (p. 17).

To facilitate upward communication Wendlinger's organization created an "Open Line" program in which employees were able to submit problems, complaints, or opinions to top management with their identities being kept completely confidential, known only to the Open Line coordinator, with a guaranteed candid written reply from management which was sent to the employee's home. The success of the program was attributed to those two factors: the employee's identity was protected, and the answers were honest. The coordinator of Open Line was given one mission: to work yourself out of a job, which means arriving at a time when free and open communication precludes the need for Open Line, where mutual trust and understanding make upward communication an easy job.

Principles of Upward Communication

Planty and Machaver (1952) identified seven principles to guide programs of upward communication. The principles seem as applicable today as when they were formulated.

1. *An effective upward communication program must be planned.* Although confidentiality and candor undergird all effective upward communication programs, supervisors and managers must stimulate, encourage, and find ways to promote upward communication.

2. *An effective upward communication program operates continuously.* Subordinates must initiate information to and request information from higher levels regardless of how things are going. Supervisors and managers must be receptive to information from subordinates and be willing to respond to what they receive when the organization is functioning smoothly as well as when things seem to be going badly.

3. *An effective upward communication program uses the routine channels.* Without denying any employee the opportunity of making contact with and being heard by managers at any level, information should flow upward through the organization following the usual, routine steps. Problems and requests for information should move upward through the organization until they reach the person who can take action; if that person can provide the information or resolve the problem, there should be little need to go beyond that point.

4. *An effective upward communication program stresses sensitivity and receptivity in entertaining ideas from lower levels.* Differences in interpretations and perceptions of events should be expected. A person's position in the organization encourages him or her to see things differently and to assign different meanings to them. Differences in values and priorities lead to differences in inferences and

conclusions. Listening in order to understand what a person means is basic to effective upward communication.

5. *An effective upward communication program involves objective listening.* Supervisors and managers must devote the time to listening to subordinates in an objective way. Reactions that distract from the seriousness of information and irritating listening habits show that upward communication is not really desired. Hearing a subordinate out, putting him or her at ease, and reducing tensions reveals a receptive intent and a willingness to hear contrary opinions, implied criticisms, and alternative points of view.

6. *An effective upward communication program involves taking action to respond to problems.* Active listening may get new ideas into the open, but a failure to take action only creates resentment and undermines the good faith in upward communication. When changes in policies or actions should be made, just listening without adjustments denies the idea of effective upward communication. If action cannot be taken, the subordinate should be informed and reasons given for why changes cannot be made.

7. *An effective upward communication program uses a variety of media and methods to promote the flow of information.* The most effective method of upward communication is daily face-to-face contacts and conversations among supervisors and subordinates. Beyond continuing interpersonal interaction within the organization and outside the workplace, the following may serve as a checklist of upward communication methods:

> Suggestion systems ("Speak Up," "Sound Off," "Open Line")
> Grievance procedures
> Attitude and information surveys
> Counseling interviews
> Rumor clinics
> Question boxes
> Employee round tables
> Manager's luncheons
> Performance appraisals
> Dial-the-Boss telephone system
> Employee letters
> Organization development activities
> Human resource development and training
> Reports and memos
> Union publications
> Grapevine

In summary, this section has reviewed the values of upward communication in an organization, discussed what kinds of information should be communicated up the line, analyzed why it is difficult to get information from lower levels to higher levels in an organization, described the climate that seems most conducive to getting information to flow upward, and listed seven principles of an effective program of upward communication.

Two directions of information flow have been considered—downward and upward. Together they constitute what is often called *vertical communication*. Information is also shared among organization members who occupy positions of approximately the same level of authority; we refer to it as *horizontal communication*.

HORIZONTAL COMMUNICATION

Horizontal communication consists of sharing information among peers within the same work unit. A *work unit* is comprised of individuals who are located at the same authority level in the organization and have the same superior. Thus at a university, a work unit may be a department. A department of communication, a department of organizational behavior, and a department of instructional science all include faculty members who are supervised by a chairperson. Communication among faculty members in one of the departments is what we call *horizontal communication*. Communication between faculty members in one department and faculty members in another department is what we shall call *cross-channel communication*—that is, information is shared across functional boundaries, or work units, and among people who are neither subordinate nor superior to one another.

Purposes of Horizontal Communication

Research and experience suggest that horizontal communication occurs for at least six reasons:

1. *To coordinate work assignments.* Members of a training and development department have a major training activity to organize and deliver. They need to meet to coordinate who will do what.

2. *To share information on plans and activities.* When ideas from several minds promise to be better than ideas from just one person, horizontal communication becomes critical. In creating the design of a training program or a public relations campaign, members of a department may need to share information on their plans and what they will be doing.

3. *To solve problems.* Recently three student interns were given assignments in the same general location. They met and engaged in horizontal communication in order to reduce the number of unnecessary trips and share rides. They were able to reduce costs and to work together to arrive at their organization assignments with fewer problems.

4. *To secure common understanding.* When changes are proposed in the requirements for an academic major, faculty must work together in order to produce a common understanding about what changes should be made. Meetings and conversations among faculty members at the same organizational level and within the same department are especially important in achieving understanding.

5. *To conciliate, negotiate, and arbitrate differences.* Individuals frequently develop preferences and priorities that eventually lead to disagreements. When this

occurs, horizontal communication among members of the work unit is essential to conciliating differences. In fact, some differences may need to be negotiated or arbitrated. It is only through horizontal communication that priorities can be accommodated and conflicts resolved.

6. _To develop interpersonal support._ Because we spend a great deal of time interacting with others on the job, we all derive some degree of interpersonal support from our colleagues. Much of our horizontal communication is for the purpose of strengthening interpersonal ties and relationships. Coworkers often have lunch together and meet at breaks to strengthen interpersonal relationships. Horizontal communication plays an important part in producing rapport among employees and encouraging a cohesive work unit. Employees at the same level who interact frequently seem to have less trouble understanding one another. Interaction among colleagues provides emotional and psychological support.

Methods of Horizontal Communication

The most common forms of horizontal communication involve some type of interpersonal contact. Even written forms of horizontal communication tend to be more casual. Thus horizontal communication occurs most often in these ways:

1. _Committee meetings._ Most coordination, sharing of information, conciliating, and problem solving takes place in meetings.

2. _Informal interaction during breaks._ Members of work units may often work individually and in somewhat isolated settings, but during breaks and at lunch time they have an opportunity to engage in horizontal communication. Faculty, for example, regularly talk in the hallway between their offices when they do not have appointments or classes.

3. _Telephone conversations._ A great deal of information is shared among employees over the telephone. Work activities are coordinated as well as some differences negotiated by means of telephone conversations. In fact, the telephone probably speeds up and increases the number of contacts with other members of the organization, especially when they are located at the end of another hallway or on the other side of the building.

4. _Memos and notes._ Handwritten or typed notes and memos are some of the most common ways of keeping in touch with coworkers. Although a subordinate may feel inhibited in sending his or her supervisor a handwritten note about a work problem, it would not be uncommon or unexpected to leave a note for a colleague.

5. _Social activities._ Bowling teams and groupings at picnics are often made up of individuals who are at the same level in the organization. Much horizontal communication occurs when coworkers gather for social activities.

6. _Quality circles._ A quality circle is a voluntary group of workers who have shared areas of responsibility. It is primarily a normal work group who produce a part of a product or service. Members of the circle meet together each week to discuss, analyze, and suggest ideas for improving their work. They are trained in the use of specific problem-solving procedures and specific techniques, such as cause-and-effect diagrams, pareto diagrams, histograms, checklists, and graphs. Circle leaders are trained in leadership skills, adult learning methods, and moti-

vation and communication techniques. Circle meetings are held on organization time and on organization premises. Quality circles are generally given full responsibility for identifying and solving problems (Yager, 1980).

Barriers to Horizontal Communication

Barriers to horizontal communication have much in common with those affecting upward and downward communication. Lack of trust among coworkers, intense concerns about upward mobility, and competition for resources can affect the way in which employees at the same level in the organization communicate with one another.

CROSS-CHANNEL COMMUNICATION

In most organizations a need exists for employees to share information across functional boundaries with individuals who occupy positions that are neither subordinate nor superior to their own. For example, departments such as engineering, research, accounting, and personnel gather data, issue reports, prepare plans, coordinate activities, and advise managers about the work of individuals in all parts of an organization. They cross functional lines and communicate with people who supervise and are supervised but who are neither superior nor subordinate to them. They lack line authority to direct those with whom they communicate and must rely primarily on selling their ideas. Nevertheless, they have considerable mobility within the organization; they can visit other areas or leave their offices just to engage in informal conversation (Davis, 1967).

Staff specialists are usually the most active in cross-channel communication because their responsibilities usually influence what occurs in several authority chains of command or positional networks. The training and development unit, for example, may have contacts with production, sales, industrial relations, purchasing, research, and engineering as well as with customers, for customer training. Staff specialists frequently have closer contact with top management which permits them to short-circuit the authoritative system. Davis (1967) rightly observes that "the results are both good and bad. Communication upward and downward tends to be improved, but lower management often waits in insecurity with the fear that it is being bypassed or criticized without an opportunity to answer" (p. 346).

Because of the potentially large number of cross-channel contacts by staff specialists and others who need to make contacts in other chains-of-command, it is important to have an organization policy to guide cross-channel communication. Fayol (1916/1940) demonstrated that cross-channel communication was appropriate, and even necessary at times, especially for employees who were lower in a channel. As shown in Figure 5.4, Employee P may save time and conserve resources by communicating directly with Employee Y. Because of the potential for undermining the authority channels and for losing control over the flow of information, two conditions must be met as part of using Fayol's Bridge:

1. Each employee who wishes to communicate across channels must secure permission *in advance* from his or her direct supervisor (in Figure 5.4, P

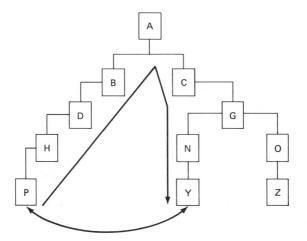

FIGURE 5.4
Fayol's Bridge for Employee P

would secure permission from Supervisor H). In some cases the permission may be granted in the form of a general policy statement indicating the circumstances that justify cross-channel communication.

2. Each employee who engages in cross-channel communication must inform his or her supervisor what happened as a result of the meeting.

The importance of cross-channel communication in organizations prompted Davis (1967) to suggest that the application of three principles would strengthen the communication role of staff specialists:

1. Staff specialists must be trained in communication skills.
2. Staff specialists need to recognize the importance of their communication role.
3. Management should recognize the role of staff specialists and make greater use of it in organizational communication.

Both horizontal and cross-channel communication involve lateral relationships that are essential to effective organizational communication. In this section we have focused primarily on *positional communication,* which involves the flow of information between people in positions in an organization. Employees often communicate from their positions. Frequently, however, organization members communicate with others without regard to their positions. This results in one or more *personal communication networks.* Positional communication is usually referred to as *formal communication;* personal communication is usually called *informal communication.* We shall briefly analyze the idea of personal or informal communication in an organization.

INFORMAL, PERSONAL,
OR GRAPEVINE COMMUNICATION

When employees communicate with one another without regard to position in the organization, the factors directing the flow of information are more personal. The direction of information flow is less stable. Information flows upward, downward, horizontally, and across channels with little, if any, regard for designated positional relationships. Since this informal, personal information emerges from interaction between people, it appears to flow in unpredictable directions, and its network is referred to as a *grapevine*. The metaphor seems apt; a grapevine seems to grow and send out shoots in all directions, capturing and hiding the fruit under a cover of heavy leaves, almost defying detection. Information that flows along the grapevine network, appears to be fickle and furtive as well. In terms of communication the grapevine has been described as "a person-to-person method of relaying secret reports which cannot be obtained through regular channels" (Stein, 1967, p. 616). Informal communication does tend to consist of "secret" reports about people and events that do not flow through official, formal channels. Information obtained through the grapevine concerns "what someone said or heard" rather than what was announced by authorities. At least the sources seem to be "secret" even if the information itself is not.

Characteristics of the Grapevine

Although research on characteristics of the grapevine is not extensive, enough has been completed over the years to suggest the following characteristics (Davis & O'Connor, 1977):

1. The grapevine functions largely through word-of-mouth interaction.
2. The grapevine is generally free of organizational and positional restraints.
3. The grapevine moves information rapidly.
4. The grapevine network is described as a *cluster chain* because each relayor tends to tell a cluster of people rather than just one other person.
5. Participants in a grapevine network tend to take one of three roles: liaisons, isolates, or dead-enders (those who usually do not pass the information on).
6. The grapevine tends to be more a product of the situation than of the people in the organization.
7. The sooner a person knows about an event after it happens, the more likely he or she is to tell others.
8. If information being told to a person concerns something in which he or she is interested, he or she is more likely to tell the information to others.
9. The predominant flow of information on the grapevine tends to occur within functional groups rather than between them.
10. Generally from 75 to 90 percent of the details of the message being transmitted by the grapevine are accurate; however, as Davis (1967) notes, "People tend to think the grapevine is less accurate than it really is because its errors

are more dramatic and consequently more impressed on memory than its day-to-day routine accuracy. Moreover, the inaccurate parts are often more important" (p. 244).

11. Grapevine information is usually somewhat incomplete, lending itself to misinterpretation even when the details are accurate.

12. The grapevine tends to exert some influence in the organization, whether for good or evil; thus an understanding of the grapevine and how it can contribute positively to the organization is important.

How to Work with the Grapevine

The number and detrimental effects of messages passed along the grapevine can be controlled by keeping the formal channels of communication open, allowing for candid, accurate, and sensitive upward, downward, horizontal, and cross-channel communication. Effective supervisor-subordinate relationships seem crucial to controlling grapevine information. Supervisors and managers should let employees know that they understand and accept information on the grapevine, especially since it reveals something about employee feelings, even if the information is incomplete and untrue.

SUMMARY

In summary, information flows in four formal directions in organizations: downward, upward, horizontally, and through cross-channels. The formal directions involve positional communication. However, organization members often communicate with one another without regard to their positions, resulting in a personal communication network. The personal communication system is often referred to as the *grapevine* and transmits informal or "secret" messages or information that does not flow through formal channels. Because the information on the grapevine is usually quite accurate but often incomplete, it may exert a powerful influence on those who are part of the system. Thus it is important for supervisors and managers to understand and help the grapevine benefit the organization.

REFERENCES

BROWN, HARRY M., and KAREN K. REID, *Business Writing and Communication.* New York: Longman, 1979.

CONBOY, WILLIAM A., *Working Together . . . Communication in a Healthy Organization.* Columbus, Ohio: Chas. E. Merrill, 1976.

DAHLE, THOMAS L., "An Objective and Comparative Study of Five Methods of Transmitting Information from Management to Business and Industrial Employees," *Speech Monographs,* 21 (March 1954), 21–28.

DAVIS, KEITH, *Human Relations at Work: The Dynamics of Organizational Behavior.* New York: McGraw-Hill, 1967.

DAVIS, WILLIAM L., and J. REGIS O'CONNOR, "Serial Transmission of Information: A Study of the Grapevine," *Journal of Applied Communication,* 5 (1977), 61–72.

FAYOL, HENRI, *General and Industrial Management,* trans. Constance Storrs. New York: Pitman Publishing Corporation, 1940. (Originally published in 1916).

HARRIMAN, BRUCE, "Up and Down the Communications Ladder," *Harvard Business Review* (September–October 1974), pp. 143–151.

HUNT, GARY T., *Communication Skills in the Organization.* Englewood Cliffs, N.J.: Prentice-Hall, 1980.

JACKSON, JAY M., "The Organization and Its Communications Problem," *Advanced Management* (February 1959), pp. 17–20.

KATZ, DANIEL, and ROBERT KAHN, *The Social Psychology of Organizations.* New York: John Wiley, 1966.

LEVEL, DALE A., JR., "Communication Effectiveness: Method and Situation," *The Journal of Business Communication,* 10 (Fall 1972), 19–25.

LEVEL, DALE A., JR., and WILLIAM P. GALLE, JR., *Business Communications: Theory and Practice.* Dallas: Business Publications, Inc., 1980.

MELCHER, ARLYN J., and RONALD BELLER, "Toward a Theory of Organization Communication: Considerations in Channel Selection," *Academy of Management Journal,* 10 (March 1967), 39–52.

MERRIHUE, WILLARD V., *Managing by Communication.* New York: McGraw-Hill, 1960.

PETERS, RAYMOND W., *Communication within Industry.* New York: Harper & Brothers, 1949.

PLANTY, EARL, and WILLIAM MACHAVER, "Upward Communications: A Project in Executive Development," *Personnel,* 28 (January 1952), 304–318.

REUSS, CAROL, and DONN SILVIS, eds., *Inside Organization Communication.* New York: Longman, 1981.

ROGERS, EVERETT M., and REKHA AGARWALA-ROGERS, *Communication in Organizations.* New York: The Free Press, 1976.

ROSENBLATT, S. BERNARD, T. RICHARD CHEATHAM, and JAMES T. WATT, *Communication in Business.* Englewood Cliffs, N.J.: Prentice-Hall, 1977.

SHARMA, JITENDRA M., "Organizational Communications: A Linking Process," *The Personnel Administrator,* 24 (July 1979), 35–43.

SIGBAND, NORMAN B., and DAVID N. BATEMAN, *Communicating in Business.* Glenview, Ill.: Scott, Foresman, 1981.

STEIN, JESS, ed., *The Random House Dictionary of the English Language.* New York: Random House, 1967.

WENDLINGER, ROBERT M., "Improving Upward Communication," *Journal of Business Communication,* 11 (Summer 1973), 17–23.

YAGER, ED, "Quality Circle: A Tool for the '80s," *Training and Development Journal* (August 1980), pp. 60–62.

6

ORGANIZATIONAL COMMUNICATION COST ANALYSIS

The analysis of what makes communication and people effective in organizations is critical, so much so that the bulk of our time is spent pondering that issue, even in this book. We must remember, however, as Thayer pointed out, that "there is always some kind of investment or expenditure whenever communication occurs" (1968, p. 154). Communicating in an organization costs. Vardaman, Halterman, and Vardaman (1970) analyzed the costs associated with written communication in an organization and concluded that "if an organization can markedly improve the handling of its written communications, it can go a long way in cutting unnecessary administrative operational costs, as well as significantly decreasing the costs of the documents themselves" (p. 1). The first step in managing communication costs, of course, is to recognize the places where costs occur. The purpose of this chapter is to describe some general perspectives and point out some useful ideas concerning the kinds of costs associated with communicating in an organization. In some areas, such as dictation (Rogers, 1979) and publications (Griese, 1978), measures of specific costs have been calculated; however, for most kinds of communicating we have little information about actual costs. Nevertheless, an awareness of potential costs of communicating may make us more sensitive to the likelihood of enormous expenditures. Hopefully our ultimate goal will be to communicate with efficiency (cost-effective) and to aid others to improve the efficiency with which communication occurs in their organizations.

DEFINITION OF COST

The cost of something is the price one pays to accomplish, acquire, or maintain it. The cost of communicating is related to what a person expends to carry out a task. Expenditures may be in various forms, including actual money or mental energy. In general we think of costs as the loss experienced in producing some-

60

thing. Hence in communicating, the costs are represented by the places where losses are experienced. The efficiency of a communication act is the ratio between how well it accomplishes a desired result and what expenditures are required to carry out the act. In other words, an efficient communication act is one that experiences little loss (as represented by expenditures of time, energy, resources) yet produces a highly desirable result. We can portray relationships among effectiveness, cost, and efficiency in the following diagram:

$$\text{EFFICIENCY} = \frac{\text{Effectiveness}}{\text{Cost}} \quad \begin{aligned} &= \text{desirable consequences} \\ &= \text{expenditures of time,} \\ &\quad \text{energy, resources} \end{aligned}$$

We can evaluate an organizational communication system in terms of the cost required to achieve a particular level of effectiveness and arrive at an index of efficiency. The index of efficiency ought to be foremost in our minds as we analyze the status and quality of any act or system of communication.

TYPES OF COSTS

One way of looking at costs is in terms of direct or financial loss, psychological expenditures, and loss in job performance (Vardaman et al., 1970). On the other hand, costs can be examined in terms of whether they relate to the individual involved, the message itself, the channels involved, the media used, or the total system (Thayer, 1968). For purposes of this analysis we shall lean heavily upon the first system but modify the categories to accommodate as wide a spectrum of communication forms and formats as possible, not just written communication. Thus we can think of three types of costs: physical resource expenditures, human resource expenditures, and production losses. We shall discuss each of these major types of costs in more detail.

Expenditures of Physical Resources

When we expend or lose physical resources, we usually see a fairly direct monetary loss, although some types of direct costs may be more difficult to measure. Thinking about the phrasing of a message takes time, which represents direct labor costs, but determining when you started to think about the message and when you stopped and whether the time was spent exclusively on thinking about the message, may be more difficult to specify than the expenditure of other types of resources. Nevertheless, an inventory of different types of physical resource expenditures may be useful. Let us look at four categories of physical resources: buildings, equipment, supplies, and labor.

BUILDINGS

Although the entire physical plant of an organization contributes to communication, some places are more communication-prone than others. Offices, for example, serve a primary communication function. The locations of some offices cost more because they are closer or farther away from central business operations. The furnishings of some offices are more expensive than others. The size of some offices is larger than others. In general the cost of an office varies with the position in the organization. Positions of higher status tend to have more expensive offices associated with them. Some offices cost more because they require more security. Secretarial spaces, exit and entrance doors, alarm systems, and corridors are often provided to enhance the security and protect the communication process and communicators from invasion or interruptions. Rooms where confidential conversations occur may cost considerably more than those where nonconfidential communication occurs. Some portion of all buildings—including offices, work rooms, and storage areas—is devoted to communication activities and represents a cost of communicating.

COMMUNICATION EQUIPMENT

A great deal of equipment in an organization has been designed and is used exclusively for communicating. Typewriters, dictating and transcribing machines, copiers, telephones, tape and video recorders, computers, calculators, and printing machinery are examples of *communication technology*. Filing cabinets, tapes, discs, desks, and storage shelves are all types of equipment used to maintain and keep messages. Television sets and teletype machines, monitors, and consoles are other types of equipment used to display messages. One of the major direct costs of contemporary organizations is the investment in communication equipment.

SUPPLIES

Even with the vast array of communication equipment available, often little can be done without the accompanying supplies. Paper, ink, fluids, punch cards, spirit masters, mag cards, pens, pencils, note pads, staples, paper clips, rubber bands, postage, and telephone services are usually referred to as *supplies and expenses*. Although some supplies may be exceptional, nearly everything listed is part of the expense of communicating.

LABOR

We usually think of communication labor costs as those involved in thinking up a message, putting the message into some proper form, distributing the message to appropriate members of the organization, and receiving, processing, and responding to messages. These costs are usually associated with the originators of messages and the receiver-interpreters of messages.

Originator Costs

Originators tend to engage in four types of activities that are associated with costs: thinking, composing, transcribing, and presenting.

Thinking

Some time is spent in just thinking about messages prior to composing them. Frequently the amount of time spent mentally reviewing ideas and alternatives is greater than the amount of time taken to write out the message.

Composing

Putting the message into some form—a speech outline, an essay, or report—also takes a great deal of time. I compose all papers, manuscripts, reports, and other written materials at a typewriter. Some people write longhand whereas others speak into a dictating machine. Rogers (1979) contends that a manager can save a considerable amount of time and money by using machine dictation rather than writing longhand or dictating to a secretary. She claims that paperwork production costs can be reduced 50 to 75 percent. She cites the figures in Table 6.1 to support her analysis. The average speed for writing in longhand is about 15 words per minute. The average speed for dictating to a secretary is about 30 words per minute. The average speed for composing using dictation equipment is about 60 words per minute. Thus a manager making $40,000 a year who spends 10 hours a week handwriting paperwork costs the organization about $9,994 each year. The same manager using dictation equipment could process paperwork four times faster, making the annual cost to the organization $2,498. Thus a single manager using dictating equipment could save the organization $7,496 in a year. There is little doubt that the costs of composing messages are a real, direct expenditure in time and salaries to an organization.

Transcribing

Transcribing refers to the process of making a copy of materials in a medium other than that in which it was originally composed. To transcribe may involve making a recording of a program, making a written or typewritten copy of orally dictated materials, or translating notes from a lecture into a manuscript. This process of reproducing a message from one form or medium into another involves considerable expense for most organizations. Rogers (1979) also calculated the cost of transcribing materials in an organization. She reported the figures and analysis in Table 6.2. The average speed at which a secretary can transcribe from handwritten copy is about 15 words per minute. The average speed at which one can

TABLE 6.1
Costs of Composing

A MANAGER'S ANNUAL SALARY OF	MAKES EVERY HOUR WORTH	AND RESULTS IN A YEARLY COST OF
$20,000	$10.25	$2,501
$25,000	$12.81	$3,126
$30,000	$15.37	$3,750
$35,000	$17.92	$4,372
$40,000	$20.48	$4,997
$50,000	$25.60	$6,246

TABLE 6.2
Costs of Transcribing

A TRANSCRIBER'S ANNUAL SALARY OF	MAKES EVERY HOUR WORTH	AND RESULTS IN A YEARLY COST OF
$10,000	$5.12	$1,250
$15,000	$7.68	$1,873

transcribe from shorthand notes is about 45 words per minute, but the average speed at which transcriptions can be made from recorded dictation is 75 words per minute. These figures show that a $15,000-a-year secretary who spends 10 hours per week transcribing handwritten drafts costs the organization $3,840 per year. The same secretary can handle the same amount of textual materials from dictation equipment nearly five times as fast, making the annual cost about $768. Thus an annual savings of $3,072 would occur just in transcribing. As you can tell, there are real costs in money involved in communicating, but there are ways of reducing costs when we are aware and working on the problem.

Presenting

Several different kinds of expenditures are considered under the category of presenting messages. The time involved in conducting meetings, giving speeches, appearing on television programs, and engaging in conversations all constitute direct costs. In addition the costs of producing written materials are part of the presentational costs of communicating. Griese (1978) reported data on the costs of producing company magazines, magapapers, newspapers, and newsletters. See Table 6.3. The figures are based purely on costs of production and exclude mailing expenses and salaries of editorial staffs. Griese cautions us that these figures may not be representative of all company publications in the categories cited, but they do suggest that communicating does constitute a major cost to organizations.

Receiver-Interpreter Costs

Receiver-Interpreters accrue similar communicating costs to those of originators of messages. We shall briefly examine four costs: receiving the message, understanding it, thinking about it, acting upon the message.

TABLE 6.3
Costs of Producing Written Materials

TYPE OF PUBLICATION	MEAN COST PER THOUSAND
All magazines	$568.06
Award-winning magazines	$413.04
Magapapers	$344.01
Newspapers	$290.23
Newsletters	$166.19

Receiving. The *reception* of a message refers to getting it physically. For a written message, reception may begin with the internal mail service and its delivery expenses, the process of sorting within a department, and opening and distributing the letters, circulars, invoices, announcements, notices, and other items to actual receivers for their handling. The reception of an oral message follows a similar pattern, including making contact with a secretary or administrative assistant, scheduling a time, waiting for the appointed time, and being escorted into the contact's office. Salespeople know the expense of "getting received" for oral communication as vividly as any group.

Goldhaber, Dennis, Richetto, and Wiio (1979) reviewed some research completed in Europe on the effects of office relocations on communication costs. Most of the costs studied concerned reception of messages: "Thorngren showed in Sweden and Goddard in England (1977) that after relocation, most workers retained 30 percent of their old communication contacts" (p. 56). Pye (1976) concluded that after an office had been relocated, "a civil servant's telephone costs would increase by about 50 pounds per year" (about $125), suggesting that economic benefits derived from the relocations did *not* offset the increased costs of maintaining contacts in the old locations.

The cost-benefit ratio (efficiency) of receiving messages may be affected by the use of newer means of transmitting and displaying images, such as videophones and microcomputer-video interactive systems (Floyd, 1980). The FYI file section of the *Training and Development Journal* listed five ways in which "video helps managers become communicators" by helping them:

Receive timely and tangible data;
Communicate specific recommendations, policies, and procedures to selected employees;
Acquire new management skills;
Eliminate redundant training and briefing tasks;
Evaluate their presentational effectiveness.

The main point being made is that video systems, whether coupled with computers or telephones, are a timely investment that can make the reception of information and contacts more cost effective. As managers often say, "The name of the game is return on investment." The truly effective manager is *not* one who simply saves money but is one who spends money wisely. The costs involved in receiving messages can be enormous. New ways for making the reception of information more efficient are being considered every day.

Understanding. The costs involved in comprehending the meaning of a message are also important. The actual amount of time that it takes to understand a message may vary from person-to-person and vary with the content and style of the message itself. The more detailed and complex the message, the greater the likelihood that the costs of understanding it will be higher. On the other hand, there are also costs associated with not understanding or with misunderstanding a message. When a message is misunderstood, additional information may be required, more time may be devoted to preparing other messages, still more time may be needed to follow up and correct the misunderstanding. Every act beyond the misunderstanding may add to the cost of communicating.

Thinking. Some time is usually desirable for pondering the consequences of each message. This time is also a cost, although it may very well be the most efficient way to spend time. Mentally rehearsing and reviewing what might be said later or how an appropriate response may be made can reduce the time and effort put into the next cycle of originator costs. Both slow and hasty responses may increase the labor and supplies costs of communication, but they also affect the next category of costs—the human factors.

In summary, expenditures of physical resources include such items as buildings, offices, meeting rooms, and work and storage areas; communication equipment such as typewriters, dictating and transcribing machines, copiers, telephones, video systems, computers, printing machinery, filing cabinets and storage cabinets, and teletype and television units; supplies that allow messages to be prepared and sent, including paper and ink, fluids, cards, pens, pencils, postage, and telephone services; and labor associated with both the originator and the receiver-interpreter of messages. Originator labor costs may be assigned to thinking, composing, transcribing, and presenting; receiver-interpreter costs are associated with physically getting a message, understanding or misunderstanding it, and thinking about the consequences of responding to it. Even though we have analyzed the expenditure of physical resources according to several categories and separately for originators and receiver-interpreters, Thayer (1968) rightly observed that the "efficiency of any message is . . . encounters-specific; it depends upon the participants, the situation, the timing, etc.—upon all of the conditions of any specific communication encounter" (p. 159).

Direct expenditures of physical resources such as office space and labor are important aspects of the costs of communication in an organization; however, the negative impact on interpersonal relationships and losses of human resource potential may be even greater communication costs than the losses associated with physical resources.

Expenditures of Human Resource Potential

Communication can have a positive and impelling effect on human beings in an organization. Communication, on the other hand, can also produce powerful negative consequences. Costs are represented by losses and expenditures of resources. The losses and expenditures of human resources occur most often as negative consequences on people in the organization. Let us look at six major losses and expenditures related to human resources.

1. *Loss of interest and motivation.* Poor communication has its quickest and most deadly cost in losses of interest and motivation among organization members. Employees fail to direct their energies toward accomplishing organization goals. They perform at minimal levels and are distracted easily. Much of what they do is only indirectly related to getting the work done, with considerable emphasis on social interaction.

2. *Loss of trust and support.* As interest and motivation disappear and disinterest and reduced levels of activity become apparent, efforts to reestablish the

former levels of interest are met with distrust and nonsupport. Modest resistance becomes apparent. Dislike and indications of withdrawal from making contacts with those who are distrusted become obvious.

3. *Interpersonal conflict.* Major signs of deteriorating interpersonal relationships create tension between people in the organization. Minor disagreements surface with angry outbursts occurring frequently. Individuals seem cross and exhibit uneven dispositions, flaring up at unpredictable times. Moderate degrees of absenteeism are noticeable. Some people refuse to engage in conversations with colleagues. On the other hand, verbal aggression substitutes for problem solving.

4. *Indiscriminate opposition.* Organization members become preoccupied with their own goals and categorically oppose suggestions without much reason. If an idea appears likely to be beneficial for them, they will support it; on the contrary, if a proposal appears to infringe on some prerogative of theirs or appears likely to not advance their cause noticeably, organization members oppose it. The merits of an idea are seldom considered.

5. *Rigidity.* Opposition leads to rigid and inflexible ways of doing things. Legalistic procedures, literal interpretations of rules and regulations, and impulsive and uncaring decisions result. Illnesses occur more frequently, and disappointments, defeat, and unhappy feelings dominate relationships.

6. *Emotional stress.* Eventually organization members begin to experience emotional stress. Minor problems and small disappointments around the office throw people into a dither—states of disorientation. Self-doubt surges. The harder people work, the less productive they are. At the end of a day the stress makes employees physically exhausted, although they have done very little physical work. Too much stress begins to have its toll on physical health. Ailments such as high blood pressure, heart disease, peptic ulcers, and some forms of arthritis strike. Stress is expensive. Good productive people have mental breakdowns and make mistakes that ultimately cost organizations millions of dollars in direct expenses.

The costs of expenditures of human resource potential are difficult to assess, but estimates of losses caused by stress-produced illness are staggering. The costs of reduced production and performance in an organization are very real.

Production Losses

Expenditures of human resource potential are nearly always reflected in losses in production and performance on the job. Conflict, opposition, distrust, rigidity, and emotional stress lead to reduced productivity. Six production losses seem apparent.

1. *Distortion of goals and objectives of the organization.* One of the major production losses that results from poor communication is the distortion of the goals of the company. Through anxiety, distrust, lack of support, rigidity, and other human resource issues, employees evolve patterns of work that facilitate the successful accomplishment of only the things they want to do. Emphasis is given to tasks that may be only partially related to the main goals of the organization. At a

college, for example, teaching may be a key goal. However, faculty members may gradually make community service or consulting more important activities, resulting in a distortion of the actual goals of the school.

2. *Misuse of resources.* Another consequence of poor communication is the misuse of both physical and human resources. Money may be budgeted for purchases that are only marginally effective, and employees may be assigned tasks that do not take full advantage of their abilities. Because of mistrust a highly competent employee may be given routine duties to perform, never allowing the employee an opportunity to make significant decisions and progress in the organization.

3. *Inefficiency in performance of duties.* Due to communication problems employees may perform their jobs with some degree of inefficiency. Through anger an employee may decide to use more paper than is necessary, to take more time than need be, or to route information along more complex channels. In each case poor communication contributes to a less efficient use of resources and contributes to inefficiency in the organization.

4. *Inept performance.* Poor communication can lead directly to doing a job badly, even to doing it wrong. Unskillful, incompetent, inept completion of a task probably contributes to waste and loss in the use of physical and human resources as often as any other cause. Although inefficiency can often be tolerated, incompetence leads more quickly to intolerable conditions than does any other form of performance. In fact, incompetence is usually grounds for dismissal. Nevertheless, much inept performance could be eliminated or at least minimized through effective communication.

5. *Lack of coordination.* Inefficiency and ineptness may be reflected in lack of coordination, or lack of coordination may result in inefficiency and incompetence. Nevertheless, the act of bringing together the elements of a situation to create a harmonious set of relationships and produce action that accomplishes a goal is so intimately connected with the quality of communication that the lack of communication or a reduction in the quality of communication that results in lack of coordination is a serious organizational loss in and of itself.

6. *Delays and work stoppages.* Although the distortion of goals, misuse of resources, inefficiency in performance, inept work, and lack of coordination all have serious effects on production and result in losses, complete work stoppages or major delays are probably the ultimate consequence of poor communication and result in the greatest amount of direct production loss. Strikes may occur over a multitude of issues, but at the heart of most differences is some degree of poor communication. The ability to resolve disagreements is also a function of the quality of communication. Merrihue (1960) has described step-by-step procedures for communicating during a strike. He points out, however, that the most effective approach was "talk based on mutual respect from careful and continuous communication within the company" (p. 276).

There can be little doubt that the consequences of poor communication are costly—costly in terms of production losses and detrimental effects on human beings.

SUMMARY

The costs of communicating in an organization are related to the price a person or organization pays to communicate. The costs of communicating affect the efficiency (cost-effectiveness) with which communication takes place and with which the organization functions. We have reviewed three basic types of costs associated with communication: expenditures of physical resources, expenditures of human resources, and losses in production. If we realize that there is always some investment or expenditure when communication occurs, we shall be more sensitive to ways of reducing the costs, thus improving the efficiency of communication in organizations.

REFERENCES

Editors, "Video Adds Effectiveness to Your Management Team," *Training and Development Journal* (December 1979), p. 8.

FLOYD, STEVE, "Designing Interactive Video Programs," *Training and Development Journal* (December 1980), pp. 73–77.

GOLDHABER, GERALD M., HARRY S. DENNIS III, GARY M. RICHETTO, and OSMO A. WIIO, *Information Strategies*. Englewood Cliffs, N.J.: Prentice-Hall, 1979.

GRIESE, NOEL L., "Cost per Thousand: Yardstick for Measuring Publication Effectiveness," *Journal of Organizational Communication* (1978), pp. 26–29.

MERRIHUE, WILLARD V., *Managing by Communication*. New York: McGraw-Hill, 1960.

PYE, R., "Effect of Telecommunications on the Location of Office Employment," *OMEGA*, 4 (3), 1976.

ROGERS, FLORENCE, "Dictation: Key to Office Effectiveness," *The Personnel Administrator* (September 1979), pp. 25–28, 34.

THAYER, LEE, *Communication and Communication Systems*. Homewood, Ill.: Richard D. Irwin, 1968.

VARDAMAN, GEORGE T., CARROLL C. HALTERMAN, and PATRICIA BLACK VARDAMAN, *Cutting Communications Costs and Increasing Impacts*. New York: John Wiley, 1970.

7

MANAGERIAL
AND
LEADERSHIP STYLES

A managerial or leadership style is the consistent patterns of behavior perceived by others when a person is attempting to influence them. As a general rule a person's managerial or leadership style develops over a long period of time and represents what many people think of as a leadership personality. Subordinates or followers expect, and feel, that they get certain types of behaviors from each leader. The behaviors are related to the content of the job or task, to personal relationships, or to some combination of both. Thus we talk about leaders whose styles lean toward getting the task done or lean toward maintaining personal relationships. Most managerial and leadership theories advanced over the last several decades have recognized the importance of these two aspects of style (Hersey & Blanchard, 1974).

The managerial or leadership styles occurring in an organization may be the result of many factors, including some that are beyond a single manager's control, such as economic conditions in the organization or in the country. Managerial style is, however, quite directly related to three elements over which a manager has some control: (1) a manager's assumptions about people and what motivates them; (2) a manager's perceptions of what he or she can do to influence others; and (3) a manager's views of the resources over which he or she has control. Thus a manager might assume that people are basically interested in their own affairs, that they work harder if one keeps a close eye on them, that the manager has the ability and time to watch their work, and that the manager has little control over the financial resources to reward them, but that the manager can submit reports to the boss about people who do not work as hard as he or she thinks they should. As a manager with those assumptions, perceptions, and controls, what might we expect to find you doing during the day? What type of leadership style might you reflect to the employees whom you supervise? How would that affect the work of the employees? The answers to these questions have their foundations in the theories of managerial and leadership styles that follow.

MANAGING AND LEADING: A CONCEPT

Contemporary organizational communication theorists tend to accept the definition of leadership offered by Tannenbaum, Weschler, and Massarik (1961), who describe leadership as *interpersonal influence, exercised in situation and directed, through the communication process, toward the attainment of a specified goal or goals.* The essence of leadership and managing, in this view, is interpersonal influence. The manager attempts to affect the subordinate through communication. Leadership is more or less effective, depending on how successful the communicative acts are in influencing the follower. Thus when a supervisor's objective is to influence someone, or when a change in a subordinate's behavior rewards the supervisor or at least reinforces or supports the supervisor's communicative attempts to influence, the supervisor is engaging in leadership (Bass, 1960).

Any member of an organization may engage in some leadership, not just a manager or supervisor. Small leadership attempts take place all of the time. Everyone tries to influence someone else from time to time; nevertheless, a supervisor or manager engages in leadership constantly. A major portion of a manager's job is to provide leadership, to be the person who communicates to influence. Leadership consists of sending and receiving influential messages between the leader and those being led. Whether a supervisor produces a change in a subordinate depends on some decision on the part of the subordinate; a supervisor cannot produce a change in a subordinate without that subordinate doing something. Positive action (successful leadership) taken by the subordinate reinforces or rewards the supervisor's leadership attempt and encourages the supervisor to try other leadership attempts. Inactivity or negative action taken by the subordinate may stifle the supervisor's leadership attempts and discourage the supervisor from exercising leadership.

From this analysis we can derive three degrees of leadership: (1) attempted, (2) successful, and (3) effective. *Attempted leadership* is when a supervisor has the intent, and is observed attempting, to influence the subordinate. *Successful leadership* is when the subordinate actually makes a change as a result of the supervisor's attempt to influence. *Effective leadership* is when the changes made by the subordinate result in attaining the goal, receiving some reward, or receiving some form of satisfaction from the change. Supervisors should generally be striving for effective leadership with all three consequences: goal attainment, reward, and satisfaction.

COMMUNICATION AND LEADERSHIP

Leadership and communication are intimately intertwined. As we are using the term, leadership consists of interpersonal influence achieved through communication. This concept excludes the use of direct physical force, since communication employs symbols to bring about influence; nevertheless, it does include directives, threats, and other verbal and symbolic forms of coercion conveyed through communication. Communication is therefore the only process by which a leader can exercise influence.

Individuals may have communication objectives other than influence. In fact, effective communication may be defined as sending a message that the receiver interprets consistently with what the communicator intended, without distortion. A leader, however, is interested in more than communicating without distortion. Moreover, a leader is usually interested in more than just producing attitude change. A leader wants action. A supervisor may communicate effectively—have a message interpreted without distortion—without being an effective leader. A supervisor may want to have a subordinate move some barrels from one location to another. The subordinate may say, "I understand that you want me to move those barrels from here to the other side of the yard," but take no action to move them. The subordinate and supervisor may have understood one another perfectly well, resulting in effective communication; however, the subordinate did not behave as the supervisor wanted, resulting in ineffective leadership.

ASSUMPTIONS ABOUT PEOPLE THAT UNDERLIE STYLES OF LEADERSHIP

A manager or leader's style of influencing subordinates or followers is grounded in some assumptions about people and what motivates them. McGregor (1960) identified two bipolar sets of assumptions or beliefs that managers and leaders have a tendency to hold. He called them *Theory X* and *Theory Y*. Most leaders probably do not embrace either of McGregor's theories in any pure sense, but the characterizations help us to visualize the mental set of an ideal type so that we can get a clear image of the thinking of a person who leans strongly in one direction or another.

Theory X

Theory X assumptions appear to be derived from a view of people as machines who require a great deal of external control. Theory X assumptions may be summarized as follows:

1. Most people think work is distasteful and try to avoid it.
2. Most people prefer to be directed.and must often be forced to do their work.
3. Most people are not ambitious, do not want to get ahead, and do not want responsibility.
4. Most people are motivated primarily by their desire for basic necessities and security-safety needs.
5. Most people must be closely controlled and are incapable of solving problems in the organization.

It is probably fair to say that leaders who hold Theory X assumptions about people think of employees as tools of production, motivated by fear of punishment or by a desire for money and security. Managers who view workers in this way probably tend to watch them closely, make and enforce strict rules, and use the threat of punishment as a means of motivating them.

Theory Y

Theory Y assumptions tend to be derived from a view of people as biological organisms who grow, develop, and exercise control over themselves. Theory Y assumptions may be summarized as follows:

1. Most people think that work is as natural as play. If work is unpleasant, it is probably because of the way it is done in the organization.
2. Most people feel that self-control is indispensable in getting work done properly.
3. Most people are motivated primarily by their desire for social acceptance, recognition, and a sense of achievement, as well as their need for money to provide basic necessities and security.
4. Most people will accept and even seek responsibility if given proper supervision, management, and leadership.
5. Most people have the ability to solve problems creatively in the organization.

Managers who base their styles on Theory Y see employees as having a variety of needs. They believe their job is to organize and manage work so that both the organization and the employees can satisfy their needs. Theory Y managers assume that personal and organizational goals may be compatible. There is some evidence, however, to suggest that both cannot be achieved within the organizational context. Some personal and some organizational goals may be quite contradictory. Nevertheless, the manager who accepts Theory Y assumptions works with employees to set goals for the organization, encourages them to share in the decision-making process, and seeks to set high standards.

KINDS OF MANAGERIAL AND LEADERSHIP STYLES

From among a multitude of models, theories, and analyses, we have chosen to examine the following six popular systems for classifying and describing managerial and leadership styles:

1. Managerial Grid Theory (Blake & Mouton)
2. 3-D Theory (Reddin)
3. Situational Theory (Hersey & Blanchard)
4. Four-Systems Theory (Likert)
5. Continuum Theory (Tannenbaum & Schmidt)
6. Contingency Theory (Fiedler)

Each of these ways of looking at leadership and managerial styles is associated with the researcher, writer, or theorist who popularized the point of view.

Managerial Grid

One of the most widely discussed theories of managerial and leadership styles is that advanced by Blake and Mouton (1964), called the *managerial grid*. The grid is derived from the basic concerns of managers: concern for the task or that which

FIGURE 7.1
Managerial Grid Styles of Leadership

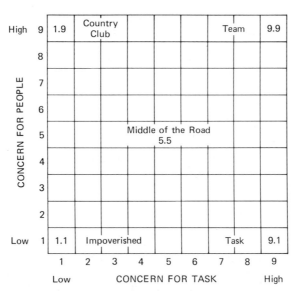

the organization is designed to accomplish and concern for the people and elements of the organization that affect people. The grid portrays the ways in which a manager's concern for the task and the people overlap and intertwine to produce styles of managing and leading. Figure 7.1 diagrams how these concerns are related to one another. The five extreme styles suggested by the grid model are presented in summary form.

1.1 *Impoverished style.* This style is characterized by very low concern for both the task and the people. The impoverished leader tends to accept the decisions of others; to go along with opinions, attitudes, and ideas of others; and to avoid taking sides. When conflict arises the impoverished leader remains neutral and stays out of it. By remaining neutral the impoverished leader rarely gets stirred up. The impoverished leader just puts out enough effort to get by. On a good day the impoverished leader may be intolerant and somewhat unfriendly, and on a bad day he or she tends to be obstinate and disagreeable.

5.5 *Middle-of-the-road style.* This style is characterized by moderate concern for both the task and the people. The middle-road leader searches for workable, although usually not perfect, solutions to problems. When ideas, opinions, and attitudes different from those of the middle-road leader develop, the middle-road leader initiates a compromise position. When conflict arises the middle-road leader tries to be fair but firm and to evolve an equitable solution. Under pressure the middle-road leader may be unsure about which way to turn to avoid tension. The middle-road leader seeks to maintain a good steady pace.

9.9 *Team style.* This style is characterized by high concern for both the task and the people. The team leader places a high value on arriving at sound, creative deci-

74

sions that result in understanding and agreement of organization members. The team leader listens for and seeks out ideas, opinions, and attitudes that are different from his or her own. The team leader has clear convictions about what needs to be done but responds to sound ideas from others by changing his or her mind. When conflict arises the team leader tries to identify reasons for the differences and to resolve the underlying causes. When aroused the team leader maintains self-control, although some impatience may be visible. The team leader has a sense of humor even under pressure and exerts vigorous effort and enlists others to join in. The team leader is able to show a need for mutual trust and respect among team members as well as respect for the job. *all american type perfection!*

1.9 *Country club style.* This style is characterized by low concern for the task but high concern for people. The country club leader places a high value on maintaining good relationships with others. The country club leader prefers to accept opinions, attitudes, and ideas of others rather than to push his or her own. The country club leader avoids creating conflict, but when it does appear, tries to soothe feelings and to keep people working together. The country club leader reacts to events in a consistently warm and friendly way so as to reduce tensions that disturbances create. Rather than lead, a country club leader extends help.

9.1 *Task style.* This style is characterized by a high concern for accomplishing tasks but a low concern for people. The task leader places a high value on making decisions that hold. The task leader is a person whose main concern is with efficiency of operations and getting the job done. The task leader tends to stand up for his or her ideas, opinions, and attitudes even though they may sometimes result in stepping on the toes of others. When conflict arises the task leader tries to cut it off or to win his or her position by defending, resisting, or coming back with counter-arguments. When things are not going just right, the task leader drives himself or herself and others.

According to Blake and Mouton, the 9.9 team style is the most desirable. A team style of leadership is based on an effective integration of both task and people concerns. In general the 9.9 leadership style assumes that people produce best when they have the opportunity to do meaningful work. Behind the 9.9 style is a commitment to involve organization members in decision making in order to use their abilities to achieve the highest possible results.

3-D Theory

Reddin (1967) builds upon the task-person grid of Blake and Mouton by adding a third dimension called *effectiveness.* The three dimensions are defined as follows:

- Task Orientation—the extent to which a manager directs subordinates' efforts toward attaining a goal.
- Relationship Orientation—the extent to which a manager has personal job relationships with subordinates characterized by mutual trust, respect for their ideas, and consideration of their feelings.
- Effectiveness—the extent to which a manager achieves the production requirements for his or her position.

The 3-D grid results in eight managerial or leadership styles. Figure 7.2 shows the three aspects of the model and the resulting styles. Four of the styles are less effective, and four of the styles are considered more effective. This implies that a low relationship orientation and a low task orientation, considered by Blake and Mouton (1.1 grid style) to be generally undesirable, may be effective when the person is viewed as being primarily conscientious about following rules and procedures in order to get the job done. A brief description of each of the eight styles follows:

MORE EFFECTIVE

Executive
High task, high relationships; seen as a good motivator who sets high standards, who treats everyone somewhat differently and who prefers to allow team management.

Benevolent Autocrat
High task, low relationships; seen as knowing what he or she wants and knowing how to get it without creating resentment.

Developer
Low task, high relationships; seen as having implicit trust in people and as being primarily concerned with developing them as harmony.

Bureaucrat
Low task, low relationships; seen as being primarily interested in rules and procedures for their own sake and as wanting to maintain and control the situation by their use; often seen as conscientious.

LESS EFFECTIVE

Compromiser
High task, high relationships where only one or neither is appropriate; seen as a poor decision maker and one who allows pressure to influence him or her too much; seen as minimizing pressures and problems rather than maximizing long-term production.

Autocrat
High task, low relationships where such behavior is inappropriate; seen as having no confidence in others, as being interested only in the immediate job.

Missionary
Low task, high relationships where such behavior is inappropriate; seen as being primarily interested in individuals.

Deserter
Low task, low relationships where such behavior is inappropriate; seen as uninvolved and passive.

Reddin (1967) explains that the four more effective styles may be equally effective, depending on the situation in which they are used. On the other hand, some managerial jobs require all four styles to be used at one time or another, whereas *other* jobs tend to demand only one or two styles consistently.

Situational Leadership

Hersey and Blanchard (1974, 1977) developed the concept of situational leadership from studies of leadership completed at Ohio State University (Stogdill & Coons, 1957) that showed, much like Blake and Mouton's, two dimensions of leadership style: consideration and initiating structure, resulting in a grid like Blake and

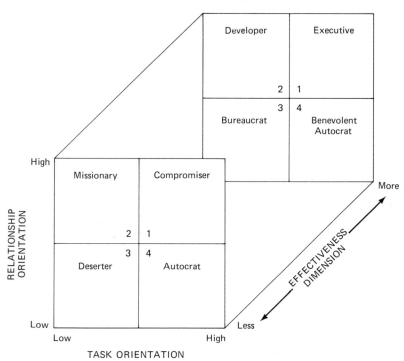

FIGURE 7.2
3-D Model of Leadership Styles

Mouton's. In addition Hersey and Blanchard identified a third variable—maturity—which functions in a way similar to Reddin's effectiveness dimension. Hence Hersey and Blanchard's model of situational leadership has an appearance like Reddin's. In fact, their interpretation of "effective" leadership is also quite similar: "The difference between the effective and ineffective styles is often not the actual behavior of leader, but the appropriateness of this behavior to the situation in which it is used" (1974, p. 6). The factor that determines effectiveness is described by Hersey and Blanchard as "the follower's level of maturity." Maturity is defined by a person's achievement-motivation, willingness and ability to take responsibility, and task-relevant education and experience. In other words, if the followers of a leader are highly mature—that is, motivated by high achievement, have high willingness and ability to take responsibility, and are experienced with the task at hand—a particular leadership style will be more effective than if the followers are less mature.

As the level of maturity of one's followers increases, the leader reduces the amount of supportive or relationship behavior accordingly. Figure 7.3 shows the patterns of leadership styles as they follow a bell-shaped curve going through the four leadership quadrants. For purposes of making quick diagnostic judgments, four styles of situational leadership are identified:

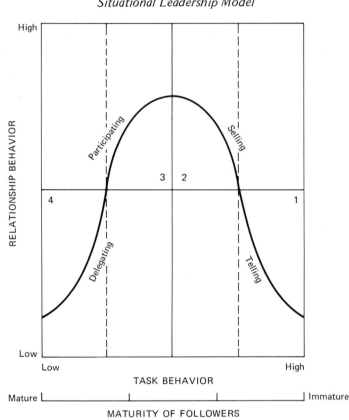

FIGURE 7.3
Situational Leadership Model

Style 1—Telling. High task, low relationship. This style is characterized by one-way communication in which the leader defines the roles of followers and tells them what, how, when, and where to do various tasks.

Style 2—Selling. High task, high relationship. This style is characterized by some effort at two-way communication, although most of the direction is provided by the leader. The leader also provides socioemotional support to get the followers to accept some responsibility for the decisions to be made.

Style 3—Participating. High relationship, low task. This style is characterized by having the leader and followers share in decision making through authentic two-way communication. The leader engages in much facilitating behavior since the followers have the ability and knowledge to do the task.

Style 4—Delegating. Low relationship, low task. This style is characterized by the leader letting the followers take responsibility for their own decisions. The leader delegates decisions to the followers since they are high in maturity, being both willing and able to take responsibility for directing their own behavior.

In contrast to both Blake and Mouton's and Reddin's theories, Hersey and Blanchard seem to regard low task, low relationship orientations as highly desirable when the followers are high in maturity. They argue that with people of high task-relevant maturity, Style 4 has the highest probability of success.

Four-Systems Theory

One of the most frequently discussed theories of managerial and leadership styles is that of Likert (1967). He devised four managerial styles or systems based on an analysis of eight managerial variables: (1) leadership, (2) motivation, (3) communication, (4) interaction, (5) decision making, (6) goal setting, (7) control, and (8) performance. Likert refers to the styles as

1. Exploitive-Authoritative
2. Benevolent-Authoritative
3. Consultative
4. Participative

We shall briefly characterize each of the four systems.

System 1—Exploitive-Authoritative. This style is based on the assumptions of McGregor's Theory X in which the manager-leader provides strong guidance and control on the premise that employees are motivated best by fear, threats, and punishments. Superior-subordinate interaction is minimal, with all decisions coming from the top and with downward communication consisting primarily of directives and orders.

System 2—Benevolent-Authoritative. This style is basically authoritarian but encourages upward communication to voice the opinions and complaints of subordinates; however, interaction between levels in the organization is through formal channels. Communication is rarely frank and candid.

System 3—Consultative. This style involves fairly frequent interaction at moderately personal levels between superiors and subordinates in the organization. Information flows both upward and downward but with slightly more emphasis on ideas that originate from the top. The manager has substantial, but not complete, trust and confidence in employees.

System 4—Participative. This style is highly supportive, with goals for the organization being set through true employee participation. Information flows in all directions, and control is exercised at all levels. People communicate freely, openly, and candidly with little fear of punishment. The participative style is similar to Blake and Mouton's 9.9 team style. Generally the informal and formal communication systems are identical, ensuring authentic integration of personal and organizational goals.

The central issue in Likert's sytems theory is decision making. System 4 (participative), with the highest level of employee participation, results in the highest level of productivity also. Likert's research indicated that most organizations prefer System 4 but regretfully actually use System 1.

FIGURE 7.4
Leadership Styles Continuum

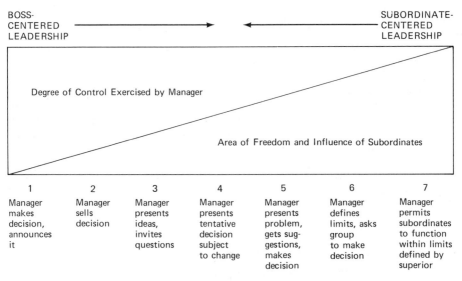

Continuum Theory

Tannenbaum and Schmidt (1957) make control over decision making the key concept in their continuum of leadership behavior. They describe seven behavior points on a continuum from boss-centered leadership to subordinate-centered leadership. The seven points characterize leader-managers in terms of those who maintain a high degree of control to those who release control to subordinates. The continuum may be diagrammed as in Figure 7.4.

Although the possible range of leadership styles may exist along a continuum as suggested, Tannenbaum and Schmidt characterize the successful leader as neither strongly control-oriented nor highly permissive. Rather, the most effective leader is one who adopts a style consistent with the demands of the situation. If direction seems appropriate, the leader gives direction; if participation in decisions is required, the leader releases control and allows the group to function in making decisions. The question generally left unanswered concerns what kinds of demands within a leadership situation call for each of the different styles. Some ideas for how to decide when to use a particular leadership style are suggested by *contingency theory.*

Contingency Theory

Many of the theories examined here implicitly, if not explicitly, acknowledge that effective leadership may be a function of or contingent upon the situation in which leadership is being exercised. Fiedler (1967) was instrumental in developing a theory of leadership styles based on the concept of contingencies. According to contingency theory the leader's effectiveness depends on the relationships within his or her style, as well as certain features of the situation. A leader's style is described in terms of variables already familiar to us: task and relationship; hence leaders are considered to be task-motivated or relationship-motivated.

The characteristics of a given leadership situation that seem most important are (1) leader-member relations, (2) task structure, and (3) leader's position power. Good *leader-member relations* exist when members like, trust, and respect the leader; this is regarded as the single most important condition for effective leadership. *Task structure* refers to the degree to which the way a job is to be done is explained in step-by-step detail; the more structured the task, the more influence the leader has over the group. *Position power* is defined in terms of the degree to which a leader can punish, reward, promote, discipline, or reprimand members; leaders have more position power when they can reward and punish.

Leader effectiveness is determined by the match between the style of leadership (task or relationship) and the favorableness of the situation. The most favorable situation exists when leader-member relations are good, the task is highly structured, and the leader has strong position power. The least favorable situation exists when leader-member relations are poor, the task is unstructured, and leader position power is weak. Of course, any situation may have varying levels of favorableness which include aspects of both better and poorer characteristics.

Table 7.1 portrays various combinations of style, characteristics, and favorableness. Eight basic contingencies result from the combinations. Research on the contingency model has shown that

1. Task-motivated leaders are more effective in highly favorable *and* highly unfavorable situations.
2. Relationship-motivated leaders are more effective in moderately favorable situations.

Thus task-motivated leaders tend to be more effective in situations in which they have either very much or very little influence. Relationship-motivated leaders tend to be more effective in situations in which they have moderate levels of influence.

Why certain leadership styles seem to be more effective in different situations is explained by looking at the requirements of favorable and unfavorable situations. In favorable situations you, as a leader, are well liked, have a clear task, and have high position power; under those conditions you obviously have everything going for you and should be able to exert influence over the group. The group should be willing to go along with your efforts to direct them, making your strongest style task-motivated. On the other hand, if you are disliked, have a vague assignment, and have little position power, then you are unlikely to have much influence over the group. In that case you should focus on the task and direct the group, relying on whatever influence you might have through the authority derived from the position. In either case—highly favorable and highly unfavorable—the task-motivated leader has the greatest likelihood of success.

Relationship-motivated leaders tend to perform most effectively in moderately favorable situations. When the situation is favorable, members do not require strong control. Tasks can be accomplished by subordinates with little task direction,

TABLE 7.1
Leadership Effectiveness

Based on a Leader Style, Situational Favorableness, and Contingencies

MOST EFFECTIVE LEADER	TASK-MOTIVATED			RELATIONSHIP-MOTIVATED			TASK-MOTIVATED	
SITUATION FAVORABLENESS	HIGHLY FAVORABLE			MODERATELY FAVORABLE			UNFAVORABLE	
Leader-member relations	Good	Good	Good	Good	Poor	Poor	Poor	Poor
Task structure	Highly structured	Structured	Unstructured	Unstructured	Structured	Structured	Unstructured	Highly structured
Leader position power	Strong	Weak	Strong	Weak	Strong	Weak	Strong	Weak
Contingency	1	2	3	4	5	6	7	8

but they need encouragement, support, and interpersonal trust, all of which are provided by the relationship-motivated leader.

SUMMARY

Leadership was defined as interpersonal influence, exercised in a situation and directed, through communication processes, toward the attainment of a specified goal or goals. Three degrees of leadership were identified: attempted, successful, and effective. Theory X and Theory Y were reviewed to assist us in visualizing the mental set underlying many of the major theories of leadership style. Six popular systems of classifying leadership and managerial styles were discussed: managerial grid (Blake & Mouton), 3-D theory (Reddin), situational theory (Hersey & Blanchard), four-systems theory (Likert), continuum theory (Tannenbaum & Schmidt), and contingency theory (Fiedler).

Most managerial and leadership theories suggest that different combinations of style and circumstances produce different levels of effectiveness. Certainly all of the theorists represented here would agree that no single style of leadership will guarantee that just the right type and amount of interpersonal influence is exercised in all situations. Interpersonal influence that results in goal attainment, rewards, and satisfaction may be communicated in a variety of ways, depending generally on the conditions identified by Fiedler—task structure, interpersonal relations, and leader power. Task-oriented leaders probably have a greater chance of being effective if the conditions are right; relationship-oriented leaders probably have an equally great opportunity of being effective if conditions are right for them.

REFERENCES

BASS, BERNARD M., *Leadership, Psychology and Organizational Behavior*. New York: Harper & Row, Pub., 1960.

BLAKE, ROBERT R., and JANE S. MOUTON, *The Managerial Grid*. Houston: Gulf Publishing Company, 1964.

FIEDLER, FRED, *A Theory of Leadership Effectiveness*. New York: McGraw-Hill, 1967.

HERSEY, PAUL, and KENNETH H. BLANCHARD, "So You Want to Know Your Leadership Style?" *Training and Development Journal* (February 1974), pp. 1–15.

HERSEY, PAUL, and KENNETH H. BLANCHARD, *Management of Organizational Behavior: Utilizing Human Resources* (3rd ed.). Englewood Cliffs, N.J.: Prentice-Hall, 1977.

LIKERT, RENSIS, *The Human Organization*. New York: McGraw-Hill, 1967.

MCGREGOR, DOUGLAS, *The Human Side of Enterprise*. New York: McGraw-Hill, 1960.

REDDIN, WILLIAM J., "The 3-D Management Style Theory," *Training and Development Journal* (April 1967), pp. 8–17.

STOGDILL, RALPH M., and ALVIN E. COONS, eds., *Leader Behavior: Its Description and Measurement,* Research Monograph No. 88. Columbus, Ohio: Bureau of Business Research, Ohio State University, 1957.

TANNENBAUM, ROBERT, and WARREN H. SCHMIDT, "How to Choose a Leadership Pattern," *Harvard Business Review,* 36 (March–April 1957), 95–101.

TANNENBAUM, ROBERT, IRVING R. WESCHLER, and FRED MASSARIK, *Leadership and Organizations: A Behavior Science Approach.* New York: McGraw-Hill, 1961.

8

MOTIVATION
AND
COMMUNICATION

why some people communicate better

Of all the issues in the fields of communication, management, and leadership, probably the most popular is that of motivation. When we talk about motivation, we are talking about reasons why people devote energy to a task. For example, we hired Sue to serve as a staff assistant to a team of six employees. Her responsibilities included answering the telephone, scheduling appointments, maintaining files, typing correspondence and reports, arranging meetings, keeping the office neat, and handling the budget, including recording receipts and expenditures. When she came to the job, she had to begin filing, typing, recording, and scheduling immediately. The previous staff assistant had taken another job on very short notice and had left the office with numerous stacks of untyped reports, correspondence, and assorted clutter. The telephone rang constantly, and team members asked for schedules and assistance in locating supplies and materials.

At the end of the third day on the job, Sue remained after office hours to assess how she might deal with the demands of everything that needed to be done. She spent an hour sorting through rough drafts of letters and reports, arranging them in a tentative order for typing. She looked through the appointment book and thought about the hours it would take to schedule the interviews and meetings. She stood by the filing cabinets and ran her fingers across the tabs in some drawers, reflecting on how the materials could be sorted and inserted so as to be found at some later time. After two hours of sorting and looking and thinking, she slumped into a chair and stared at the floor.

The next morning she arrived at work before 7:00 A.M. and typed several short items before other employees began to stop at her office. Throughout the morning she typed, answered the telephone, and filled requests. During the lunch hour, between bites of a sandwich and sipping a soda, Sue stacked and filed papers. After lunch she completed a report and several pieces of correspondence. By closing time she had made good progress on the pile of typing. For an hour after everyone else had left the building, Sue sorted and filed papers. She arrived at the office at about 7:00 A.M. the next day.

A CONCEPT OF MOTIVATION

Sue was motivated. She was willing to devote large amounts of both physical and mental energy into performing the job. Of course, individuals differ in the amounts of energy, enthusiasm, and persistence they are willing to invest in their work. Nevertheless, the more energy a person puts into a job, the more we say that person is motivated. The question that has puzzled managers for a long time is, "Why do some people work hard whereas others do as little as possible?" The answer lies in the degree to which people are willing to direct their behaviors toward some goal. Sue was willing to direct her behaviors toward a goal; she was motivated. Motivation was inside her. No one motivated Sue; she motivated herself.

FOUR THEORIES OF MOTIVATION

The most common theories of motivation refer to needs and goals as the driving forces of human behavior. We shall review four explanations of how needs and goals function to motivate people:

> Hierarchy theory
> ERG theory
> Motivator-Hygiene theory
> Expectancy theory

A *need* is something that is essential, indispensable, or inevitable to fill a condition. The term *need* is used to refer to the lack of something. Thus the concept of a need is something that is lacking and must be filled. We are told that all behaviors are responses to satisfy needs. What kinds of needs do we try to satisfy?

Hierarchy Theory

Maslow (1943, 1954) proposed that our needs fall into five categories: physiological, safety or security, belongingness or social, esteem, and self-actualization, as portrayed in Figure 8.1. These needs, according to Maslow, develop in an hierarchical order, with physiological needs being the most prepotent until satisfied. A prepotent need has great influence over other needs as long as it is unsatisfied. For example, it is difficult, although not impossible, to give full attention to saving for the future when you feel strong hunger pains. As someone observed, it is tough to be concerned about mosquitoes when you are standing up to your waist in alligators. Thus physiological needs urge to be satisfied before all others. Nevertheless, a lower-order need might not have to be completely satisfied before the next higher one be-

FIGURE 8.1
Maslow's Needs Hierarchy

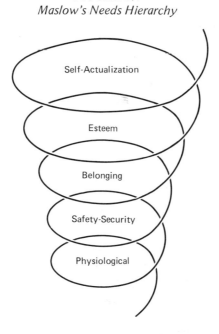

comes active, as suggested by the overlapping lines of the spiral. You might very easily be concerned about your safety even if you seem fatigued. However, it is quite likely that a major portion of the prepotent need will have to be satisfied before the next order becomes a strong motivator. The concept of prepotency postulates also that a satisfied need is no longer a motivator. Only unsatisfied needs impel people to action, to direct their behaviors toward a goal.

The five sets of needs are arranged in an hierarchical order, with physiological being the lower order, safety and security next, belonging in the middle, esteem needs higher, and self-actualization needs being the highest order. Once bodily needs are satisfied, a person seeks satisfaction for safety and security needs; then when a person feels secure, he or she is motivated by the next level of needs—esteem. When a worker is able to satisfy all of the lower needs, what he or she considers most important or satisfying is to be able to feel that he or she is doing something of value and is being fulfilled as a person.

On the job we tend to be motivated at the lowest level of need for which we have little satisfaction. When our need for security has been satisfied by a decent income or our need for esteem has been satisfied by good working conditions, improvements in those areas do not increase motivation. Since most people working in organizations have basic satisfaction of lower-level needs, the most appropriate means of motivation is through satisfaction of higher-level needs. The overlapping of needs orders is expressed by Ralph Waldo Emerson's observation that "our chief want in life is somebody who shall make us do what we can. This is the service of a friend. With him we are easily great."

Research on Maslow's hierarchy of needs has *not* supported the five orders of needs particularly well. Wahba and Bridwell (1976) reviewed the literature on Maslow's model and concluded that a two-level hierarchy of lower-level and higher-level needs may exist but that the specific categories identified by Maslow were not verified. The idea of prepotency has also failed to be strongly supported by empirical research reviewed by Wahba and Bridwell. The evidence suggests that a person may very well have strong belonging, esteem, and self-actualization needs at the same time. It may be that the research was just unable to make fine distinctions between orders of needs and prepotencies.

ERG Theory

Alderfer (1972) identified three categories of needs, in comparison to Maslow's five levels of needs. The three types of needs are *existence* (E), *relatedness* (R), and *growth* (G). Existence includes physiological needs such as hunger, thirst, and sex, and material needs such as compensation and a desirable work environment. Relatedness needs involve relationships with those who are important to us, such as family members, friends, and work supervisors. Growth needs concern our desires to be productive and creative so as to achieve our potential. These three needs areas are similar to Maslow's and, in fact, span the entire range of needs as suggested by Maslow. In general the ERG needs concept is a refinement of Maslow's needs system, but they differ in two respects. First, although the order of the needs is similar, the idea of hierarchy is not included. Alderfer argues that if the existence needs are not satisfied, their influence may be strong, but the other need categories may still be important in directing behaviors toward goals. Second, he also claims that even though a need may be satisfied, it may continue as a dominant influence in decisions. You may, for example, have a reasonably good salary and a secure job but continue to seek raises, even though existence needs seem fairly well satisfied. In that case a satisfied need may continue to be a motivator. On the other hand, relatedness and growth needs may increase in intensity as they are satisfied. The more you discover ways to be productive and creative, the more you want to be increasingly productive and creative.

Motivator-Hygiene Theory

Herzberg (1966) attempted to determine what factors influence worker motivation in organizations. He discovered two sets of activities that satisfy a person's needs: (1) those related to job satisfaction and (2) those related to job dissatisfaction. The factors affecting job satisfaction are called *motivators*. These include *achievement, recognition, responsibility, advancement or promotion, the work itself,* and *the potential for personal growth*. All of these are related to the job itself. When these factors are responded to positively, employees tend to experience satisfaction and seem motivated. However, if these factors are *not* present in the work, employees will lack motivation but will not be dissatisfied with their work.

Those factors related to dissatisfaction are called *maintenance* or *hygiene* factors. Maintenance or hygiene factors include *pay, supervision, job security, working conditions, administration, organizational policies,* and *interpersonal relationships* with peers, superiors, and subordinates on the job. These factors are related to the environment or context of the job, rather than the job itself. This is why programs to motivate employees using Herzberg's system refer to it as "motivation through the work itself." When these factors are responded to positively, employees do not experience satisfaction or seem motivated; however, if they are not present, employees will be dissatisfied.

Motivators are related to job satisfaction but not to dissatisfaction. Hygiene factors are related to job dissatisfaction but not to satisfaction. Thus to retain or maintain employees, managers should focus on the hygiene factors; however, to get employees to devote more energy to their jobs, managers should focus on the motivators. Managers adjust the job itself to motivate employees and adjust environmental factors to prevent dissatisfaction. For example, a supervisor who does a good job of creating positive relationships with employees will be disappointed if he or she thinks that those employees will be motivated to work harder as a result. Since supervisory relations is a hygiene factor, employees will most likely not be dissatisfied. To motivate employees, the supervisor will need to find ways to give employees greater freedom and more responsibility in doing their work, or at least give them more recognition for work done well. If employees do not get recognition, they will not necessarily be dissatisfied with their jobs, but they will not be motivated to work harder.

Comparison of Maslow's, Alderfer's, and Herzberg's
Needs Categories

There is a great deal of similarity among these three ways of talking about motivation. Each system describes self-actualization, growth, and motivators in similar terms. Maintenance or hygiene factors tend to satisfy needs at the physiological and security levels as well as to satisfy the existence needs. Interpersonal relations and supervision might be considered ways to satisfy relatedness, belonging needs, and esteem needs. Figure 8.2 portrays relationships among the three approaches.

FIGURE 8.2
Three Categories of Needs

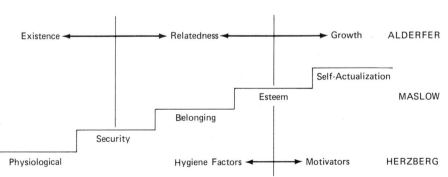

DIFFERENCES BETWEEN SUPERVISORS AND EMPLOYEES
ON WHAT MOTIVATES WORKERS

Although a great deal has been written on the topic of motivation, managers often base their decisions about employee motivation on erroneous information about what actually motivates employees. The sad truth is that supervisors frequently are out of touch with what employees want from their jobs. Kovach (1980) argues that employee attitudes and actual factors that motivate employees change more rapidly than does a supervisor's knowledge about what motivates workers. He claims that most theories of motivation are outdated by the time they are implemented. To support his claim, Kovach replicated the 1946 study completed by the Labor Relations Institute of New York in which first-line supervisors and employees who worked directly for them ranked ten items that provide motivation on the job. The results indicated that a gap existed between what employees wanted from their jobs and what supervisors thought employees wanted. Kovach administered the 1946 questionnaire to a group of over 200 employees and their immediate supervisors to see if the results were similar. The findings of the 1946 study and Kovach's 1979 study are shown in Table 8.1. An analysis of the results indicates that with the exception of the ranking of "sympathetic help with personal problems," the gap between supervisors and their employees has not been narrowed. For example, the items *security* and *wages* were ranked by employees in 1946 as having intermediate importance for them and were ranked by supervisors as having high importance for employees, whereas *appreciation of work* and *feeling in on things* were ranked as having high importance for employees yet supervisors perceived those items as being of low importance to employees. The same discrepancies were discovered by

TABLE 8.1
What Motivates Employees*

	1946		1979	
	Employee	*Supervisor*	*Employee*	*Supervisor*
Full appreciation of work done	1	8	2	8
Feeling of being in on things	2	9	3	10
Sympathetic help with personal problems	3	10	9	9
Job security	4	2	4	2
Good wages	5	1	5	1
Interesting work	6	5	1	5
Promotion and growth in the organization	7	3	6	3
Personal loyalty to employees	8	6	8	7
Good working conditions	9	4	7	4
Tactful discipline	10	7	10	6

*Rankings range from 1 to 10—1, most important; 10, least important.

the 1979 study. Differences in perceptions between supervisors and employees on what motivates employees still appear to exist.

Some of the differences between what employees feel motivates them and what supervisors feel motivates employees may be found in changing attitudes and values. However, most people have choices to make between different ways of satisfying needs and between degrees of effort they will exert toward accomplishing a particular goal. A person's actual motivation (effort directed toward a goal) may be a function of his or her expectations that a certain investment of energy will result in the accomplishment of a particular goal. Vroom's expectancy theory of motivation helps to explain how what a person's values and what a person expects can have an effect on motivation.

Expectancy Theory

Vroom (1964) has developed a theory of motivation based on the kinds of choices a person makes in seeking to achieve a goal, rather than on internal needs. Expectancy theory has three key assumptions:

1. Every individual believes that if he or she behaves in a particular way, he or she will get certain things. This is called an *outcome expectancy.* For example, you may believe (or have an expectancy) that if you score at least an 85 on the next test, you will receive a passing grade in the course. Also, you may have the expectancy or belief that if you receive at least a B grade in a class, members of your family will approve of what you are doing. Thus we may define an outcome expectancy as *a person's subjective assessment of the probability that a particular outcome will result from that person's actions.*

2. Every outcome has a value, worth, or attractiveness for a specific person. This is called a *valence.* For example, you may value a title or the opportunity for advancement, whereas someone else may value a retirement program or nice working conditions. The valence or value of some aspect of the job usually results from internal needs, but the actual motivation is a more complex process. Thus we may define a valence as *the value a person places on an expected outcome.*

3. Every outcome has associated with it a perception of how hard it will be to achieve the outcome. This is called an *effort expectancy.* For example, you may have the perception that if you study the textbook very hard, you will be able to score an 85 on the next test, but that you will have to devote an exhausting amount of effort to this course in order to score a 90. Thus we may define an effort expectancy as *the probability that a person's effort will lead to accomplishing a particular goal.*

Motivation is explained by combining these three principles. A person will be motivated when he or she believes that (1) a particular behavior will lead to a particular outcome, (2) the outcome has a positive value to him or her, and (3) the outcome can be achieved by the effort he or she is willing to exert. Thus a person will choose, when he or she sees alternatives, that level of performance that has the highest motivational force associated with it. When faced with one or more choices about how to behave, you will ask yourself a series of questions such as, "Can I perform at the expected level if I try?" "If I perform at the expected level, what will happen?" "Do I value those things that will happen?" You will then decide to do those things that seem to have the best chance of producing a positive, desired outcome. In other words, you will be motivated. You will be willing to devote the energy to accomplishing the tasks that you feel will lead to a positive outcome with the amount of effort you are willing to exert. A person's ability to perform a particular task plus the effort that a person is willing to exert to perform the task determines the level of performance. If you do not feel that you have the ability, it may not be worth the effort to try to accomplish the task. Motivation, in expectancy theory, is the decision to expend effort.

Nadler and Lawler's (1976) analysis of expectancy theory suggests some specific ways in which managers and organizations ought to handle their affairs in order to achieve the maximum motivation from employees:

1. *Determine what kinds of outcomes or rewards have value for employees.* It is easier to find out what people want than it is to change people to want what you have to offer. Thus the skillful manager emphasizes needs analysis, not necessarily changing individual employees.

2. *Define precisely, in observable and measurable behaviors, what is desired from employees.* For example, tell them to "write three term papers" rather than "be a good student."

3. *Make certain that the outcomes are attainable by the employees.* If a person feels that the expected level of performance is higher than he or she can reasonably achieve, the motivation to perform will be low.

4. *Link desired outcomes to desired levels of performance.* For example, if an employee values external rewards, then you should emphasize promotion, financial gain, and recognition. Thus in expectancy theory, environmental factors such as salary may in fact be motivation. If the employee values internal rewards, then increased responsibility, challenge, and achievement should be stressed. We should not forget, however, that people's perceptions, not reality, determine their motivation. Motivation occurs only if an employee sees a relationship between rewards and expectations.

5. *Make sure that rewards are large enough to motivate* significant behavior. Trivial rewards, it is said, result in trivial effort.

6. *High performers should receive more of the desired rewards* than do low performers. Seek an equitable system of rewards, not an equal one. People and organizations usually get what they reward, not what they would like.

In Chapter 7 we looked at specific managerial and leadership styles that affect the decisions that employees make about devoting their energies to accomplishing tasks. Motivation may be the single most important goal of managing and leading in an organization.

SUMMARY

In this chapter we have briefly outlined the features of four theories of motivation. Maslow's hierarchy of needs theory postulates five internal needs which are arranged according to an order of prepotency. Thus physiological needs must be satisfied before safety-security needs motivate a person, and belonging and esteem needs must be satisfied before self-actualization needs become effective. Alderfer's existence-relatedness-growth theory appears to encompass a range of needs similar to those of Maslow, but it discounts the idea of hierarchy and argues that a satisfied need may continue to be a motivator. Herzberg's motivator-hygiene theory postulates two sets of needs, those concerning job satisfaction and those concerning job dissatisfaction. Satisfiers or motivators are primarily related to the job itself, whereas dissatisfiers or hygiene factors are related primarily to the environment. Vroom's expectancy theory of motivation suggests that a person will devote the energy to accomplishing a task if he or she believes that actions will lead to an outcome, that the outcome has a positive value for him or her, and that the effort he or she is willing to exert will achieve the outcome. All four of these theories contribute to our understanding of why people make the decision to expend energy to accomplish a task.

REFERENCES

ALDERFER, C. P., *Existence, Relatedness, and Growth: Human Needs in Organizational Settings*. New York: The Free Press, 1972.

HERZBERG, FREDERICK, *Work and the Nature of Man*. New York: Collins Publishers, 1966.

KOVACH, KENNETH A., "Why Motivational Theories Don't Work," *S.A.M. Advanced Management Journal* (Spring 1980), pp 54–59.

MASLOW, ABRAHAM H., "A Theory of Human Motivation," *Psychology Review*, 50 (1943), 370–396.

MASLOW, ABRAHAM H., *Motivation and Personality*. New York: Harper & Row, Pub., 1954.

NADLER, DAVID A., and EDWARD E. LAWLER III, "Motivation: A Diagnostic Approach," *Harvard Business Review* (February 1976), pp. 26–38.

VROOM, VICTOR H., *Work and Motivation*. New York: John Wiley, 1964.

WAHBA, M.A., and L.G. BRIDWELL, "Maslow Reconsidered: A Review of the Research on the Need Hierarchy Theory," *Organizational Behavior and Human Performance*, 15 (1976), 212–240.

9

ORGANIZATIONAL COMMUNICATION RELATIONSHIPS

One of the most distinctive features of organizational communication is the concept of relationship. Goldhaber (1979) defines an organization as a "network of interdependent relationships" (p. 14). When things are interdependent, this means that they both affect and are affected by each other. Organizations consist of people in positions who have a variety of interdependent connections between and among them. The relationships are affected by the people in the organization, and the people in the organization are affected by the relationship. Like the relations people have generally, organizational relations can be divided into two classes: (1) the person in relation to the physical environment and (2) the person in relation to other people; that is, person-to-thing and person-to-person relationships. This chapter focuses on the person-to-person aspects of organizational life.

DEFINITION OF RELATIONSHIP

A *relationship* is some type of emotional connection. Emotions arise when people care for one another. *Caring* means placing some value on people. Thus a relationship is a connection between individuals in which they *value* one another and *care* for each other (Pace & Boren, 1973). Only a cold, unfeeling person can look at another human being and be unconcerned about what happens. Relationships may exist between people and things—some people love their cars and have an emotional connection with them—or between people and people; individuals may work together and have only a relation, a connection, without the emotional dimension, without caring. D'Aprix, speaking of the importance of showing employees and coworkers that they have dignity and value to you, said: "You don't have to like them, but you do have to show them you care for them" (Goldhaber, 1979, p. 198).

We have identified three types of relationships that usually exist in organizations: interpersonal, positional, and serial. Let us study the characteristics of each of them for a moment.

INTERPERSONAL RELATIONSHIPS

The most intimate relationships we have with other people on a personal, friend-to-friend, peer-to-peer level are usually referred to as *interpersonal.* Our closest friends in an organization, on the job, in church, or at the club tend to care for us more than others. It is with them that we have our most satisfying interpersonal relationships. With them we *resonate, vibrate,* and *jibe,* indicating that we care for them. Hoopes (1969) has observed that "the alienated are those people who have been excluded or who have excluded themselves" (p. xii). In authentic interpersonal relationships no one is excluded, nor does anyone want to exclude others.

What are some characteristics of effective interpersonal relationships? My own analysis (Pace & Boren, 1973) of interpersonal relationships suggests that you will be successful if you do the following:

1. Maintain close personal contact without having feelings of hostility develop.
2. Define and assert your own identity in relation to others without having disagreements develop.
3. Pass information on to others without having confusion, misunderstanding, distortion, or other unintended changes occur.
4. Engage in open problem solving without provoking defensiveness or breaking off the process.
5. Help others to develop their own effective personal and interpersonal styles.
6. Participate in informal social interaction without engaging in tricks or ploys or devices that put a damper on pleasant communication.

Although you may think of other general goals to be achieved through effective interpersonal relationships, these will suffice to illustrate the direction of our thinking on this issue. Much of the content of later chapters will address the question that usually looms large at this point: How does one achieve those goals? I have suggested elsewhere (Pace, Boren, & Peterson, 1975) that interpersonal relationships tend to improve when both parties do the following:

1. Communicate feelings directly and in a warm, expressive manner.
2. Communicate what is happening in their private worlds through self-disclosure.
3. Communicate a warm, positive understanding of each other by giving relevant, understanding responses.
4. Communicate a genuineness toward each other by expressing acceptance both verbally and nonverbally.
5. Communicate an ongoing and unconditional positive regard for each other through nonevaluative, friendly responses.
6. Communicate why it may be difficult or even impossible to agree with each other in nonevaluative, accurate, honest, constructive confrontation.

Clearly interpersonal relationships exert a powerful and pervasive influence over organizational affairs. Where the conditions for good interpersonal relationships exist, there also we tend to find positive responses to supervisors, responsiveness to personal and organizational needs, sensitivity to employee feelings, and a willingness to share information, all prerequisites for effective upward and downward communication. Sometimes increased productivity is also found. *Quality circles* represent a way of utilizing improved interpersonal relationships to facilitate increased productivity, but their success is contingent upon an organizational climate that may be very difficult to produce generally (see Zemke, 1980). To better understand the important but fragile nature of interpersonal relationships in organizations, we shall look at the second type of relationship: positional.

POSITIONAL RELATIONSHIPS

Positional relationships are defined by the authority structure and functional duties of members of the organization. The rationale for creating an organization based on positional relationships was presented in an earlier chapter on *classical* theories of organization. However, nearly all theories of organization place the concept of positional relationships at their center. Koontz and O'Donnell (1968) highlight these relationships in a chapter called *Making Organizing Effective*. They cite a dozen common mistakes that thwart the effective and efficient performance of individuals in the organization. We shall refer to a few of the mistakes they develop at some length. For example, the first mistake is the failure to plan properly. Part of failing to plan properly is "organizing around people" (p. 407), rather than positions. Organizing around people leads to several problems that positional relationships avoid. In the first place, they suggest, you can never be sure that "all the necessary tasks will be undertaken" (p 407). In the second place, a danger arises that "different people will desire to do the same things, resulting in conflict or multiple command" (p. 407). In the third place, through retirement, resignation, promotion or death, "people have a way of coming and going in an enterprise . . . which makes organizing around them risky" (p. 407), making their duties hard to recognize and to fill easily. Koontz and O'Donnell cite "failure to clarify relationships" as the second mistake in organizing. They explain that failure to clarify organization relationships accounts for jealousy, friction, insecurity, inefficiencies, and buck-passing more than any other mistake in organizing. Jackson (1959) in discussing the communication problems of organizations, makes a similar observation: "I can think of nothing which would facilitate more the free and accurate flow of communication in an organization than consensus about questions of work, authority, prestige, and status relationships" (p. 20). Those elements are, of course, intimately tied in with positional relationships. For effective and efficient organization functioning, positional relationships are probably the most critical to specify and clarify.

Superior-Subordinate Relationships

The most common positional relationship, and probably the most crucial to efficient and effective organizational functioning, is that of superior to subordinate. Positions in an organization are arranged in hierarchical order creating a series of superior-subordinate relationships throughout the organization. In fact, except for the very top and the very bottom of the organization, all positions, and the people in them, have a subordinate relationship to some positions and a superior relationship to other positions. Thus regularities and patterns in superior-subordinate communication have implications for almost the entire organization. Where superior-subordinate relationships can be strengthened, the human resources of the entire organization can be strengthened.

The concept of superior-subordinate relationships rests firmly on differences in authority, which are translated into differences in status, privilege, and control. The superior is perceived, at least, as having higher status, more privileges, and certain areas of control over a subordinate. The subordinate has a lower status, fewer privileges, and is dependent on the superior. Although the subordinate is dependent on the superior and frequently defers to the superior, the superior is also dependent on the subordinate. The supervisor must depend on the subordinate to go along with the directives and suggestions, to complete the work, to accept instructions, to inform the superior of problems, and to relay information to others. The way in which a subordinate responds to a superior, according to research and observation (Sanford, Hunt, & Bracey, 1976), is contingent upon such factors as how much the subordinate *trusts the superior,* much as we suggested in our discussion of interpersonal relationships, and how badly the subordinate wants to move up in the organization—*upward mobility aspirations.* Jackson (1959) suggested, for example, that employees are "always communicating as if they were trying to improve their position" and that they communicate with people "who will help them achieve their aims." That suggests, of course, that the quality of communication between a superior and a subordinate may very well be a function of the interpersonal relationship established between them and how the relationship satisfies the subordinate's needs.

Jablin's (1979) synthesis of superior-subordinate communication identified nine categories of issues: (1) interaction patterns, (2) openness, (3) upward distortion, (4) upward influence, (5) semantic-information distance, (6) effective versus ineffective superiors, (7) personal characteristics of dyads, (8) feedback and (9) effects of systemic organizational variables on the quality of superior-subordinate communication. Figure 9.1 summarizes a few of the major findings on each of the nine issues of superior-subordinate communication.

The research on subordinate-to-superior communication indicates that subordinates tend to tell superiors what they think the superior wants to hear, or what the subordinate wants the superior to hear, and to send superiors information that reflects favorably on the subordinate or, at least, does not reflect badly on the subordinate (Krivonos, 1976; Maier, Hoffman, & Read, 1963; Mellinger, 1956; Pelz, 1952; Read, 1962). These consequences appear to be related to the nature of positional relationships in organizations and especially to the inherent hierarchical, superior-subordinate relationship that comes from the structure of organizations. On the other hand, the hierarchy may be essential and inevitable in handling large numbers of people, in controlling interaction, and, in fact, in getting the work done. In spite of this seeming anomaly, the hierarchy and superiors and subordinates tend to create workable relationships and occasionally to engage in effective communication. One explanation for these positive experiences may lie in an understanding of communication rules and how they affect superior-subordinate relationships.

FIGURE 9.1
A Summary of Some Findings
on Superior-Subordinate Communication

Interaction Patterns

1. Between one-third and two-thirds of a supervisor's time is spent communicating with subordinates.
2. The dominant mode of interaction is face-to-face discussion.
3. The majority of interactions is about task issues.
4. Superiors are more likely than subordinates to initiate interaction.
5. Superiors are less positive toward and less satisfied with interactions with subordinates than with their superiors.
6. A subordinate's job satisfaction is positively correlated with estimates of communication contact with superiors.
7. Superiors think they communicate more with subordinates than subordinates think they do.
8. Subordinates feel they send more messages to their supervisors than the supervisors think they do.
9. Superiors who lack self-confidence are less willing to hold face-to-face discussions with subordinates.
10. Role conflict and role ambiguity on the part of superiors are correlated with direct interactions with subordinates.
11. Subordinates seek informal help in their work setting more from their superiors than from peers or subordinates.
12. Superiors are more likely to serve as liaisons about production rather than maintenance or innovation issues.

Openness in Communication

13. Subordinates are more satisfied with their jobs when openness of communication exists between superiors and subordinates.
14. Openness of communication appears to be related to organizational performance.
15. The willingness of superiors and subordinates to talk as well as the actual talk on a topic is a function of the perception of the other's willingness to listen.
16. Superiors and subordinates prefer supervisor responses that are accepting and reciprocating rather than neutral-negative (unfeeling, cold, or nonaccepting).
17. Subordinates dislike disconfirming responses from a superior and prefer those that provide positive relational feedback.

Upward Distortion of Communication

18. In superior-subordinate relationships when one person does not trust the other, the nontrusting person will conceal his or her feelings and engage in evasive, compliant, or aggressive communicative behavior and under-or overestimate agreement on issues.
19. Subordinates will tend to omit critical comments in their interaction with superiors who have power over them.

FIGURE 9.1 (cont.)

20. Mobility aspirations and low trust tend to have a negative influence on the accuracy of communication between subordinates and superiors; however, even if the subordinate trusts his or her superior, high mobility aspirations reduce the likelihood of communicating potentially threatening information.

21. Subordinates seem to feel less free to communicate with superiors who have held the subordinate's position.

22. Subordinates tend to see greater appropriateness, expect fewer harmful consequences, and have a greater willingness to disclose important, yet personally threatening, information to superiors in organic as compared with mechanistic organizational climates.

23. Subordinate tendencies to distort upward communication can be reduced by increasing the superior's consideration or by increasing the accuracy with which the superior transmits downward information.

24. Intrinsically motivated subordinates tend to distort messages less than do extrinsically motivated subordinates.

Upward Influence of a Subordinate's Superior, or the Pelz Effect

25. Supervisors who exercise influence upward with their own superiors are more likely to have subordinates with high levels of satisfaction, although extremely high influence may separate subordinates from superiors.

26. Subordinates who see their superior as having high upward influence also have a high desire for interaction with, high trust in, and a high estimation of accuracy of information received from the superior.

27. Subordinate confidence and trust in a superior are positively related to the superior's success in interactions with higher levels of management.

Semantic-Information Distance

28. The larger the semantic distance between superior and subordinate, the lower the subordinate's morale.

29. Superiors tend to overestimate the amount of knowledge subordinates possess on given topics.

30. Significant semantic distances exist between union and management personnel and between union leadership and their members.

31. Serious semantic distances are frequent between superiors and subordinates.

Effective versus Ineffective Superiors

32. More effective superiors tend to enjoy talking and speaking up in meetings, are able to explain instructions and policies, and enjoy conversing with subordinates.

33. More effective superiors tend to be empathic listeners, responding understandingly to silly questions; they are approachable and listen to suggestions and complaints.

34. More effective superiors tend to ask or persuade rather than tell or demand.

FIGURE 9.1 (cont.)

35. More effective superiors tend to be sensitive to the feelings and ego needs of subordinates.

36. More effective superiors tend to be more open in passing information along by giving advance notice of changes and explaining the reasons for policies and regulations.

37. Supervisory effectiveness tends to be contingent on such factors as task structure, superior-subordinate relations, and superior-position power.

Superior-Subordinate Personal Characteristics

38. Subordinates who have tendencies toward an internal locus of control see their superiors as more considerate than do external-control subordinates and are more satisfied with participative superiors.

39. Superiors who have tendencies toward internal locus of control tend to use persuasion to obtain subordinate cooperation, whereas externals tend to use coercive power more.

40. Superiors tend to rate subordinates as competent when they have values similar to those of the superior.

41. Superiors who are apprehensive communicators are not particularly well liked by subordinates.

42. Authoritarian subordinates seem most satisfied when they work for directive superiors.

43. Subordinate satisfaction with his or her immediate superior is related to the subordinate's perception of the superior's credibility.

Feedback from Superiors and Subordinates

44. Subordinate feedback responsiveness is greater when subordinates are told what needs to be done with completed assignments, when the superior makes the assignment to the subordinate, and when the subordinate feels that he or she can secure clarification about assignments from the immediate superior.

45. Positive feedback to a superior tends to make the superior more task-oriented.

46. The performance of superiors tends to improve after feedback from a subordinate.

47. Feedback from a superior that shows a lack of trust results in subordinate dissatisfaction and aggressive feelings.

The Effects of Systemic Organizational Variables on Superior-Subordinate Communication

48. The technology of an organization tends to affect superior-subordinate communication.

49. Upper-level superiors tend to involve their subordinates more in decision making than do lower-level superiors.

50. Organizations with flat structures tend to reward superiors who favor sharing information and objectives with more rapid advancement than do organizations with tall structures.

Communication Rules

The behavior of people in organizations, you will recall from our discussion of the characteristics of organizations, is governed by general but definite *rules*. Rules do lots of things in organizations: protect and restrict; facilitate effort and block it; encourage excellence and provide sanctuary for the inept; maintain stability and retard change; permit diversity and create conformity. Rules constitute both the organizational memory and the means for changing the organization (Perrow, 1972). We need to answer the questions: What are rules? How do they influence relationships? How does one function effectively by using the rules? Since we are concerned directly with rules that affect relationships, and especially positional relationships, we shall concentrate on what are popularly known as *communication rules* (see Farace, Monge, & Russell, 1977).

Definition of Rules

Ⓘ A *rule* is a principle designed to govern conduct, action, procedure, or arrangements of some sort. In the same sense a rule is the statement of some expectation or norm or a description of some appropriate form of behavior. Often we regard the customary or normal practice of something to be the rule—that is, because something is done regularly, we assume that there is some principle governing the way in which it is done. Thus we say that a person's behavior is rule governed when it occurs regularly and seems consistent with some principle that can be stated.

Some organizational rules are stated explicitly, such as when a person is to come to work and go home. Such rules are generally regarded as official and are usually written down in policy manuals or handbooks. We call them *formal* rules. Other organizational rules are not stated formally. We learn about them by living in the organization, by watching and violating the rules. We call them *informal* rules. The formal rules may be consistent or they may be inconsistent with the informal rules. Part of every employee's time is devoted to learning the rules and in deciding which rules take priority. In any case the rules tell us what to do and how to do it.

Ⓘ Communication rules indicate to us what we should communicate and how it should be communicated. Rules that indicate expectations of what should be communicated are called content rules; rules that indicate how the content should be communicated are called procedural rules (Cushman & Whiting, 1972). In the analysis of superior-subordinate relationships in organizations, the rules must be applied to clearly identifiable positional relationships—that is, the rules are assumed to govern the communicative behavior of a pair of organizational members who have a specific positional relationship. The content rules govern what the superior-subordinate pair will talk about, and the procedural rules govern how the interaction will take place.

For a particular superior-subordinate pair, content rules might indicate that they can talk freely about problems of getting the work done, that they can talk about some topics, such as employee benefits, company products, and their functions in relation to other departments, but that they may not discuss such topics as salary raises, promotion opportunities, company earnings, and union relations. On the other hand, content rules may indicate that some topics may be discussed at appropriate times, such as union relations right after collective bargaining sessions have ended or company earnings right before a stockholders' meeting. Content rules also apply to whether the personal problems of the employee are discussed with the supervisor and to what degree of openness, and whether mistakes, criticism, bad news, or other sensitive topics can be introduced into conversations.

Procedural rules indicate such actions as who starts a conversation—can the subordinate initiate interaction or must the subordinate wait for the supervisor to contact him or her—how delays are treated, how long a conversation will last, how frequently they will meet, who will terminate the meeting, how the conversation will be stopped, how interruptions will be handled, where the conversation will take place, who establishes the mood of the meeting, and who will decide what topics will be discussed. Procedural rules tend to govern how the parties in a conversation will be addressed. Slobin, Miller, and Porter (1968) studied the forms of address used in an organization. Their results showed that subjects always reported using *first names* (FN) in addressing subordinates (S), subordinates' subordinates (SS), and fellow workers (FW). There was a decrease in the use of first names when referring to the boss (B), but there was a large decrease in using first names when referring to the boss's boss (BB). In the case of upper management they all reported using first names within the firm. Persons of higher status reported being referred to by title and last name (TLN), whereas they used first-name references when communicating downward. The general manager and strangers from other departments were called by title and last name by persons of relatively lower status, such as those in the steno pool. The rule appeared to be *use title and last name in addressing persons of higher status or less intimacy, and use first name when addressing those of lower or equal status.* If you want to test the strength of this rule in an organization of which you are a member, just violate the rule. Address people differently from what the rule dictates. You'll see.

Satisfaction with Rules

A relationship represents a connection with some form of emotional dimension. When you seek to understand a relationship, knowing the rules and expectations that govern a person's behavior is often helpful. Most of the time, however, you need to know how satisfied the individuals in the relationship are with the rules. In a superior-subordinate relationship it is helpful to know that the superior operates by the rule that lets the superior interrupt the subordinate. An answer to the question of whether the subordinate, or the superior for that matter, is satisfied with that arrangement may tell us a great deal about the quality of the relationship. For almost any rule you can learn much by knowing how satisifed the parties are with it.

Co-orientation on Rules

Often the most important information about rules comes from determining the co-orientation on the rules of those involved in the relationship. *Co-orientation* depends on whether the superior and the subordinate see things the same way. That is, on a rule about who interrupts whom, do the subordinate and the superior

TABLE 9.1
Four Possible Combinations of Agreement and Accuracy

		Accuracy	
		Low	High
Agreement	High	Ignorance	Consensus
	Low	False consensus	Dissensus

see the superior as the one who does the interrupting? If so, we say they have *agreement* on that rule. That is one part of co-orientation. Both parties react in the same way to how the rule is violated. Another part of co-orientation involves empathy or how well one person can predict how the other person feels. If the subordinate is able to predict what the superior says about a particular rule, we say that the subordinate has an *accurate* perception of the rule in operation. In a relationship we are looking for both parties to have accurate perceptions of how each other responds to communication rules. If there is a high level of agreement and a high level of accuracy, we say there is *consensus* on those rules, or a high level of co-orientation. In instances where each party disagrees with the other but understands why they disagree, we say that there is *dissensus*. This represents the attitude of agreeing to disagree. Occasionally a superior and subordinate do not really agree on a rule, but they are equally unable to predict that they do not agree. This leaves them in a situation of disagreeing and not knowing it. This is called *false consensus*, because what they thought was agreement turned out not to be the case. Sometimes the superior and subordinate agree on a rule but have low accuracy—that is, the superior and subordinate agree, but they do not know that they agree. This is called *ignorance*. They agree but don't know it. One can diagram these four possible combinations of agreement and accuracy in a two by two table like Table 9.1 (Scheff, 1967).

Looking at superior-subordinate, positional relationships in terms of co-orientation on communication rules can lead to what Wilmot (1975) calls a dyadic unit—when two people are aware that the other person understands them—"Each person sees the other seeing them" (p. 8). In other words, the superior and the subordinate say of one another, "I see that you see me behaving consistent with the rules," or "I see that you see me violating a rule." Under those conditions the superior is aware that the subordinate is aware of him or her, and the subordinate is aware that the superior is aware of him or her. When both persons can say that, a dyad is created. When this occurs between a superior and a subordinate, we have a positional relationship.

Communication Competence

Knowledge and understanding of communication rules is often necessary for survival in many modern organizations; however, competence in using rules is a necessity for advancement in the organizational world. Several different levels of competence in dealing with rules have been described by Harris and Cronen (1970):

Minimally competent. This person has a knowledge of the rules necessary for day-to-day interaction in doing a job. The minimally competent person, however, does not know what to do to impress superiors in order to move up in the organization.

Satisfactorily competent. This person seeks out the rules of the organization and internalizes them as his or her own; however, this person is unable to initiate actions beyond those consistent with the organization's current operations. This makes the person an ideal employee, equipped for accomplishing short-term goals but inadequate for organizational leadership. This type of competence has been called *satisficing.* A satisficer makes a set of requirements rather than exceeds the standard by seeking to understand the complexity of a decision. Satisficers are not skilled at seeking and using information necessary for obtaining long-term benefits for the organization or for the individual.

Optimally competent. This person has the ability to know the rules of the organization, to see alternatives to the rules, and to recognize the likely consequences of each. The optimally competent person is able to detect contradictions and ambiguities in rules and is sensitive to multiple meanings stemming from differences in content and procedural rules.

Organization members, of course, vary in their communication competence. One may know what is wrong with a rule but may not be able to make any changes. Another may know the rules for participating in a staff meeting but may not know the rules for getting a contract signed.

SERIAL RELATIONSHIPS

People have interpersonal and positional relationships in organizations, as we have seen. In addition they have serial relationships. Information is transmitted throughout formal organizations by a process in which the person at the top of the hierarchy sends a message to a second person who, in turn, reproduces the message for a third person. The reproduction of the first person's message becomes the message of the second person, and the reproduction of the reproduction becomes the message of the third person (Haney, 1962). Situations in which information is disseminated by means of this person-to-person-to-person format are referred to as *serial.* Three individuals are involved: the person who originates the message, the person who relays the message, and the person who terminates the sequence (Pace, 1976). The key figure in this system is the *relayor* (Pace & Hegstrom, 1977).

Relayor Functions

Smith (1973) points out that some communicators are senders, some are receivers, and some are in between. The people in the middle are messengers; they are relayors. The relay person, he says, is a "very common figure in communication processes" (p. 313). John Alden, for example, was a relayor for Miles Standish who wanted to ask Priscilla Mullens to marry him. A librarian, a concert pianist, an actor, a reporter, a professor, a manager, and a supervisor are all relay persons at one time or another. The relayor receives a message and carries it part of the way toward some terminal point in much the same way as a "relay of fresh horses carries the riders along the route, and a relay man carries the baton onward in a track meet" (p. 314). In organizations, messages are carried forward by means of these serial relationships in which a relay passes the word from a superior to a subordinate downward or from a subordinate to a superior upward. The relayors carry the message along and thereby hold the organization together.

Smith (1973) identified four basic functions served by relay persons: to link, to store, to stretch, and to control. We shall summarize and briefly characterize each of these functions in order to better understand the serial or relayor relationship in organizations.

Linking

A supervisor tries to link an operative with a manager; the union steward connects union members with management; a line on an organization chart links one organization member to another. Although they may look simple, the links are more complicated than they appear.

Linking processes have at least three troublesome characteristics: they connect and disconnect; they make adjustments for the parties being linked; and they vary along several dimensions, including the distance, physically and psychologically, from the people they link.

Supervisors are links between management and workers. They can connect those parts of the organizational system, or they can disconnect them. They can send information forward, or they can hold it. Relayors, as communicators in the middle, can bring the ends together or they can untie the connections. A human relay functions much like a transmission system in a car. The relay connects two independent moving parts. Like a transmission, the relayor adjusts the inertias of one part to that of the other. Such adjustments avoid lurching, burning rubber, and breaking the system apart. A mediator, for example, adjusts labor and management to one another, using gears and clutches to speed up or slow down, to ease into a situation, or to shift into high gear on the open road. Finally, relayors vary in terms of the physical and psychological distance they maintain between those they link. Most professors, for instance, are closer to their books than to their students; some supervisors are closer to the workers than to management. This linking function, Smith argues, creates an ethic in which relayors value adjustment and assimilation of points of view above all else. Since the relayor must work with powerful forces on both sides of him or her, the task is one of bringing the forces together, of linking them so as to use the power of both. However, the linker cannot be assimilated by either of the sides and still be a person in the middle. The relayor must remain in the middle and not conform wholly to either side.

Storing

Storing is the second function of the relayor. When a section head receives a message from a manager to send on to an operator, he or she must store the message. If the section head forgets the message on the way, he or she would be unable to deliver it and would not be a relayor. Storing accomplishes a number of purposes beyond that of just holding the message. For about the same reason that a farmer stores hay in a barn, the relayor stores messages—to adapt to the needs of sender and receiver, to buffer against fluctuations in what the receiver wants to hear and what the sender wants said. Storing spans the tie space between the producer of a message and the consumer of a message. Storing implies a conservative ethic, because the relayor who stores preserves the system. As a storer, the relayor values the status quo.

Stretching

The process of adapting the parts of a system to one another involves making some changes. Stretching is a form of change involving the enlargement or amplification of the message. In this sense Paul Revere's ride stretched the light from his lamp from the belfry of a Boston church to Lexington. Reporters stretch the words of a speaker in New York all the way to Los Angeles. This is a matter of distance. Relayors also stretch, up to a point, the meanings associated with a message. They amplify the meaning of a message. At a political convention in 1980, reporters stretched and amplified the meaning of a statement about whether former President Ford would be the vice presidential candidate. In fact the meaning may have been stretched and amplified to such a point that it was mutilated. The relayor has to stretch, or amplify, meanings without mutilating, or distorting, them. Former President Ford was not the person selected to run as the vice presidential candidate; television reporters stretched and overinterpreted to the extent that they may have created a new message of their own. Some relayors underinterpret and lose some of the message. The ethic of the relayor is between the under- and the overinterpretation of a message. The relayor analyzes meaning, makes meanings apparent that seem obscure, internalizes meaning, resulting in some changes; however, the analysis, the revelations, and the internalizing are all part of preparing the message for relaying.

Controlling

Linking, storing, and stretching are the foundations of the relayor's fourth function —controlling. The first thing that a relayor controls is the *means* by which links are made. A teacher, as a relayor, has control over the means by which the lesson will be presented in order to link the student with the source of the lesson. The reporter controls how the message will be presented. The travel agent controls information about airline routes. The manager controls how official information will be transmitted to workers. The relayor controls channels and media as well as information itself.

Relayors are the in-between people; they are in between senders and receivers. They link the units of a system together by adjusting them to one another. In adjusting and adapting to the units, the relayors change messages. Change is often necessary to produce harmony between units in the system, yet change is opposed to the ethic of preserving and conserving the system. Nevertheless, by regulating the transmission, the storage, and the interpretation of messages, the relayor has control over the communication system. In the end the relayor may no longer be the intermediary; the relayor may become master of the system. In the end, you remember, it was John Alden who married Priscilla.

Likert (1961) recognized the central role of the relayor in organizations when he described the linking pin structure of organizations. In his model, almost every organization member is a relayor, serving as the link between the upper unit and the lower unit.

SUMMARY

Three types or relationships tend to occur in organizations: interpersonal, positional, and serial. Interpersonal relationships are based on caring, concern, kindness, and responsiveness. Positional relationships are based on authority, work, prestige, and status. The most common form of positional relationships is that of superior and subordinate. Communication rules describe expected and acceptable behaviors in organizations. Serial relationships are based on the need for people to serve as relayors of information in organizations.

REFERENCES

CUSHMAN, DONALD, and GORDON C. WHITING, "An Approach to Communication Theory: Toward Consensus on Rules," *The Journal of Communication,* 22 (September 1972), 217–238.

FARACE, RICHARD V., PETER R. MONGE, and HAMISH M. RUSSELL, *Communicating and Organizing.* Reading, Mass.: Addison-Wesley, 1977.

GOLDHABER, GERALD M., *Organizational Communication* (2nd ed.). Dubuque, Iowa: Wm. C. Brown, 1979.

HANEY, WILLIAM V., "Serial Communication of Information in Organizations," in *Concepts and Issues in Administrative Behavior,* ed. S. Malick and E. H. Van Ness. Englewood Cliffs, N.J.: Prentice-Hall, 1962.

HARRIS, LINDA, and VERNON E. CRONEN, "A Rules-Based Model for the Analysis and Evaluation of Organizational Communication," *Communication Quarterly* (Winter 1979), pp. 12–28.

HOOPES, NED E., ed., *Who Am I?: Essays on the Alienated.* New York: Dell Pub. Co., Inc., 1969.

JABLIN, FREDERIC M., "Superior-Subordinate Communication: the State of the Art," *Psychological Bulletin,* 86 (1979), 1201–1222.

JACKSON, JAY M., "The Organization and Its Communication Problem," *Advanced Management* (February 1959), pp. 17–20.

JACOBSON, EUGENE, and STANLEY E. SEASHORE, "Communication Practices in Complex Organizations," *Journal of Social Issues,* 7 (1951), 28–40.

JOHNSON, DAVID W., *Reaching Out: Interpersonal Effectiveness and Self-Actualization.* Englewood Cliffs, N.J.: Prentice-Hall, 1972.

KOONTZ, HAROLD, and CYRIL O'DONNELL, *Principles of Management* (4th ed.). New York: McGraw-Hill, 1968.

KRIVONOS, PAUL, "Distortion of Subordinate to Superior Communication." Unpublished paper presented at a meeting of the International Communication Association, Portland, Oregon, 1976.

LIKERT, RENSIS, *New Patterns of Management.* New York: McGraw-Hill, 1961.

MAIER, NORMAN, L. HOFFMAN, and W. READ, "Superior-Subordinate Communication: The Relative Effectiveness of Managers Who Held Their Subordinates' Positions," *Personnel Psychology,* 16 (1963), 1–11.

MELLINGER, GLEN D., "Interpersonal Trust as a Factor in Communication," *Journal of Abnormal and Social Psychology,* 52 (1956), 304–309.

PACE, R. WAYNE, "A Model of Serial Communication." Unpublished paper presented at the fall meeting of the New Mexico Communication Association, Las Cruces, New Mexico, November 1976.

PACE, R. WAYNE, and ROBERT R. BOREN, *The Human Transaction.* Glenview, Ill: Scott, Foresman, 1973.

PACE, R. WAYNE, ROBERT R. BOREN, and BRENT D. PETERSON, *Communication Behavior and Experiments: A Scientific Approach.* Belmont, Calif.: Wadsworth, 1975.

PACE, R. WAYNE, and TIMOTHY G. HEGSTROM, "Seriality in Human Communication Systems." Unpublished paper presented at the annual conference of the International Communication Association, Berlin, 1977, pp. 1–54.

PELZ, DONALD C., "Influence: A Key to Effective Leadership in the First-Line Supervisor," *Personnel,* 29 (1952), 209–217.

PERROW, CHARLES, *Complex Organizations: A Critical Essay.* Glenview, Ill.: Scott, Foresman, 1972.

READ, WILLIAM, "Upward Communication in Industrial Hierarchies," *Human Relations,* 15 (1962), 3–15.

REDDING, W. CHARLES, *Communication within the Organization.* New York: Industrial Communication Council, 1972.

SANFORD, AUDREY C., GARY T. HUNT, and HYLER J. BRACEY, *Communication Behavior in Organizations.* Columbus, Ohio: Chas. E. Merrill, 1976.

SCHEFF, T., "Toward a Sociological Model of Consensus," *American Sociological Review* (1967), pp. 32–46.

SLOBIN, D. I., S. H. MILLER, and L. W. PORTER, "Forms of Address and Social Relations in a Business Organization," *Journal of Personality and Social Psychology,* 8 (1968), 289–293.

SMITH, ALFRED G., "The Ethic of the Relay Men," *Communication: Ethical and Moral Issues,* ed., Lee Thayer. London: Gordon and Breach Science Publishers, 1973.

WILMOT, WILLIAM W., *Dyadic Communication: A Transactional Perspective.* Reading, Mass.: Addison-Wesley, 1975.

ZEMKE, RON, "Honeywell Imports Quality Circles as Long-Term Management Strategy," *Training* (August 1980), pp. 91–95.

10

INTERPERSONAL
STYLES
IN
ORGANIZATIONAL
COMMUNICATION

Jim Bitter, a supervisor over a team in the wing assembly unit, entered the conference room for a meeting with other supervisors and the manager of quality control. Ann Moran called the meeting to order and focused immediately on a problem with fasteners on a panel. Bitter immediately challenged Moran's interpretation of the source, arguing that fasteners did not meet specifications. Although another supervisor tried to comment that the manager was only attempting to introduce the meeting by making reference to this one issue, Bitter addressed the entire group with an air of confidence, a tinge of condescension, and quickly reviewed the exact number of fasteners that did not meet specifications, where they had come from, and what needed to be done to meet specifications. The manager of quality control slumped in her chair with a glare.

Bitter was right, and he knew it; the manager and other supervisors knew it. There was no question that Bitter was on his way up. Jim Bitter was accustomed to getting his way in meetings by using data, being highly persuasive, and bearing directly on the issue. He could throw aside superfluous comments and reduce those who questioned him to a fearful quiver. Regretfully many of his suggestions were not followed. Subordinates complained about his lack of patience, his antagonism, and his powerful intellect. Bitter's lack of humor and sensitivity showed both on the job and off; his racquetball games were competitive and intense. At home, at the club, in church, at Rotary, Bitter was the bane of others—he puzzled, frustrated, enraged, and confused. Levinson (1978) describes Bitter as a person with an *abrasive personality*.

DEFINITION OF COMMUNICATION STYLE

The abrasive personality, along with a number of other types, is recognized because it involves a consistent, regular way of communicating. The abrasive personality, like the amiable, dynamic, passive, or assertive type, exhibits a recognizable style of communicating. *A communication style is a particular, distinctive, or characteristic mode, manner, or tone of expressing and responding.* There is mounting evidence that a person's communication style is especially important in the way in which he or she manages interpersonal relationships as well as contributes to total organizational effectiveness. Tubbs and Gritzmacher (1979) reviewed eight studies involving the communication of managers in organizations. They concluded that the results of the eight studies taken together "provide consistent and strong support for the assumption that management communication behaviors do play a significant part in contributing to or detracting from total organizational effectiveness" (p. 7). In one study the factor called *communication style* accounted for 17 of 22 percent of the variance.

The importance of interpersonal communication style has been argued in both scholarly and popular literature. Lynch (1977), for example, described the work of Dr. Paul Mok, who "contends . . . that every person has his own very visible 'communicating' style" (p. 28). Four primary communicating styles were identified: intuitor, thinker, feeler, and sensor. The characteristics of each communicating style and a brief quiz to give a person a clue to his or her own style has been described (Mok & Lynch, 1978). Problems in an organization, they argue, stem from a poor mix of communicating styles rather than from a conflict between styles; however, conflict is reduced and understanding is improved when the styles of those engaged in interaction are similar. The idea is to identify your own communicating style so you know what is important to you, then to recognize the other person's communicating style. The final step is to adjust your style to be compatible with the other person. Mok said that "by knowing our own communicating style, we get to know ourselves better. And we get along with others better as we develop the ability to recognize—and respond to—their styles" (Mok & Lynch, 1978, p. 107).

Norton (1978), on the other hand, has developed what he calls a *communicator style construct.* Communicator style is defined as "the way one verbally and paraverbally interacts to signal how literal meaning should be taken, interpreted, filtered, or understood" (p. 99). Nine variables or aspects of communicator style were identified. Figure 10.1 provides short phrases that characterize the nine dimensions (Sypher, 1980).

FIGURE 10.1
Short Phrases That Characterize
Nine Variables in Norton's Communicator Style Construct

1. Dominates, takes charge
2. Dramatizes, jokes, and exaggerates
3. Argumentative, enjoys heated discussions
4. Uses expressive gestures and facial expressions
5. Makes immediate impression, leaves impression
6. Calm, relaxed, and easygoing
7. Attentive listener, empathetic
8. Open with feelings and emotions
9. Friendly, encouraging, and tactful

Sypher's (1980) extensive analysis of the data from a number of research studies using Norton's instrument revealed two dimensions of style: The first, anchored by *attentive and friendly* components at one end and *dominant and contentious* components at the other, suggests a "continuum ranging from nondirective communicative activity to directive communicative activity." The second "seems to be anchored at one end by dramatic and animated communicative activity which requires energy expenditure and allows tension release, and at the other end by relaxed communicative activity which conserves energy and reflects a state of already released tension" (p. 109).

Ganster, Petelle, Baker, Dallinger, and Backus (1981) reported a factor analytic study using the items from Norton's communicator style measure and semantic differential scales in which two factors emerged: an evaluative one and a dynamism one. Ganster et al.'s factors seem close to the two dimensions identified by Sypher. Both reflect continua along evaluative and activity scales. Although not fully confirmed as yet, the empirical analysis of communication styles holds promise in identifying basic components of interpersonal communication styles.

The effectiveness of staff specialists, supervisors, or managers is greatly dependent upon how well they work with others. Our contact with other people is through our interpersonal communication styles. There is an atmosphere of cooperation, mutual confidence, and accomplishment when people work well together, make good decisions, and take effective actions. We can all remember times when those with whom we work seem slow to listen, reluctant to act, and uncooperative. Often success is achieved only by continuing to communicate in spite of the difficulties. Bramson has estimated that only about ten percent of an organization's members are persistent troublemakers ("Troublemakers in the Office," 1980). He described five such types, each with identifiable communication styles: hostile-aggressives, complainers, indecisives, unresponsives, and know-it-alls; any or all of these types may fit the description of an abrasive person. By understanding these predictable and typical communicative styles, we can learn to adjust to, respond to, and cope with difficult communicators.

In this chapter we shall explain and analyze two ways of talking about interpersonal styles of communicating. This review will, hopefully, assist you in recognizing or discovering your natural style of communicating and some of the potential styles of others. Nevertheless, with this information, you may broaden your repertoire of communication styles so that you can, for at least short periods of time, adapt effectively in order to build, rebuild, maintain, or strengthen interpersonal relationships through sensitivity to interpersonal communication styles.

TRANSACTIONAL ANALYSIS

The first system for describing interpersonal communication styles which we shall review is based on the philosophy and principles of existentialist psychiatry advanced by Eric Berne of *The Games People Play* fame. Existentialism asserts, in simplified form, that people are basically good but that their behavior is sometimes unacceptable. When people are given enough information about their behavior, they can recognize differences and difficulties. People can, when they recognize difficulties, take control of their behaviors and change them. They have the power and abilities within them to control and change themselves.

Control over a person's interactions with others is accomplished by recognizing which of three dominant ego states or psychic personalities is active in an individual during a given set of interpersonal transactions. Berne used the personal terms of *Parent, Adult,* and *Child* to refer to the basic ego states. To bring about change, the first task is to clarify in your mind which behaviors are associated with the Parent ego state, the Adult ego state, and the Child ego state. The second task is to gain control over your behaviors by means of the Adult.

Ego states may be regarded as realities that are identified primarily by observing the verbal and nonverbal behaviors of individuals as they engage in interactions. The primary objective is to become aware of the ego state or states that serve as the foundation of your behaviors. Once the ego states can be identified, a study of various transactions with others can be conducted to determine whether interaction will continue, stop, or be ulterior.

An *ego state* is the combination of habits, ways of thinking, and feelings that a person has acquired and has imprinted on his or her brain over time. The recordings on the brain associated with ego states are called *tapes.* The Parent and Child ego states are permanent recordings in the brain that can never be erased, but they can be updated by the Adult ego state (Anderson, 1973).

PARENT EGO STATE

The *Parent ego state* is that body of recordings stored in the brain that come from observations of what your parents (mother, father, or other authority figures) say and do. The implication is that you carry around with you recordings of how you think the "big people" in your life behaved; the recordings are based on what happened during the first five or six years of your life. Your Parent lectures, moralizes, points its finger in an accusing way, teaches, and corrects. These behaviors are your script. A life script resembles a theatrical script. Jongeward and James (1973) state that "most people, often without knowing it, design their behavior, their facial expressions, even their words as though they were 'on stage' either as a main character or in a supporting role" (p. 3). The world certainly seems like a stage, with people playing the parts called for in the script.

ADULT EGO STATE

The *Adult ego state* is that aspect of your personality that figures things out by looking at the facts. The Adult processes data and computes the likelihood of a person being able to deal effectively with the outside world. The Adult is unemotional, like a computer, and is concerned with what is most useful or expedient or what fits the circumstances. The Adult ego state is not related to age but is oriented to reality and the objective gathering of information. An Adult script is a recording or voice that says,"On the basis of the available information . . ." or asks, "Should I do this . . . ?" or states, "This looks practical." The Adult also identifies from which ego state you are operating. One of the goals of learning transactional analysis is to strengthen the Adult so that you can recognize more clearly and easily when your Parent or Child ego state is dominant in the transaction.

CHILD EGO STATE

The *Child ego state* represents that body of recorded information that comes from how you responded when you were a little child. These recordings include what you heard, saw, and felt. Since a child's vocabulary is usually limited, most of the reactions are feelings, and the conclusions about yourself are based on those feelings. The primary feelings include frustration, anxiety, helplessness, and inadequacy, but they also include joy, spontaneity, curiosity, imagination, and excitement. When you look, sound, and act like a child, you are probably communicating from your Child ego state, regardless of your age. Your Child script is that recording which says, "Wow! Great! Rotten!" Your Child's voice cries, "I want that! Try and make me do that."

The structure of your personality is diagrammed like this:

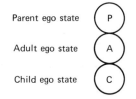

Parent ego state   P

Adult ego state   A

Child ego state   C

You can become acquainted with your PAC by listening to your recordings. You may hear distinct words or you may infer states from the feelings rumbling inside you. In addition you can become skilled in recognizing the PAC of other people by watching for clues in the behavior of others.

Six Communication Styles

Each ego state produces some recognizable communication styles. Six basic communication styles appear in organizations, according to Wofford, Gerloff, and Cummins (1977), and spring from the three basic ego states.

Controlling (Parent). Controllers limit and direct the behavior—actions—of others. They tell people what to do and what not to do. They use their authority to persuade and influence to secure compliance with their directives. Control can be achieved in harsh or pleasant ways. Gentle urgings, explicit statements uttered with a smile, comments offered first in a conversation, and indirect observations about what would be preferable ways of doing things are all ways of expressing a controlling style.

Structuring (Parent). Structurers have a neutral way of expressing themselves, appearing objective, while focusing on the order of events. They influence what others do by applying procedures, rules, schedules, goals, and standards to their activities. Pleasantly, but without intense emotional expression, structurers guide behavior by discussing the most desirable ways of doing things. They defer to the customary ways and the socially acceptable procedures. Like the controlling style, structuring is a common and positive style to use in organizations. In fact, little focus and task accomplishment would take place without the use of these styles, on occasion.

Egalitarian (Adult). Egalitarians express acceptance and equality of relationship in what they say more frequently than do controllers or structurers. Egalitarians stimulate others to respond, to talk back as it were, in an effort to encourage personal initiative. They show a genuine concern for others and are more relaxed and informal in their interactions. This style tends to produce closer personal relationships in the organization and consensus decision making. Egalitarian influence stems more from personal relationships than from positional authority or organizational rules.

Dynamic (Adult). Dynamicists have a highly active and even somewhat aggressive or outspoken style of communicating. Their expressions tend to be brief and direct, candid and open, with little evasion or indirectness. A dynamicist's comments are usually directed toward immediate problems and the pragmatics of getting them solved. The dynamicist's statements are frank and action-oriented. This is the style of movers, those who get action quickly and in an adult manner.

Relinquishing (Child). Relinquishers express ideas in order to subordinate themselves to others. Relinquishers are receptors more than directors; they show interest in others, they prefer to support, they defer to the interests of others. A relinquisher communicates confidence in others, making the relinquishing style ideal for counseling and building competence in others. On the other hand, dependent and truly subordinate individuals often respond to the relinquisher as weak and indecisive, and develop some resistance, frustration, and resentment with the communicative style.

Withdrawing (Child). Withdrawers express a desire to reduce interaction with others. They communicate the message that they do not wish to influence others. Withdrawers engage in avoidance behaviors and give few verbal responses. They make comments about not wanting to get involved and not being interested in issues and problems. When pressed to participate in decision making, withdrawers may become emotional and verbally attack others as a way of indicating that they do not wish to become part of the conversation. More often than not, aggressive withdrawal expressions create a barrier to effective communication.

Wofford et al. (1977) appropriately argue that "no single style is preferred for every situation." They suggest that organizational members should develop flexibility in the use of communication styles so that they can adapt to particular situations in the most effective manner (p. 163).

Transactions

A *transaction* is a unit of interpersonal interaction in which one person, talking to another, provides a stimulus and the other, in return, gives a behavioral response that is related to the original stimulus. The idea is that Person A says something (stimulus) and Person B reacts (response) to the stimulus. The stimulus behavior (talking or actions) may evolve from any one of the three basic ego states (Parent, Adult, Child) and be expressed by any one of the six communicative styles (controlling, structuring, egalitarian, dynamic, relinquishing, withdrawing). Likewise, the response may be produced from any one of the ego states and be expressed by any one of the communicative styles.

There are three different types of transactions: complementary, crossed, and ulterior. They can be understood most directly through diagrams, the analyst's method of explaining how transactions take place.

COMPLEMENTARY TRANSACTIONS

The first type of transaction is called *complementary* because the response is compatible with or complementary to the stimulus. In a diagram the lines are parallel. The basic principle on which complementary transactions are based is that when the lines are parallel, communication can continue; it may proceed with difficulty, but it can continue. Figure 10.2 portrays complementary transactions involving Parent to Parent, Adult to Adult, Child to Child, and Child to Parent ego states.

You might recognize clues to the six communication styles in the examples in Figure 10.2. The Parent transaction shows the two parties telling one another and others what to do and what the preferred ways of doing things are. The Adult transaction demonstrates direct, open, and brief comments, all of which are characteristic of egalitarian and dynamic styles. The Child transaction expresses the joy and excitement of the child's reactions; the reactions could just as well have been emotion, aggressive, and withdrawing. The Child to Parent transaction indicates

FIGURE 10.2
Complementary Transactions

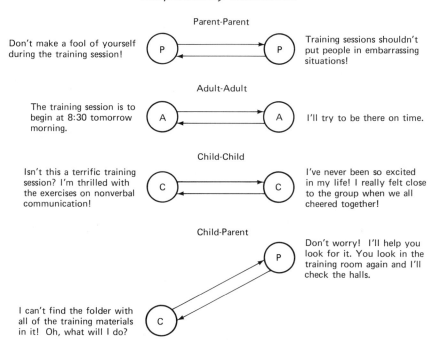

Parent-Parent

Don't make a fool of yourself during the training session!

Training sessions shouldn't put people in embarrassing situations!

Adult-Adult

The training session is to begin at 8:30 tomorrow morning.

I'll try to be there on time.

Child-Child

Isn't this a terrific training session? I'm thrilled with the exercises on nonverbal communication!

I've never been so excited in my life! I really felt close to the group when we all cheered together!

Child-Parent

Don't worry! I'll help you look for it. You look in the training room again and I'll check the halls.

I can't find the folder with all of the training materials in it! Oh, what will I do?

the helplessness of the child and the controlling and structuring comments of the parent styles.

In the examples the responses are compatible and relate to the stimulus comments. The lines of communication are basically open, and interaction can continue as long as the two parties wish to offer complementary messages. Complementary transactions do not always mean that the conversation will lead to productive ends; it may mean only that the two parties are able to continue talking. Being able to engage in communication may be extremely important for getting things done later, although it may involve being adaptable, mollifying emotional reactions, and encouraging others without making much progress in the short run.

CROSSED TRANSACTIONS

Some transactions, on the other hand, involve reactions that are uncomplementary or evolve from ego states that are different from what was intended. These are called *crossed transactions* because the lines cross each other in the diagram. A second principle of transactional analysis is that when the lines are crossed,

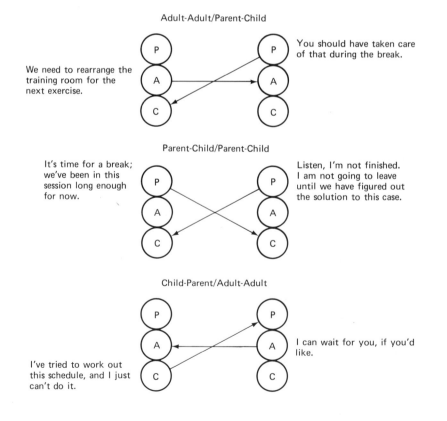

FIGURE 10.3
Crossed Transactions

Adult-Adult/Parent-Child

We need to rearrange the training room for the next exercise.

You should have taken care of that during the break.

Parent-Child/Parent-Child

It's time for a break; we've been in this session long enough for now.

Listen, I'm not finished. I am not going to leave until we have figured out the solution to this case.

Child-Parent/Adult-Adult

I've tried to work out this schedule, and I just can't do it.

I can wait for you, if you'd like.

communication stops—that is, understanding ceases to be a major factor in the transaction although the parties may continue to make expressive sounds and actions toward one another. Many crossed transactions are innocuous, but some may be explosive; all of them, however, result in defensiveness, unwillingness to continue communicating, or some form of irritation. Few of the results are helpful to understanding the people or the situation.

Crossed transactions are those in which the response to the stimulus is unexpected. An ego state is activated that was not anticipated, and the lines of the diagram cross one another. Figure 10.3 illustrates some of the ways in which transactions are crossed. In the first case a request is made from the Adult ego state to rearrange the room, but the response is an accusation from the Parent ego state to the Child which crosses over the Adult-Adult transaction. The second transaction involves a Parent stimulus directed toward a child but receives a Parent response directed toward a Child, crossing over the initial Parent-Child intent. The final example shows the first party initiating a stimulus from a Child ego state, expecting a Parent response, but getting an Adult to Adult reaction. Help was requested, but only a direct, frank, and Adult response was received.

ULTERIOR TRANSACTIONS

The third type of transactions occur in the organization, in social situations, and at home, but involve a hidden meaning. These are called *ulterior transactions.* The diagram of an ulterior transaction involves three or more ego states as shown in Figure 10.4, with dotted lines showing the hidden meaning. The example shows that the transaction appears on the surface to be Adult to Adult, but the hidden meaning indicates that the student is giving an ulterior Child stimulus and receives an ulterior Parent response. Because the ulterior meaning is often expressed by very subtle nonverbal behaviors, it is possible to miss ulterior messages or to impute them when they are not intended. The ulterior message is the basis of all psychological games (Morrison & O'Hearne, 1977). "Games," Goldhaber and Goldhaber (1976) write, "are crooked, dishonest ways of manipulating yourself and other people into providing you with your desired payoff (usually in the form of a favorite feeling)" (p. 136). For some people, however, one value of a game is that the real meanings involved in interpersonal communication can be hidden in ulterior

FIGURE 10.4
Adult-Adult Social Transaction;
Child-Parent Ulterior Transaction

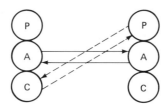

transactions, allowing them to engage in interpersonal interaction without becoming intimate and close to others.

An understanding of transactional analysis may aid you in matching styles and transactions so as to facilitate complementary relationships. When you have the opportunity to select responses for stimulus messages of others, you might choose a style that promotes better interpersonal relationships.

ASSERTIVENESS

The second system of identifying interpersonal communication styles which we shall discuss is grounded in contemporary behaviorism. A behaviorial approach focuses on observable behaviors rather than on inferred, internal, or underlying ego states. The claim of behaviorists is that successes or failures in learning from various experiences can account for a person's current behaviors. Changes from a nonassertive style of communicating to an assertive style of communicating may be produced by using the principles of operant conditioning, the ground rules of behaviorism. Operant conditioning makes changes in behavior directly, by providing contingencies (positive or negative reinforcements) when the appropriate styles are expressed. Thus many of the techniques for developing a more assertive communication style depend on providing rewards after assertive behaviors have been demonstrated (Williams & Long, 1975).

One of the early books that described assertiveness communication styles was that of Alberti and Emmons (1974). They explain that their book was written to help people "overcome personal powerlessness" (p. 13). They were critical of styles of communicating that failed to recognize and affirm the value of each individual. They cite the civil rights movement of the 1960s as the impetus for interest in assertive styles of communicating. The particular philosophy and methods, however, evolved out of the theory of radical behaviorism attributed to John B. Watson and amplified by B. F. Skinner and Joseph Wolpe (Craighead, Kazdin, & Mahoney, 1976). Craighead et al. mention that "one of the first attempts by behaviorial clinicians to improve the social skills of clients was related to . . . assertive training" (p. 364). They indicate that clinical work on assertiveness training focused first on the expression of irritations and angry feelings, but that it now includes the ability to communicate praise, affection, and approval. Assertiveness training now tends to refer to developments in any socially acceptable expression or to communication of some form of personal right or feeling by a person.

Three Communication Styles

The literature on assertiveness identified three basic communication styles, variously referred to as passive or timid, aggressive or overpowering, and assertive or confident. Although there are some similarities between aspects of the Parent, Adult, and Child styles as described by transactional analysis, the differences help to expand the concept of interpersonal styles of communicating and to provide enriching contrasts. We shall briefly characterize the three basic styles described in the assertiveness literature.

PASSIVE

This style represents a pattern of communication showing a fairly low level of adequacy. The person rarely expresses feelings and demonstrates little self-confidence. The passive style of communicating involves not speaking up, being inhibited, feeling hurt and anxious, allowing others to decide what you should do and say, and going along with an idea when you do not want to. The passive person feels timid, looks timid, and acts timid. When you exhibit a passive communication style, you tend to agree with others regardless of how you feel. You avoid expressing your opinions when you feel you should. You tend to walk and speak somewhat hesitantly, maintaining a fearful type of demeanor, and assuming a self-deprecating posture and bearing (Pace, Peterson, & Burnett, 1979).

AGGRESSIVE

The person using this style sounds, and often looks, hostile toward others. The aggressive communication style is recognized by loud speaking and vigorous, abusive, and vehement statements of feelings and opinions. The aggressive style is intense, giving the impression that the speaker thinks badly of others and has the right to hurt them. Persons who use the aggressive communication style suggest that they are inadequate in their personal lives and have difficulty handling relationships. Aggressors tend to produce defensive and self-protecting behaviors on the part of those with whom they interact.

ASSERTIVE

The assertive style of communicating conveys a sense of confidence and a positive attitude toward others. The person who behaves assertively speaks in a conversational tone (neither passive nor aggressive), at a moderate rate, but with firmness and determination. The assertive person speaks to the issue and expresses feelings and opinions directly and openly.

The assertive communication style is revealed through the tone of the voice, vocal inflections, volume, and fluency; it is also expressed through eye contact, posture, gestures, and facial expressions.

The assertive person's eye contact is direct, steady, and relaxed, with occasional looking away; however, an assertive style involves looking directly at the other person, rather than at the floor, ceiling, or walls. His or her posture is erect, although when sitting, the assertive person may lean slightly toward the other person, rather than slumping or leaning away. His or her gestures are relaxed and calm, rather than jabbing and intense. Gestures are consistent with the seriousness of the conversation. His or her facial expressions support the importance and urgency of the request. They reflect dignity and positive feelings, rather than sarcasm or disgust. His or her vocal tones convey a feeling of confidence, at a rate that is neither too slow nor too rushed. His or her voice expresses calmness and resolve to handle the conversation in a mature fashion. A lower-pitched voice is usually associated with the assertive communication style; however, the volume, even with a low pitch, is controlled and loud enough to be heard easily. An assertive person is heard and regarded.

.   The assertive communication style is characterized as the consistently most desirable one. In close interpersonal situations involving spouses and children or relatives; in situations involving consumer relations, such as getting a haircut or buying items in a store; at work when asked to stay late or when a subordinate has made an error or is tardy; in school during discussions involving topics about which you are concerned and even disagree; and in social settings, such as making a date or meeting strangers, the assertive style indicates that you are in control and know what you are doing; it also enhances your personal worth and allows you to be of greater service to yourself and others.

An interesting way of distinguishing among passive, aggressive, and assertive styles is to see and hear responses to the same situation given in the different styles. Figure 10.5 presents three situations, each with three different responses. After reading three situations, each with three different responses, classify each response by indicating whether it is generally passive, aggressive, or assertive. When you've finished, study back over the responses and decide which ones seem closer to how you would like to react in contrast to how you actually react in similar situations. By matching your actual responses with the styles illustrated, you may discover something about your own interpersonal style.

Read each of the responses aloud to get a sense of how comfortable you feel saying them. Exaggerate the vocal tones and movements to simulate the passive, aggressive, and assertive styles. Now compare your choices with the following key:

Situation 1	Situation 2	Situation 3
a. Aggressive	a. Assertive	a. Passive
b. Passive	b. Passive	b. Assertive
c. Assertive	c. Aggressive	c. Aggressive

As you reflect on which style you seem to use most frequently and which seems most comfortable, you may decide that you need to look into ways of strengthening or even changing your interpersonal style. Bolton (1979) points out, however, that most people tend to rely on one style more than others but that all of us might very well be *situationally* passive, aggressive, or assertive. This means that with some people in some situations, we may be passive, but with other people in other situations, we may be assertive or aggressive. Nevertheless, if you are situationally passive or aggressive, you will feel most comfortable using the dominant style in the majority of situations, even though you may be able to behave assertively on occasion.

James and Jongeward (1971) offer transactional analysis as a means for helping human beings become significant, thinking, aware, creatively productive people-winners. They argue for an integrated interpersonal style that draws upon the charm and openness of the Child, the morality and courage of the Parent, and the objectivity, personal attractiveness, and responsibility of the Adult. The "integrated Adult" is the fully developed person, the self-actualizing person who is in touch with his or her potential. The integrated Adult has "the honest concern and a commitment toward others that are characteristic of a good parent, the intelligence to solve problems that are characteristic of an adult, and the ability to create, express awe and show affection that are characteristic of a happy and healthy

FIGURE 10.5
*Examples of Passive, Aggressive and Assertive
Interpersonal Responses*

RECOGNIZING PASSIVE, AGGRESSIVE, AND ASSERTIVE INTERPERSONAL STYLES

1. You made a mistake on some aspect of your job. Your supervisor discovers it and lets you know rather harshly that you should not have been so careless.

   a. _____ You bristle up and say that he has no business criticizing your work. You tell him to leave you alone and not bother you in the future because you're capable of handling your own work.

   b. _____ You say you are sorry that you were stupid; overapologizing, you say you'll never let it happen again, how silly of you to make such a mistake.

   c. _____ You agree that you made the mistake and say that you are sorry and will be more careful next time. You add that you feel that your supervisor is being somewhat harsh and you see no need for it.

2. You are being asked by your boss to head the United Fund Charity collection at work for the third straight year. You didn't mind doing it the first two years but now feel that it's time someone else did it. You say,

   a. _____ "No, I've enjoyed the experience, but this year it is important to me that someone else gets the responsibility."

   b. _____ "OK, but this is the last year I can do it."

   c. _____ "No, I'm sick and tired of doing the work for the whole office. Let somebody who doesn't have anything else to do organize it."

3. You and your spouse have an evening engagement which has been planned for several weeks. Today is the date, and you plan to leave immediately after work. During the day, however, your supervisor explains to you that you are to stay late this evening to work on a special assignment that has just come in.

   a. _____ You say nothing about your important plans and simply agree to stay until the work is finished.

   b. _____ You tell your supervisor, talking in a firm but pleasant voice, that you have important plans and will not be able to stay this evening. You then ask the supervisor what other alternatives are available.

   c. _____ You say, in a nervous, abrupt voice, "No, I will not work late tonight." Then you criticize the boss for not planning the work schedule better.

child" (p. 271). The goals of transactional analysis and its accompanying integrated Adult interpersonal style makes it especially appealing as a model for the development of effective interpersonal communication styles.

Bolton (1979) argues persuasively that the advantages of developing an assertive interpersonal style are threefold:

1. Assertive people like themselves and feel good about themselves.
2. Assertiveness fosters fulfilling relationships and allows a person to release positive energy toward others.
3. Assertive behaviors reduce a person's fears and anxieties and allows a person to get what he or she wants out of life.

"A major goal of assertion training," Bolton says, "is to enable people to take charge of their own lives. It helps them break out of ruts and away from stereotyped or compulsive behaviors. At its best, assertion helps people develop the *power of choice* over their actions" (p. 137). Nevertheless, the end result of developing an assertive interpersonal style is the ability and strength to select the appropriate way of behaving in each individual situation, not just to behave assertively in all situations. An assertive interpersonal style enables you to take control of your life.

SUMMARY

Interpersonal communication style was defined, in this chapter, as a particular, distinctive, or characteristic mode, manner, or tone of expressing and responding. Research on a communicator style construct developed by Norton suggests that interpersonal style consists of two dimensions—behaviors that range from attentive and friendly to dominant and contentious and behaviors that are dramatic and animated in contrast to those that are relaxed and conserve energy.

Two systems of categorizing interpersonal styles were discussed: transactional analysis, which is grounded in the philosophy and principles of existential psychiatry and reveals six communication styles springing from the three basic ego states of Parent, Adult, and Child; the six styles are controlling, structuring, egalitarian, dynamic, relinquishing, and withdrawing. Assertiveness, which is based on contemporary behaviorism, recognizes three fundamental ways of relating and communicating with others—passively, aggressively, and assertively; the three corresponding interpersonal styles may be applied situationally, but the assertive style is considered the generally most useful for taking control of one's life in order to acquire the power of choice over their actions.

REFERENCES

ALBERTI, ROBERT E., and MICHAEL L. EMMONS, *Your Perfect Right: A Guide to Assertive Behavior* (2nd ed.). San Luis Obispo, Calif.: IMPACT, 1974.

ANDERSON, JOHN P., "A Transactional Analysis Primer," in *The 1973 Annual Handbook for Group Facilitators,* ed. J. Williams Pfeiffer and John E. Jones. Lajolla, Calif.: University Associates Publishers and Consultants, 1973.

BERNE, ERIC, *The Games People Play*. New York: Grove Press, Inc., 1964.

BOLTON, ROBERT, *People Skills*. Englewood Cliffs, N.J.: Prentice-Hall, 1979.

CRAIGHEAD, W. EDWARD, ALAN E. KAZDIN, and MICHAEL J. MAHONEY, *Behavior Modification: Principles, Issues, and Applications*. Boston: Houghton Mifflin, 1976.

GANSTER, DANIEL C., JOHN PETELLE, DOUGLAS BAKER, JUDITH DALLINGER, and DENCIL BACKUS, "Leader Communication Style: Toward the Development of a Multi-Dimensional Model." Unpublished paper, Departments of Management and Speech Communication, University of Nebraska–Lincoln, 1981.

GELLERMAN, SAUL W., *The Management of Human Relations*. New York: Holt, Rinehart & Winston, 1966.

GOLDHABER, GERALD M., and MARYLYNN B. GOLDHABER, *Transactional Analysis: Principles and Applications*. Boston: Allyn & Bacon, 1976.

JAMES, MURIEL, and DOROTHY JONGEWARD, *Born to Win*. Reading, Mass.: Addison-Wesley Publishing Company, 1971.

JONGEWARD, DOROTHY, and MURIEL JAMES, *Winning with People: Group Exercises in Transactional Analysis*. Reading, Mass.: Addison-Wesley, 1973.

LEVINSON, HARRY, "The Abrasive Personality," *Harvard Business Review* (May–June 1978), pp. 86–94.

LYNCH, DUDLEY, "In Sync with the Other Guy," *TWA Ambassador* (March, 1977), pp. 28–31.

MACKENZIE, R. ALEC, "The Management Process in 3-D," *Harvard Business Review* (November–December 1969), pp. 80–87.

MOK, PAUL, and DUDLEY LYNCH, "Easy New Way to Get Your Way," *Reader's Digest* (March 1978), pp. 105–109.

MORRISON, JAMES H., and JOHN J. O'HEARNE, *Practical Transactional Analysis in Management*. Reading, Mass.: Addison-Wesley, 1977.

NORTON, ROBERT W., "Foundation of a Communicator Style Construct," *Human Communication Research*, 4 (Winter 1978), 99–112.

NORTON, ROBERT W., "The Illusion of Systematic Distortion," *Human Communication Research*, 7 (Fall 1980), 88–96.

PACE, R. WAYNE, BRENT D. PETERSON, and M. DALLAS BURNETT, *Techniques for Effective Communication*. Reading, Mass.: Addison-Wesley, 1979.

SYPHER, HOWARD E., "Illusory Correlation in Communication Research," *Human Communication Research*, 7 (Fall 1980), 83–87.

"Troublemakers in the Office," *Time*, March 17, 1980, p. 72.

TUBBS, STEWART L., and KAREN J. GRITZMACHER, "Supervisory Communication and Organizational Effectiveness: Past, Present, and Future Research Issues." Unpublished paper presented at the Speech Communication Association convention, November 1979.

WILLIAMS, ROBERT L., and JAMES D. LONG, *Toward a Self-Managed Life Style*. Boston: Houghton Mifflin Company, 1975.

WOFFORD, JERRY C., EDWIN A. GERLOFF, and ROBERT G. CUMMINS, *Organizational Communication: The Keystone to Managerial Effectiveness*. New York: McGraw-Hill, 1977.

11

ORGANIZATIONAL COMMUNICATION CLIMATE, SATISFACTION, AND INFORMATION ADEQUACY

Have you ever had the experience of working on a job, having your supervisor come by and watch what you're doing for a few moments, and then kind of shrug and say, "Huh"? You ask, "Is there something wrong?" The reply you hear is, "Oh, nooo." Your supervisor walks away. Later you're taking a break, and two guys working in your area saunter up to the drink dispenser where you are standing. They just look at you and lean against the wall with their backs to you. You decide to stop at the personnel office and check on your overtime. Although you've been in the personnel office many times, the clerk asks your name and where you work. The clerk thumbs through the file drawer, looks at you, and shakes his head in a puzzled way. He says, "What did you say your name is?" You reply, "Never mind!" and frown deeply as you slam the door on your way out. Under your breath you mutter, "What is the matter with this place?" You look up at the sky expecting to see dark clouds signaling a thunderstorm. The sun is bright, and the sky is a beautiful blue. You wonder. Your mind storms. "It's the climate," you say. "We have a terrible climate in this organization!"

DEFINITION OF CLIMATE

Just as the weather creates a physical climate for a region, the way in which people communicate creates a "psychological" climate for an organization. A climate is the generally prevailing weather conditions of an area. The physical climate is a composite of temperature, air pressure, humidity, precipitation, sunshine, cloudiness, and winds throughout the year that is averaged over a series of years. The *communication climate* is a composite of human behaviors, perceptions of events, responses of employees to one another, expectations, interpersonal conflicts, and opportunities for growth in the organization throughout the year that is averaged over a series of years. You may experience a pattern of weather conditions that give you an inaccurate impression of the physical climate of a region; in the same way you may receive an inaccurate impression of the communication climate of an organization based on a short visit or some unusual interpersonal interactions. Sometimes, however, the weather on a particular day gives you a good picture of the physical climate just as a few interpersonal contacts can give you a clear picture of the communication climate.

IMPORTANCE OF CLIMATE

Is the physical climate of an area important? Is the communication climate of an organization important? Blumenstock (1970) explains that the physical climate "affects our way of life": the clothing we wear, the food we raise, the houses we construct, the transportation we use, the kinds of plants and animals in the area. In a similar fashion the communication climate of an organization affects the way we live: to whom we talk, whom we like, how we feel, how hard we work, how innovative we are, what we want to accomplish, and how we seem to fit into the organization. Redding (1972) states that *"the 'climate' of the organization is more crucial than are communication skills or techniques (taken by themselves) in creating an effective organization"* (p. 111).

The distinction between the overall climate of an organization and the communication climate of an organization is not easy to make, but the difference is important enough to try.

ORGANIZATIONAL CLIMATE

A definition by Goldhaber, Dennis, Richetto, and Wiio (1979) describes the idea of organizational climate; they suggest that organizational climate consists of the perceptions of organization members about

1. how they can act or behave, and about
2. what seems responsible for the way others act or behave.

This suggests that organization members sense or feel or perceive that certain aspects of the organization influence how they can behave in the organization. Organization members also explain why other members of the organization act the way they do in terms of the forces that influence their behavior. The literature on organizational climate (James & Jones, 1974; Taylor & Bowers, 1972; Waters, Roach, & Batlis, 1974) suggests that six aspects of organizational life have a strong effect on perceptions that lead to conclusions about the overall organizational climate.

1. *The importance of human beings in the organization.* The more organization members feel that they can act the way they do because human beings are considered important in the organization, the more highly they tend to rate the overall

organization climate. If they believe that human beings are considered to be unimportant in the organization, then the overall organization climate will be considered less desirable. The logic of the overall organization climate is about the same for the five other aspects of the organization.

2. *The flow of information in the organzation.* The more organization members feel that they can act the way they do and others can act they way they do because the flow of information is adequate, the more highly they tend to rate the overall organization climate. If the flow of information is inadequate, the organization climate tends to be rated lower.

3. *Practices related to motivating employees.* If organization members view motivational practices in a positive way and feel that they behave and others behave in response to the motivational practices, they tend to rate the organization climate more highly. If the motivational practices (such as incentives, compensation, work conditions, benefits) are viewed as negative, then the organization climate will be rated lower.

4. *Decision-making practices.* The more that organization members feel that their actions and the actions of others are caused by positive decision-making practices, the more positively the overall organization climate is rated. If decision-making practices are viewed negatively and seem to be the cause of their behavior, organization members tend to rate the organization climate lower.

5. *Technology and work resources.* If organization members consider the materials, procedures, and equipment to be up to date and well maintained, making them able to perform their work well, they tend to consider the organization climate to be higher than if they feel that the equipment and materials are holding them back from performing their jobs effectively.

6. *Upward influence.* The organization climate tends to be rated more highly if organization members feel that they have some influence on what happens in their departments, and the organization climate tends to be rated lower if organization members feel they are unable to influence those who supervise them.

The overall climate of an organization consists of perceptions by organization members of six dimensions of organizational life, which includes information flow and some practices involving communication; however, some perceptions directly involve the climate in which communicating occurs. This is called the *organizational communication climate.*

ORGANIZATIONAL COMMUNICATION CLIMATE

The climate of communication in an organization is a composite of evaluations and reactions to certain activities that take place in an organization. The organizational communication climate involves three interacting parts, as shown in Figure 11.1.

Thus the climate in which communication occurs is a consequence or result of how *organization members perceive* (hold attitudes and expectations about or are satisfied with) such *organizational features* as its policies, information flow, work to be done, pay and benefits, promotions, coworkers and supervisors in terms

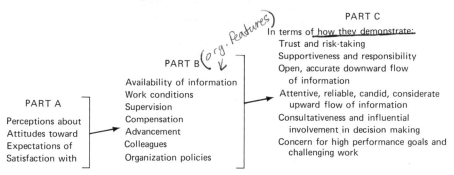

FIGURE 11.1
The Interacting Parts
of Organizational Communication Climate

PART A

Perceptions about
Attitudes toward
Expectations of
Satisfaction with

PART B (org. features)

Availability of information
Work conditions
Supervision
Compensation
Advancement
Colleagues
Organization policies

PART C

In terms of how they demonstrate:
Trust and risk-taking
Supportiveness and responsibility
Open, accurate downward flow
  of information
Attentive, reliable, candid, considerate
  upward flow of information
Consultativeness and influential
  involvement in decision making
Concern for high performance goals and
  challenging work

of *how they demonstrate* to the organization members that the organization *trusts* them and allows them the freedom to take risks, *supports* them and gives them responsibility in doing their jobs, is *openly* providing accurate and adequate information about the organization, *attentively* listens and gets reliable and candid information from subordinates, actively *consults* organization members so that they see that their involvement is influential in decisions in the organization, and has a concern about *high standards* and challenging work (Goldhaber, 1979; Goldhaber et al., 1979; Jablin, 1980; Sanford, Hunt, & Bracey, 1976; Timm, 1980).

The existence of a phenomenon such as "organizational communication climate" is often criticized until some way of measuring it has been developed. Dennis (1974) reported creating a questionnaire that measured five important components of communication climate. Peterson and Pace (1976) developed the *OA Communication Climate Inventory* (CCI) designed to measure the six dimensions of climate mentioned here which were derived from the analysis of managerial climate completed by Redding (1972). Bednar (1977), Baugh (1978), and Applbaum and Anatol (1979) have used the instrument in research. Tests of the CCI's internal reliability show coefficients ranging from .80 to .97, which are generally considered very satisfactory. Factor analysis of the CCI indicates the emergence of one main factor. Applbaum and Anatol (1979) reported that the CCI "may be a valid index of overall organizational communication climate" (p. 10).

We now need to identify relationships between the communication climate in organizations and other organizational variables such as structure, regulations, morale, and interpersonal relationships. In that way we can recognize those dimensions of communication that ought to be scrutinized in order to improve the overall organization climate and ultimately the effectiveness and efficiency of the organization. We shall discuss some ways for identifying problem areas and making improvements in the organizational communication system in later chapters.

Organizational and communication climate are important, as we mentioned earlier. It is so important, in fact, that some organizations base their recruiting and investment appeals on having high ratings of climate. The Kollmorgen ad (see Figure 11.2) illustrates the high regard held for a great organization climate.

FIGURE 11.2
The Kollmorgen Ad

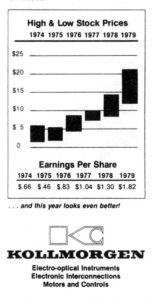

If your boss really trusted you, would you work harder?

Some companies are run like dictatorships; some like democracies. At Kollmorgen, we trust people. We think freedom and respect for the individual are the best motivators of man, especially when innovation and growth are the objectives, as they are at our company.

Kollmorgen is a fast-growing, high-technology company, and we intend to continue to grow by giving people the freedom to grow as individuals. We want them to feel free to try out their bright ideas and, if the free market buys them, to share in the rewards. So far the system has worked extraordinarily well. Freedom has paid off handsomely for our investors and our employees, from top to bottom.

Would you like to work for us? Would you like to invest in our stock (it's listed as KOL on the New York Stock Exchange)? If you would like to know more about a company that puts trust, responsibility, and the free market system to work helping people prosper, write for our annual report to Robert L. Swiggett, president, Kollmorgen Corporation, 66 Gate House Road, Stamford, CT 06902.

High & Low Stock Prices

1974 1975 1976 1977 1978 1979

$25
$20
$15
$10
$ 5
0

Earnings Per Share

1974	1975	1976	1977	1978	1979
$.66	$.46	$.83	$1.04	$1.30	$1.82

. . . and this year looks even better!

KOLLMORGEN

Electro-optical Instruments
Electronic Interconnections
Motors and Controls

Another construct or idea that has surfaced from research on organizational issues, particularly those surrounding the idea of productivity and employee satisfaction, is that of communication satisfaction. Downs (1977) reported that communication satisfaction has several identifiable dimensions itself and that instruments can measure it.

ORGANIZATIONAL COMMUNICATION SATISFACTION

According to Redding (1972), the term *communication satisfaction* has been used to refer to "the over-all degree of satisfaction an employee *perceives* in his total communication environment" (p. 429). The construct of *satisfaction* enriches the idea of communication climate. Climate includes the organization member's satisfaction with the availability of information. Satisfaction, in this sense, refers to how well the available information fulfills the organization member's requirements or demands for information, from whom it comes, the ways in which it is disseminated, how it is received and processed, and what kinds of responses one receives. Satisfaction is concerned with differences between what a person would like in terms of communication in an organization and what a person has in that regard. The organizational communication climate should clearly be affected by perceptions of how well the communicative activities of an organization satisfy a person's demands.

Satisfaction with communication is a function of what one gets compared with what one wants. Satisfaction should *not* be tied to any conception of message (displaying or interpreting) effectiveness. If the communication experience meets a requirement, it is likely to be regarded as satisfying, although it may not be particularly effective as far as standards of creating, displaying, and interpreting messages is concerned. You may feel a need for certain kinds of information or for having information presented to you in a particular way. When information is communicated in ways consistent with what you feel you would like, then you should experience satisfaction with communication.

The items that contribute most to satisfaction with communication in an organization are not fully identified, but the work of Wiio (1978), Downs and Hazen (1977), and Beckstrom (1980) suggest some dimensions. From Wiio's and Downs and Hazen's research Beckstrom constructed a questionnaire designed to measure ten factors of organizational communication satisfaction which were generally held in common by the earlier researchers. A factor analysis of responses revealed eight factors accounting for 55.1 percent of the variance. The factors that comprise satisfaction with organizational communication appear to be a combination of the following:

1. *Satisfaction with the person's job.* This included items about pay, benefits, promotion, and the work itself. Apparently satisfaction with aspects of the job contributes to satisfaction with communication.

2. *Satisfaction with the adequacy of information.* This factor included items about the degree of satisfaction with information about policies, new techniques, administrative and staff changes, future plans, and personal performance. Satisfaction with information received about the organization seems important to a concept of organizational communication satisfaction.

3. *Satisfaction with a person's ability to suggest improvements.* This factor included items such as places where communication ought to be improved, notification of changes for purposes of improvement, and the specific strategies used in making changes. Satisfaction with the kinds of changes being made, how the changes are to be made, and being informed about the changes appears to have relevance to satisfaction with organizational communication.

4. *Satisfaction with the efficiency of various channels of communicating.* This factor included items about the ways in which information is disseminated through an organization, including house organs, bulletins, memos, and other written materials. Communication satisfaction appears to be related to a person's view of how efficiently the media of an organization are used to disseminate information.

5. *Satisfaction with the quality of media.* Items related to this factor involved concerns about how well written materials were phrased, the value of the information when received, the balance and availability of information, and the promptness of the arrival of information. This suggests that concerns about the appearance, appropriateness, and availability of information have an effect upon a person's satisfaction with communication in an organization.

6. *Satisfaction with the way in which coworkers communicate.* This factor included items about horizontal and informal communication and about the degree of satisfaction derived from discussing problems and getting information from coworkers. This factor implies that satisfaction with communication in an organization is related in part to satisfactory relationships with peers.

7. *Satisfaction with communication involving the organization as an entity.* This factor included items involving relationships with the organization, support from the organization, and information from the organization. It appears that satisfaction with communication in the organization is affected by aspects of the organization often associated with communication climate, such as trust, support, and high performance goals.

In discussing communication satisfaction research, Downs (1977) observed that subjects tended to see a relationship between communication and satisfaction in the organization, with comments about communication climate and relationships with supervisors being most prominent. Such relationships suggest that supervisory styles have a powerful influence in both perceptions of climate and perceptions of satisfaction. We discussed supervisory styles in Chapter 7.

Closely related to the idea of communication satisfaction is the issue of *actual level of information* that any given member of the organization has about organization affairs. Redding (1972) referred to this as *information adequacy.* Beyond having adequate information about the organization, the question arises concerning whether having information is related in any way to goals of the organization—such as productivity, satisfaction, and employee development.

INFORMATION ADEQUACY

Information adequacy represents the actual amount of information accurately understood by a given group of organization members, plus their perceptions of whether they feel adequately informed (Redding, 1972). A cloud hanging over this issue concerns *what organization members ought to be told.* Usually decisions about what employees should know are made by top management of the organization. However, when lower-level employees report that the information they receive is inadequate, those decisions are made by the employees themselves. In any case information adequacy depends on some definition of what information ought to be known.

In a research program on measuring the effectiveness of employee communications being conducted at Southern Illinois University, Bateman and Miller (1979) reported developing the following list of topics on which employees might like to be informed:

fringe benefits
division products
employee hobbies
news about company
cartoons and jokes
how division products are used
employee recreational news
charity funds and drives
departmental features
savings bond programs
business trends affecting company
all products
executive promotions
employee safety
news about retirees
how company products are used
compensation
new or improved products
sales progress
free enterprise system
recipes and cooking hints

They also developed a checklist of subjects that employees might like to discuss with their supervisors; the list included

machine or job-related problems
time off
state of the division
potential layoffs
performance evaluation
procedures
fringe benefits
the company in general
overtime

tools and equipment
incoming orders
vacation time
plant or office procedures
how well the employee is doing
pay and pay increases

For purposes of their study Bateman and Miller chose six areas over which to develop a multiple-choice, objective examination to measure information adequacy. The areas were

wages and benefits
corporate diversity
business issues and problems
overseas business
acquisitions and growth
safety

Whether these are the best areas and the kinds of information that an employee ought to know has not been answered by any research reported at this time. The issue seems to be a substantial one for organizations, because, as Walton (1962) observed: "If each employee really mastered *all* the communications humming about him, he would have precious little time for anything else but that" (p. 22). Nevertheless, the general rule seems to be one of general and widespread ineffectiveness of downward communication, at least as far as information adequacy is measured by actual informational tests (Redding, 1972).

SUMMARY

In this chapter we have discussed the idea of organizational communication climate, organizational communication satisfaction, and information adequacy. We pointed out that the climate of an organization consists of how members of the organization can act and what they feel is responsible for the way others act. The climate in an organization, we also suggested, may be more important in creating an effective organization than are communication skills or techniques. The communication climate of an organization consists of the perceptions by organization members of characteristics of the organization in terms of how they demonstrate such behaviors as trust, supportiveness, and consultativeness. *Organizational communication satisfaction* refers to how well the available information fulfills the requirements of organization members for information and how it is handled. *Information adequacy* refers to what organization members ought to be told and whether the available information meets the need.

REFERENCES

APPLBAUM, RONALD I., and KARL W. E. ANATOL, "An Examination of the Relationship between Job Satisfaction, Organizational Norms, and Communication Climate among Employees in an Organization." Paper presented at meetings of the Communication Association of the Pacific, Honolulu, 1979.

BATEMAN, DAVID N., and JEFFREY L. MILLER, "Measuring the Effectiveness of Employee Communications." Paper presented at the annual meeting of the American Business Communication Association, December 1979.

BAUGH, STEVEN, "Communication Climate in a School District." Unpublished doctoral dissertation, Brigham Young University, 1978.

BECKSTROM, MARK R., "Measuring Communication Satisfaction in an Organization: The Design of a Measurement Instrument, Testing Its Reliability and Validity." Unpublished master's thesis, Brigham Young University, 1980.

BEDNAR, DAVID A., "The Measurement of Communication Climate in Organizations: The Reliability of a New Inventory." Unpublished master's thesis, Brigham Young University, 1977.

BLUMENSTOCK, DAVID I., "Climate," The World Book Encyclopedia, Vol. IV, pp. 520-524. Chicago: Field Enterprises Corporation, 1970.

DENNIS, HARRY S., "The Construction of a Managerial Communication Climate Inventory for Use in Complex Organizations." Paper presented at the annual meeting of the International Communication Association, New Orleans, 1974.

DOWNS, CAL W., "The Relationship between Communication and Job Satisfaction," in Readings in Interpersonal and Organizational Communication, ed. R. C. Huseman, C. M. Logue, and D. L. Freshley, pp. 363-376. Boston: Holbrook Press, Inc., 1977.

DOWNS, CAL W., and MICHAEL D. HAZEN, "A Factor Analytic Study of Communication Satisfaction," The Journal of Business Communication, 14, No. 3 (1977), 63-73.

GOLDHABER, GERALD M., Organizational Communication (2nd ed.). Dubuque, Iowa: Wm. C. Brown, 1979.

GOLDHABER, GERALD M., HARRY S. DENNIS, III, GARY M. RICHETTO, and OSMO A. WIIO, Information Strategies: New Pathways to Corporate Power. Englewood Cliffs, N.J.: Prentice-Hall, 1979.

JABLIN, FREDERIC M., "Organizational Communication Theory and Research: An Overview of Communication Climate and Network Research," Communication Yearbook 4. New Brunswick, N.J.: Transaction Books, 1980.

JAMES, A. P., and L. R. JAMES, "Organizational Climate: A Review of Theory and Research," Psychological Bulletin, 81 (1974), 1096-1112.

LEVEL, DALE A., "A Case Study of Human Communication in an Urban Bank." Unpublished doctoral dissertation, Purdue University, 1959.

PETERSON, BRENT D., and R. WAYNE PACE, "Communication Climate and Organizational Satisfaction." Unpublished paper, Brigham Young University, 1976.

REDDING, W. CHARLES, Communication within the Organization: An Interpretive Review of Theory and Research. New York: Industrial Communication Council, Inc., 1972.

SANFORD, AUBREY C., GARY T. HUNT, and HYLER J. BRACEY, Communication Behavior in Organizations. Columbus, Ohio: Chas. E. Merrill, 1976.

TAYLOR, J. C., and D. G. BOWERS, *Survey of Organizations.* Ann Arbor: Institute for Social Research, University of Michigan, 1972.

TIMM, PAUL R., *Managerial Communication: A Finger on the Pulse.* Englewood Cliffs, N.J.: Prentice-Hall, 1980.

WALTON, EUGENE, "Project: Office Communications,"*Administrative Management,* 23 (August 1962), 22–24.

WATERS, L. K., D. ROACH, and N. BATLIS, "Organizational Climate Dimensions and Job-Related Attitudes," *Personnel Psychology,* 27 (1974), 465–476.

WIIO, OSMO A., *Contingencies of Organizational Communication.* Helsinki: Institute for Human Communication, 1978.

12

GROUP PROCESSES
IN
ORGANIZATIONAL
COMMUNICATION

*communication among members
of cliques*

Network analysis has shown us that organizations consist of individuals who communicate more or less exclusively with one another; we call these *cliques* (Middlemist & Hitt, 1981, p. 186; Rogers & Rogers, 1976, p. 113). In the popular literature of our time, cliques are often referred to as *groups*. Cliques may meet the requirements of face-to-face groups, but some cliques are simply a number of individuals who communicate with one another. In both cases—cliques or groups—forces are at work that affect how members participate in the organization and contribute to their own well-being and the welfare of the organization. We call those forces *group processes*. This chapter is about group processes in organizations.

THE CONCEPT OF A CLIQUE

The term *clique* refers to different collections of people, but all cliques have the following common elements:

1. A number of individuals (more than two, which we call a *dyad* rather than a clique);
2. who interact with one another (as opposed to interacting with those who are not members of the clique); and
3. who perceive themselves as sharing some common interests, likes or dislikes, attitudes, or goals as members of a group.

This definition does not preclude individuals who interact with one another over the telephone or by computer printout from being members of a clique. Nevertheless, it does distinguish between a collection of people watching a baseball game who do not interact with one another from being called a clique, even though they appear to share some common interests. Just because someone is employed by an organization does not make him or her a member of a clique or a group. In fact, some employees feel that they are isolates in a large organization because they have little regular interaction with a manageable number of other employees and do not perceive themselves to share many likes or dislikes with a small number of their colleagues. When a person begins to identify with the likes or dislikes of a few other individuals, at least that person feels as if he or she is a member of a clique. That is the beginning of group membership.

GROUP FORMATION AND DEVELOPMENT

If you are to affect groups and work to help them achieve social and organizational goals, it is desirable to understand the reasons that led to their creation. You may be able to influence the groups to become a positive value to the organization, thereby avoiding potential problems. Some of the work of professionals in human resource development is directed toward building productive groups and teams of employees.

Group Formation

People appear to have a natural proclivity for joining with others as a means of satisfying some of their interpersonal needs.

FORMING GROUPS THROUGH NEED SATISFACTION

The idea of interpersonal needs is based on the assumption that people want to have associations with other people. All of us must satisfy to some degree certain interpersonal needs. Schutz (1958) described three needs that constitute his theory of interpersonal relations called *FIRO* (fundamental interpersonal relations orientation): (1) the need for inclusion, (2) the need for control, and (3) the need for affection.

INTERPERSONAL NEEDS

Inclusion is the need to interact with other people. Some people like a lot of contact, whereas others prefer to work alone and maintain their privacy. Each person, to some degree, is trying to interact with others while attempting to maintain a certain amount of solitude. We seek to have other people initiate contact with us, but we also want to be left alone.

Control is the need to have power and influence. We all vary in terms of the degree to which we want to be controlled by others versus the degree to which we wish to control them. You may know someone who wants to be controlled completely by a friend or spouse. On the other hand, you may know, or be, a person who has strong feelings about being independent and in control of your own decisions.

Affection is the need to have warm, close, personal relationships with others.

TABLE 12.1
Matrix of Scores on the FIRO-B Inventory

	Inclusion I	Control C	Affection A
Express (E)			
Want (W)			

At the other extreme is the situation in which a person prefers impersonal and distant rather than close relationships with other people. Each of us has our preferences. One person may want others to show warmth and affection toward him or her but find it difficult to express affection toward them.

The description of each interpersonal need has suggested that there are two parts to each one: *the expressed behaviors,* or the behaviors a person initiates toward other people, and *the wanted behaviors,* or the behaviors a person prefers that others express toward him or her. Your fundamental interpersonal relations orientation (FIRO) is your usual approach to interpersonal relations in terms of the three needs (inclusion, control, and affection) and the degree to which you want and express behaviors relevant to each need. Schutz (1958) developed a questionnaire called FIRO-B (for "behavior") that allows individuals to be located in a matrix on the basis of scores in each need area. Table 12.1 shows the matrix.

FORMING GROUPS THROUGH ASSIGNMENT

There is little doubt that groups are created through voluntary association in response to the impelling motivation of interpersonal needs. In fact, most of us will join a number of groups over the years as a subtle way of satisfying those interpersonal needs. Nevertheless, we ought to recognize that in organizations, group membership is often brought about by the assignment of individuals to positions, committees, or teams. A considerably larger amount of interaction occurs as a consequence of assignment to some task in an organization rather than as a result of fulfilling some interpersonal need to belong. Assignment to a team helps to satisfy our need to be part of a group, but the team is formed through assignment. However, the very assignment to a team or formal group or promotion to a supervisory or managerial position allows for the development of group ties that strengthen and satisfy our interpersonal needs.

Assignment to a work group in the organization provides for opportunities to participate in group problem solving, information sharing, and informal interaction. People who are in close proximity to one another tend to interact more, and interaction tends to help develop feelings of attraction. Assignment to a committee or work team gives you a chance to experience emotional reactions that aid in unifying a group. People are usually attracted to others who share common emotional experiences. The accomplishment of a particular task often leads to positive emotional experiences and strengthens group cohesiveness.

137

Group Development

An important theoretical and practical discovery about group processes is that every group, regardless of its purpose of composition, proceeds through four phases of development if given adequate time. For a group to progress from one phase to another, it must arrive at a general understanding, frequently called *consensus,* of both interpersonal relationships and task aspects of group processes. If consensus has not been reached at one stage prior to proceeding to another, a regression often occurs later. What is particularly important to remember is that groups need to go through each of the stages. If they do not, the group is frequently stymied right when it should be accomplishing its objectives.

Several systems for describing stages have been created over the years (Bales & Strodtbeck, 1951; Bennis & Shepard, 1956; Fisher, 1970), but we shall use Tuckman's (1965) general system. It reflects the major stages identified in the research and represents a systematic way of thinking about stages in group development. The four stages and the interpersonal relation and task function issues associated with each stage in the model are summarized in Table 12.2.

Stage 1: Forming. At Stage 1 the task function is to make sure that individual group members are oriented to the work to be done—why they are there, what they are supposed to do, and how they are going to do it. Group members may be instructed on these points, or they may evolve the goals and orientation through interaction. On the interpersonal relations side, members must resolve a number of dependence-independence issues, such as the extent to which the designated leader will provide direction, the ground rules on which the group will operate, and the agenda that will be followed. At this stage group members are getting oriented to one another and the task to be accomplished.

Stage 2: Storming. Different feelings about authority, rules, the agenda, and leadership surface in the form of interpersonal conflict. Resolving those differences is critical to movement to the next stage. Unresolved conflict tends to deter the group from becoming a smooth functioning team. In task functions the group is seeking to answer questions about who is going to be responsible for what tasks, what the work rules are going to be, and what the rewards will be. The creation of assignments and rules to govern work and interaction imposes organization and structure on the group.

TABLE 12.2
Stages in Group Development

STAGE	INTERPERSONAL RELATIONS ISSUES	TASK FUNCTION ISSUES
1. Forming	Dependence/independence	Orientation
2. Storming	Interpersonal conflict	Organization/structure
3. Norming	Cohesion	Information sharing
4. Performing	Interdependence	Problem solving

Stage 3: Norming. As the differences are resolved and the group acquires structure, individuals begin to experience a sense of cohesion and a feeling of catharsis at having resolved interpersonal conflicts and survived the main interpersonal issue. They begin to share ideas and feelings, give feedback to one another, solicit feedback, explore actions related to completing the task, and share information, the primary task function. Group members begin to feel good about what is going on. There is an emerging openness with regard to the task, and some playfulness even occurs. Groups that get stuck at this stage experience high levels of pleasantness about interacting with other members and evolve into what has been called a happy circle or a group with high morale and intense levels of interaction. Unfortunately the feelings of cohesiveness often stall the group and keep it from moving to the performing stage.

Stage 4: Performing. At this stage members are both highly task- and highly person-oriented. They work singly, in subgroups, and as a total unit. Group members both cooperate and compete; there is support for experimenting with alternative ways of making decisions and solving problems. In interpersonal relations group members feel highly interdependent, but neither dependent nor independent. The task function is one of problem solving. Harmony for its own sake is replaced by individual freedom and a strong emphasis on productivity.

In real-life working groups, of course, the interpersonal relations issues and the task issues are dealt with jointly and simultaneously. Although we separated them at times for convenience, organizational groups cope with interpersonal problems and task problems as if they were pretty much the same. The ability to recognize some differences, however, may allow you to catch thorny issues that may be stalling the group, to separate interpersonal relations issues from the task issues, and to effectively aid the group in being productive.

All too often the major emphasis of the group is on trying to solve a specific problem without considering how group processes might be improved to solve problems more efficiently in the long run. Some attention should be paid to how the group itself functions, to what behaviors help the group accomplish its work. Groups, especially work groups, seldom examine how they operate. Except for the expletives uttered when something goes wrong later on, the group members focus almost exclusively on difficulties with the task. It may be that the group has interpersonal problems that interfere with the way in which it works. If a little time were devoted to trying to discover why the team functioned so badly, it might be making a solid investment with great dividends in the future.

GROUP DYNAMICS

A group usually serves three functions for its members: (1) it satisfies interpersonal needs, (2) it provides support for individual self-concepts, and (3) it protects individuals from their own mistakes (Hampton, Summer, & Webber, 1973). Besides helping individual members in those three areas, the group takes on an identity, or self-concept, of its own. The group acquires some goals of its own. Occasionally individual goals conflict with group goals; sometimes group goals differ from those

⑤ of the organization, but sometimes they are all very similar. The way in which the group progresses through the four stages from getting organized to being productive is related to how the group copes with three important aspects of group life: (1) the roles or activities performed by group members, (2) the norms and differences in status that develop as members interact, and (3) the conflict that evolves from pressures to behave competitively rather than cooperatively (Huse & Bowditch, 1973). The interaction among individual needs, group goals, and the roles, norms, and conflict of group functioning is what we shall call the *dynamics* of a group. Let us now look at the three aspects of group life and how they contribute or detract from the way in which groups accomplish their goals.

Individual Group Roles

⑥ The types of behaviors, activities, and roles that take place in a group may be analyzed in terms of three goals: (1) what it takes to get the job done, (2) what it takes to keep the group together, and (3) what it takes to satisfy irrelevant personal needs (Benne & Sheats, 1948). The first type is usually called *task roles,* the second type is referred to as *maintenance roles,* which are both considered to be contributors to the effectiveness of a group, and the third type is called *self-serving roles,* which more often than not actually hinder effective group functioning. Self-serving roles represent ineffective behavior in groups and become the observable manifestations of interpersonal conflict.

Task roles. Behaviors such as offering ideas, suggesting methods and plans, asking for information and opinions, prodding people along, and handling procedural activities, such as distributing papers and recording ideas, all contribute to the smooth functioning of a group. These types of behaviors help to get the job done.

Maintenance roles. Behaviors such as providing praise, expressing warmth and support, mediating differences, listening to others, accepting group decisions, introducing some humor to relax the group, and bringing in group members who might not otherwise speak also contribute to the smooth functioning of a group. These types of behaviors keep the group together.

Self-serving roles. Behaviors such as attacking the status of others, opposing group ideas stubbornly and for personal reasons, asserting superiority to control and interrupt others, using flattery to patronize group members, clowning and engaging in horseplay and ridicule, and staying off the subject under discussion to avoid making a commitment represent ways to thwart the progress of the group. These types of behaviors prevent the group from getting the job done and discourage them from staying together.

Figure 12.1 lists and defines some typical functional and nonfunctional roles which you might review in order to recognize desirable behaviors that are not being enacted in a group and undesirable behaviors that occur too frequently and deter the group from accomplishing its goals.

FIGURE 12.1

Typical Functional and Nonfunctional Individual Roles in Groups

FUNCTIONAL OR EFFECTIVE BEHAVIOR IN GROUPS

Task Roles

1. *Initiating:* suggest goals, methods, and procedures; starts the group moving.

2. *Information seeking:* asks for data, factual statements, reports, and experiences.

3. *Information giving:* gives estimates, personal experiences, reports, ideas, and facts.

4. *Opinion seeking:* asks for beliefs, values and expressions of feelings.

5. *Opinion giving:* offers own beliefs, attitudes, values and feelings.

6. *Clarifying:* interprets issues, elaborates on ideas, gives examples and illustrations.

7. *Summarizing:* pulls together related ideas, restates suggestions, demonstrates relationships among ideas.

8. *Procedure facilitating:* passes out papers, arranges seating, runs projector, records ideas on paper, chart, or chalkboard.

Maintenance Roles

1. *Energizing:* prods group to action, stimulates more activity.

2. *Supporting:* praises others, expresses solidarity and togetherness.

3. *Gatekeeping:* brings in nonparticipators, prevents dominance by one or two, helps everyone interact.

4. *Harmonizing:* conciliates feelings of others, mediates disagreements between others.

5. *Tension relieving:* diverts attention of others from tense situations, relaxes others, introduces relevant humor.

6. *Following:* listens to others, goes along with group decisions.

7. *Compromising:* offers alternative ideas that improve member status, admits errors, and modifies position to aid progress.

8. *Consensus testing:* checks to see if the group is close to a decision or tries a trial idea.

NONFUNCTIONAL OR INEFFECTIVE BEHAVIOR IN GROUPS

Self-Serving Roles

1. *Blocking:* constantly raises unreasonable objections, insists that nothing can be done.

2. *Attacking:* expresses disapproval and ill will, deflates status of others, uses barbed jokes.

3. *Dominating:* interrupts and orders people around, gives directions in a superior tone, controls through flattery and other patronizing behaviors.

4. *Recognition seeking:* boasts, calls attention to own accomplishments, seeks sympathy or pity, claims credit for ideas of others.

5. *Clowning:* engages in horseplay and ridicule, disrupts with cynical remarks, diverts attention of group to tangents.

6. *Playboying:* shows lack of involvement, abandons group while being there physically.

7. *Confessing:* engages in personal catharsis, uses group as audience for talking about mistakes.

8. *Special-interest pleading:* supports personal projects and interests and presses others for support, advocates interests not related to task.

Group Norms and Status

As a group progresses through the stages in group development, it begins to acquire a life of its own, a history and culture, that is revealed through the expression of similar feelings, beliefs, and values among group members. A commonality of feelings and beliefs is often referred to as a *norm,* or standard of appropriate and acceptable behavior. The tendency to associate with people who share your feelings, beliefs, and values; to listen to and accept their ideas; and to defend their points of view also strengthens group solidarity and exerts pressure on group members not to deviate from group decisions.

If you happen to belong to a group whose values are different from yours or those of other groups of which you are a member—such as family, church, or consciousness-raising association—you will probably find yourself in a position in which you must decide whether (1) to accept the new values, (2) to try to bring about a change in the values of the group, or (3) to leave the group. Employment may bring you into an organization in which the values of the business are different from yours. You will have to decide how to cope with the norms of acceptable behavior in that organization.

Although norms in a group are strong influences toward conformity or similarity in behavior, they also reveal differences among members. Once you have established yourself in a group and demonstrate that you are able to behave according to group norms, a conflicting need often emerges: the need for *status* or prestige. Even within small work groups some subtle differences in status are usually apparent. The norms that indicate how we should behave in your presence define your status: the "respect or disrespect, familiarity or unfamiliarity, reserve or frankness" we are to show in your presence indicates how you are different from the rest of the group (Hampton, Summer, & Webber, 1973). If you fail to treat people with the appropriate degree of respect or disrespect, you may be subject to punishment for violating group norms.

The factors that accord individuals status in any particular group vary from group to group. A person's family background, name, or relatives may provide status in some organizations. In some jobs education, seniority, age, sex, or ethnic background may contribute to higher status. Such personal characteristics as physical size, dress and general appearance, sociability, friendliness, self-confidence, and status in another group (such as an athletic club) may all influence perceptions of status. On the job a person's title, job description, compensation, privileges, freedom from direct supervision, office location, furnishings, and potential for upward mobility may be considered when others assign status to you. Regardless of what elements determine status in your group, you can be pretty certain that the best positions will be occupied by high-status individuals.

Competition and Conflict within the Group

Individual group roles and group norms and status affect the way in which group members communicate with one another. In addition most group members have occasion to cooperate and to compete with each other. A situation in which rewards are limited so that when one group member gets the rewards other group members lose them is usually called one of *competition.* If group members believe, on the other hand, that no one will be rewarded unless they all contribute to the task, the situation will usually be called one of *cooperation.*

In a work group some external authority determines how the rewards are to be distributed among group members. The boss creates or works within a system in which pay, recognition, promotions, and other rewards are given according to conditions established by the organization. Thus whether the group members are to function in a competitive or a cooperative atmosphere is decided by the organization. For example, the organization could have a policy that the lowest producer on the team each month is to be fired, regardless of how well the team does. The consequence would most likely be a fairly competitive climate. A single member of a team might create a competitive atmosphere even if the organization was attempting to have groups work cooperatively. By monopolizing the time, using more space than others, consuming a large number of supplies, or traveling more than other group members, one individual can be viewed as taking something that is scarce but of value to all group members. If the resource is considered limited, the one member can make competition an inevitable consequence of being a group member just by getting more than his or her share.

Most groups, of course, have some cooperative activities and some competitive ones. In order to accomplish a task, they may be required to cooperate. Nevertheless, the group members may still compete for personal rewards such as admiration, approval, affection, and power. Few rewards, whether personal or material, are distributed equally. Differences in roles and status lead to perceptions that rewards will be distributed competitively.

EFFECTS OF COMPETITION

When group members view their roles as highly competitive, they tend to listen less to what other members say, to understand less well what was actually said, become less interested in high achievement, tend to help one another less, have more difficulty coordinating their group's efforts, are more likely to duplicate the efforts of others in order to do the work themselves, tend to be less efficient, and tend to do lower-quality work. In addition they may not like what they have accomplished, the group with whom they worked, or each other as individuals as much.

EFFECTS OF COOPERATION

When group members view their roles as highly cooperative, they tend to show more coordination of their efforts. There is greater diversity of contributions per group member, with more subdivision of activities. Group members tend to be more attentive, have higher mutual comprehension of information, and make more common appraisals of information. Cooperative groups tend to exhibit a clearer orientation and orderliness with more pressures toward achievement. The interaction seems more friendly, and the group and its products are evaluated more favorably.

Not all jobs demand the same degree of competition and cooperation. Some kinds of work require creative performances that may receive strong stimulation from competition; other work requires the careful and complete cooperation of every team member in order to be successful. The ideal balance between competition and cooperation is a continuing issue and relates directly to the type of work that is being done. Regardless, competition and cooperation have different effects on team work. Competition is more likely to lead to conflicts within the group.

CONFLICT

It is possible to analyze conflict from a number of different communicative levels, such as the intrapersonal, interpersonal, intergroup, or interorganizational. We have chosen to look at conflict in a group setting since conflicts at both the intrapersonal and the interpersonal levels may be demonstrated in the group. Later in this chapter we shall briefly analyze intergroup processes and intergroup conflict.

Conflict has been defined as an "expressed struggle between at least two inter-dependent parties, who perceive incompatible goals, scarce rewards, and interference from the other party in achieving their goals" (Frost & Wilmot, 1978, p. 9). In this view the "struggle" represents differences between the parties that are expressed, recognized, and experienced. For conflict to occur, the difference must be com-municated. Conflicts may be expressed in different ways, from very subtle nonverbal movements to all-out physical brawling, from subtle sarcasm to all-out verbal attack.

The concept of struggle is related to efforts designed to achieve goals, to secure resources, and to get rewards that are also being sought after by the other party. The implication is that people want to do different things and they also want to have the same things. These are the concepts of incompatible goals and scarce rewards. Early signs of conflict may be identified by an increase in the rate of dis-agreements among group members. Previously neutral comments take on an un-friendly tone. As the tension continues, more explicit signs of disagreement surface. The conflict is expressed through sighs, uneasy twitches in facial muscles, faltering silences, lapses in attention, slouching, doodling, turning away, and curt verbal utterances.

If members of a group have common goals, the likelihood of conflict develop-ing is lowered. Goals involve a wide variety of desires that people would like to achieve, some of which are real and tangible and others of which are imagined and intangible. The goal of a company to reduce costs may in fact be quite incompat-ible with the goal of an employee to increase his or her income. However, some superordinate goal may encompass both of the incompatible goals to allow conflict to be managed to the advantage of both the company and the employee.

Rewards are of different kinds. Most of us are familiar with salaries, bonuses, promotions, corner offices, and vacations, but more personal reactions such as respect, time together, warmth, pride, listening and love are also rewards. Frost and Wilmot (1978) argue that in interpersonal conflict, "regardless of the content issue involved, the parties usually perceive a shortage of power and/or self-esteem reward" (p. 12). Thus conflicts may often be averted by showing that those rewards are less scarce than supposed.

PERSONAL CONFLICT STYLES

There seems to be general agreement that people have preferred ways of han-dling conflict, or at least habitual ways of dealing with conflict (Filley, 1975; Frost & Wilmot, 1978). A habitual way of behaving is one that is somewhat fixed and resistant to change because it is comfortable and natural. When two people come together expecting to claim their share of scarce resources, they somewhat habitually think about themselves and the other person. Thus conflict styles appear to be some combination of the amount of concern you have about accomplishing your own goals and the amount of concern you have about the other person accomplishing his or her goals. These concerns can be portrayed by two axes running from low concern to high concern. The resulting cells with mixtures of concern for accomplishing personal goals and concern for allowing or even helping the other person accomplish his or her goals represent styles that people have for dealing with conflict. Figure 12.2 identifies five personal conflict styles which we shall briefly characterize. The terms used to label the styles are derived from the writings of Hall (1969), Blake and Mouton (1970), and Kilmann and Thomas (1975).

1. *Competitor or tough battler.* The person who employs this style pursues his or her own concerns somewhat ruthlessly and generally at the expense of other members of the group. The Tough Battler views losing as an indication of weakness, reduced status, and a crumbling self-image. Winning is the only worthwhile goal and results in accomplishment and exhilaration.

2. *Collaborator or problem solver.* The person who employs this style seeks to create a situation in which the goals of all parties involved can be accomplished. The Problem Solver works at finding mutually acceptable solutions. Winning and losing are not part of his or her way of looking at conflict.

FIGURE 12.2
Personal Conflict Styles

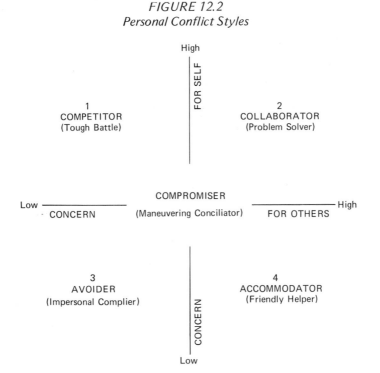

3. *Compromiser or maneuvering conciliator.* The person who employs this style assumes that everyone involved in a disagreement stands to lose, and he or she works to help find a workable position. A pattern of "giving in" often develops.

4. *Accommodator or friendly helper.* The person who employs this style is somewhat nonassertive and quite cooperative, neglecting his or her own concerns in favor of those of others. The Friendly Helper feels that harmony should prevail and that anger and confrontation are bad. When a decision is reached, the Accommodator may go along and wish later that he or she had expressed some reservations.

5. *Avoider or impersonal complier.* The person who employs this style tends to view conflict as unproductive and somewhat punishing. Thus the Avoider gets away from an uncomfortable situation by refusing to be concerned. The result is usually an impersonal reaction to the decision and little commitment to future actions.

Unfortunately when conflict occurs we have tendencies to do and say things that perpetuate the conflict rather than reduce or eliminate it. Although frequently very difficult to do, there are usually a few actions that can be taken to start the deescalation of conflict. Disagreements seldom resolve themselves. In small groups conflict is usually handled best through the process of *integration*—the combination of each person's ideas into a group idea (Barnlund & Haiman, 1960).

INTEGRATION

The goal of integrative decision making is to achieve consensus. The philosophical basis underlying consensus is that differences in thinking, feeling, and behaving are best resolved by incorporating the points of view of all parties into the decisions or plans. Cooperative effort is achieved by finding, isolating, and clarifying areas of agreement and disagreement, thus systematically narrowing the area of difference and enlarging the area of acceptability (Pace, Peterson, & Burnett, 1979). Two areas of difference need to be managed: differences in understanding and differences in feelings.

Differences in understanding may be determined in three ways: (1) By discovering what the other person or party means. Many times a simple statement of what a person means prevents disagreements from escalating. (2) By checking the validity of evidence and reasoning. Disagreements and conflicts often develop because it is possible for two people to reason from the same data and arrive at totally different conclusions. You might want to locate the source of evidence in order to determine how accurate it is. (3) By identifying a more basic value or goal, sometimes called a *superordinate goal.* When a disagreement is based on differences in preferences or values, understanding may be increased by identifying a more basic value that is acceptable to all parties.

Differences based on feelings may be determined in five ways: (1) By increasing the self-esteem of those with whom you have the disagreement. A basic source of emotional resistance is loss of face. No one wants to appear foolish, illogical, or misdirected. Reduce disagreements based on feelings by providing ego support and ways of strengthening self-esteem. (2) By creating an atmosphere of inquiry. Get group members to probe into the issue by asking open-ended questions. Resistance often occurs because all alternatives have not been explored. (3) By involving each member of the group in the discussion. Emotional barriers and negative feelings flare up when we feel uninvited or discouraged from making contributions. Avoid squelching anyone, regardless of what they have said. (4) By using summaries to show the group where it has been and where it is going. Summaries can help objectify comments and reduce excessive generalizing and overstatement. Group members are allowed to respond to a more objective summary rather than the original emotional comments. (5) By providing for the release of feelings. Participants should have the opportunity to make highly emotional statements without argument or refutation. Many disagreements can be resolved simply by letting the other person dissipate the underlying feelings (Pace, Peterson, & Burnett, 1979).

The use of integrative decision making to reduce disagreements capitalizes on a merger of information, logic, and feelings to achieve the best collective judgment of the entire group. Conflict is used creatively and constructively.

INTERGROUP PROCESSES

So far in this chapter we have examined the processes involved in the formation, development, and maintenance of groups. In this final section we shall extend the discussion to issues surrounding communication between groups and the processes and factors that produce conflict between groups in the organization. Most large organizations consist of many small groups that can be distinguished on the basis of who belongs to them, the goals they have to achieve, the space they occupy, and their leadership. These groups ought to cooperate to achieve the goals of the parent organization, but they often end up fighting or at least competing vigorously among themselves for resources, power, status, and other rewards, in the same way that individuals compete against one another. Groups, like individuals, tend to protect, maintain, and enhance their own positions within the organization. They resist others whom they perceive as threats to what they value and possess. The result is often intergroup conflict (Coffey, Athos, & Reynolds, 1975).

One of the most important aspects of organizational life concerns relations among groups within the organization (Schein, 1969). The symptoms of bad relations are often somewhat easy to recognize. A breakdown in the flow of work or lack of coordination between groups usually stands out. Poor communication or a failure to exchange information adequately may be a symptom that accompanies lack of coordination. Delays and mistakes often lead to tensions and negative feeling. If groups must rely on one another to get their work done, the symptoms are often more dramatic. Conflict between groups is expressed in much the same way that interpersonal conflict is. "Criticisms, bickering, snide remarks, and intentional ignoring of others are clear indicators of difficult relations, just as the opposites indicate satisfying ones" (Coffey et al., 1975).

Intergroup Conflict

When one or more groups feel frustrated because they are being kept from accomplishing their goals, intergroup conflict occurs. Some groups look for the source of frustration inside their group—their own skills, methods, equipment, and procedures.

Other groups look for the source of their frustrations outside their group. When they think they have found the source of their frustrations in some other group, a downward spiral of conflict develops. Seven stages seem to characterize the cycle:

1. Beginnings of doubt and distrust appear, and the climate between the groups deteriorates.
2. Perceptions of the outside group become distorted or stereotyped and polarized, with verbal comments dividing the "good" groups from the "bad" ones.
3. Cohesiveness and related feelings such as friendliness, attractiveness, closeness, and importance within each group increase.
4. Adherence to group norms and conformity also increase in each group.
5. Groups ready themselves for more authoritarian leadership and direction.
6. Hostile behaviors, reduced communicative contacts, and other signs of negative intergroup relations become apparent.
7. Complete separation is mutually desired, and any form of positive collaborative effort ceases (Coffey et al., 1975).

What happens to the competing groups when a decision is made and one is the winner and the other is the loser? Schein (1969) indicates that the winning group retains its cohesiveness and may even increase in that area. It also experiences a letdown and becomes complacent and casual. Along with the loss of its fighting spirit, the winning group experiences higher intragroup cooperation and concern for its members with an accompanying decrease in concern for task accomplishment. The winning group tends to feel that its positive image and the negative stereotype of the other group have been confirmed.

The losing group looks for an explanation for its loss in some external source such as the decision makers or dumb luck. When the group accepts its loss, it begins to splinter, internal fights break out, and unresolved internal conflicts surface. The losing group becomes more tense, gets ready to work harder, and appears desperate to find something to blame for the loss. The losing group places a high concern on recouping its losses by working harder, with less concern for member needs. The losing group tends to learn something about itself because its positive image was upset by the loss, forcing a reevaluation of the group's perceptions. Once the loss has been accepted realistically, the losing group tends to become more cohesive and more effective.

Reducing Intergroup Conflict

Huse and Bowditch (1973) suggest five ways for minimizing conflict within the existing organizational framework:

1. Make certain that information for solving problems is discovered and held in common by the groups involved. Representatives of different groups might meet regularly to study problem areas and to develop joint recommendations.
2. Rotate people among different groups. This suggestion implies the Buck Roger's era of organization theory with temporary work groups and project management. Some groups are too specialized to use this method of reducing conflict, but some work areas are well suited for rotating members.

3. Bring groups into close contact with one another. Bring the opposing groups together to clear the air and allow them to share perceptions.
4. Locate a common enemy. A competing company, the government, or some other group may allow the groups in conflict to join forces and cooperate to repel the invader. This may bring the groups into closer contact and dissipate the conflict.
5. Identify or develop a common set of goals. This is the idea of locating a superordinate objective that both groups have in common.

SUMMARY

In this chapter we have discussed group processes in the organization. Both intragroup and intergroup activities and conflicts have been examined. A group, or clique, was defined as a number of individuals who interact with one another and who perceive themselves as sharing some common interests. This definition allows individuals who interact over the telephone or by computer printout to be members of a clique. Group formation was analyzed in terms of Schutz's three-needs theory of interpersonal relations: inclusion, control, and affection. Schutz's instrument, called FIRO-B, was mentioned as a way to locate individual need levels and determine their compatibility. A short discussion of the effects of forming groups through assignment rather than through satisfaction of interpersonal needs indicated that such a procedure simply accelerated the need to understand stages in group development. Four stages in the development of effectively functioning groups were discussed: forming, storming, norming, and performing. Four interpersonal relations issues and four task function issues were also analyzed.

The dynamics of group processes were discussed in terms of individual group roles or activities, group norms and status, and competition and conflict within groups. Eight task roles, eight maintenance roles, and eight self-serving roles were listed and defined. Cooperation and competition were characterized. Five personal conflict styles were discussed: the Competitor, the Collaborator, the Accommodator, the Compromiser, and the Avoider. Ways of resolving conflict through the process of integration were also analyzed. Finally, intergroup processes and conflict were examined. A seven-stage cycle of frustration leading to intergroup conflict was explained. The effects on groups of winning and losing in competition and five ways of reducing intergroup conflict were discussed.

REFERENCES

BALES, ROBERT F., and F. L. STRODTBECK, "Phases in Group Problem Solving," *Journal of Abnormal and Social Psychology*, 46 (1951), 485–495.

BARNLUND, DEAN C., and FRANKLYN S. HAIMAN, *The Dynamics of Discussion*. Boston: Houghton Mifflin, 1960.

BENNE, KENNETH, and P. SHEATS, "Functional Roles of Group Members," *Journal of Social Issues*, 4 (1948), 41–49.

BENNIS, WARREN G., and H. A. SHEPARD, "A Theory of Group Development," *Human Relations*, 9 (1956), 415–437.

BLAKE, ROBERT R., and JANE S. MOUTON, "The Fifth Achievement," *Journal of Applied Behavior Science,* 6 (1970), 413–426.

COFFEY, ROBERT E., ANTHONY G. ATHOS, and PETER A. RAYNOLDS, *Behavior in Organizations: A Multidimensional View* (2nd ed.). Englewood Cliffs, N.J.: Prentice-Hall, 1975.

FILLEY, ALAN C., *Interpersonal Conflict Resolution.* Glenview, Ill.: Scott, Foresman, 1975.

FISHER, B. AUBREY, "Decision Emergence: Phases in Group Decision-Making," *Speech Monographs,* 37 (1970), 53–66.

FROST, JOYCE HOCKER, and WILLIAM W. WILMOT, *Interpersonal Conflict.* Dubuque, Iowa: Wm. C. Brown, 1978.

HALL, JAY, *Conflict Management Survey.* Austin, Tex.: Teleometrics, Inc., 1969.

HAMPTON, DAVID R., CHARLES E. SUMMER, and ROSS E. WEBBER, *Organizational Behavior and the Practice of Management* (revised). Glenview, Ill.: Scott, Foresman, 1973.

HUSE, EDGAR F., and JAMES L. BOWDITCH, *Behavior in Organizations: A Systems Approach to Managing.* Reading, Mass.: Addison-Wesley, 1973.

KILMANN, RALPH, and KENNETH THOMAS, "Interpersonal Conflict-Handling Behavior as Reflections of Jungian Personality Dimensions," *Psychological Reports,* 37 (1975), 971–980.

MIDDLEMIST, R. DENNIS and MICHAEL A. HITT, *Organizational Behavior: Applied Concepts.* Chicago: Science Research Associates, Inc., 1981.

PACE, R. WAYNE, BRENT D. PETERSON, and M. DALLAS BURNETT, *Techniques for Effective Communication.* Reading, Mass.: Addison-Wesley, 1979.

ROGERS, EVERETT M., and REKHA AGARWALA-ROGERS, *Communication in Organizations.* New York: The Free Press, 1976.

SCHEIN, EDGAR H., *Process Consultation: Its Role in Organization Development.* Reading, Mass.: Addison-Wesley, 1969.

SCHUTZ, WILLIAM, *FIRO: A Three Dimensional Theory of Interpersonal Behavior.* New York: Holt, Rinehart and Winston, 1958.

TUCKMAN, B. W., "Developmental Sequence in Small Groups," *Psychological Bulletin,* 63, (1965), 384–399.

13

NETWORKS, PATTERNS, AND ROLES

the flow of information
in organizations

The accomplishment of most organizational tasks is related to how well information is communicated to people in all parts of the organization. The process of making information available to organization members and securing information from them is referred to as the *flow of information.*

DEFINITION OF FLOW

To describe something as a *flow,* it must move or proceed continuously. Water in a stream "flows" because it issues from some source and proceeds along its course. Any continuous movement may be called a flow. Thus we think of information flowing throughout an organization because, at least perceptually, it issues from some source and appears to move somewhat continuously from person to person. Technically, information *does not* literally flow. In fact, information itself does not move. What does seem to happen is the display of a message, the interpretation of the display, and the creation of another display. The creation, display, and interpretation of messages is the process by which information is distributed throughout organizations.

The concept of *process* implies that events and relationships are moving and changing continuously, that events and relationships are dynamic. A dynamic relationship or event is one involving energy and action. Thus what we call the flow of information in an organization is actually a dynamic process in which messages are constantly and continuously being created, displayed, and interpreted. The process is ongoing and constantly changing—that is, organizational communication is not something that happens and stops. Communication takes place all the time.

Organizational communication may be thought of as a "happening"—an experience that started before you entered the process and continues after you make an exit. To begin communicating means that you are aware that the experience is happening. As an event, communication always has something that precedes it and something that follows it. You step into the process not knowing very precisely what came before or what will take place after and being somewhat vague about what is actually taking place at the moment.

Guetzkow (1965) has appropriately pointed out that the flow of information in an organization may occur in one of three ways: simultaneously, serially, or in some combination of the two. We shall examine the meanings of these ways of disseminating information in organizations.

SIMULTANEOUS MESSAGE DISSEMINATION

A great deal of organizational communication is person to person, or dyadic, involving only a source and an interpreter as the final destination. However, it is also fairly common for a manager to want information to get out to more than one person, such as when changes in a work schedule need to be made or when a group needs to be briefed on a new procedure. Frequently messages—called memos or memorandums—are sent to many individuals in an organization. On occasion, such as a university-wide faculty meeting, the top executive or president wishes to send a message to all members of the organization. Many organizations publish a house organ—a magazine or a newsletter that is mailed to all members of the organization. When all members of a particular unit—a department, college, or division—are to receive information at about the same time, we call the process *simultaneous message dissemination* (Figure 13.1).

When the same message needs to arrive at different locations at the same time, plans should be made to use a simultaneous message dissemination strategy or technique. The selection of a dissemination technique on the basis of timing (simultaneous arrival) necessitates thinking about dissemination methods a little bit differently than we usually do. For example, one of the main concerns is whether the message can be distributed at the same time. You might think of a written memo as a sure-fire way of sending a message to all members of an organization at the same time. However, the mail service might delay receipt of the memo for some individuals, and some individuals may not pick up their mail for several days. On the other hand, a meeting might be a way of getting information to everyone in the organization

FIGURE 13.1
Simultaneous Message Dissemination

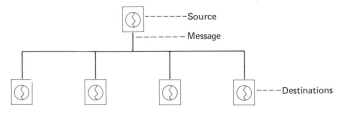

at the same time, but, as you can appreciate, the schedule of some individuals may not permit them to attend a meeting, especially if they must travel to attend. The memo is a written medium whereas a meeting is an oral, face-to-face medium. Either or both methods may facilitate the simultaneous dissemination of information to a particular group of organization members; either or both may be ineffective.

With the development of telecommunication media, the task of disseminating information to everyone on a simultaneous basis has been simplified for some organizations. At a given time widely located employees may all tune in to a designated channel on their television monitors and simultaneously see and hear the chief executive officer provide information. Occasionally a large proportion of the population of the United States is able to listen and visually respond to a message from the President by seeking access to a television set. Television allows a single speaker to make contact with all members of an organization on an individual basis, without the necessity of them coming together or having a printed document delivered to them. With the development of more sophisticated cable and telephone systems coupled with video images, it may be possible for entire organizations to have visual and vocal contact with one another while remaining at their individual places of work. Simultaneous message dissemination may be more common, more effective, and more efficient than other ways of facilitating the flow of information in an organization.

SERIAL MESSAGE DISSEMINATION

Haney (1962) has explained that a considerable amount of information is disseminated in chain-of-command organizations—business, industry, hospitals, military, government agencies—by means of serial communication. Rogers and Shoemaker (1971) noted that researchers on the diffusion of innovations—new farm practices, new medicines—"found that ideas usually spread from a source to an audience of receivers via a series of sequential transmissions . . ." (p. 13). When information is disseminated by means of a series of one-to-one-to-one contacts in which the originator of a message displays the message for a second person who in turn interprets and reproduces the message for a third person, the process is called *serial message dissemination* (Figure 13.2). Strictly speaking the "flow" of information in an organization occurs in this serial, successive, reproductive sequence. Haney (1962) notes that "serial transmission is clearly an essential, inevitable form of communication in organizations" (p. 150).

The serial dissemination of information involves the extension of the dyad so that a message is relayed from Person A to Person B to Person C to Person D to Person E in a series of two-person transactions in which each individual beyond the originator first interprets and then displays a message for the next person in the sequence.

As you can determine by examining Figure 13.2, serial message dissemination represents a pattern of "who talks to whom." It has, as one of its most significant features, a pattern of dissemination. When messages are disseminated in a serial fashion, information spreads on an irregular time schedule, thereby arriving at different destinations at different times. Individuals tend to be aware of information

FIGURE 13.2
Serial Message Dissemination

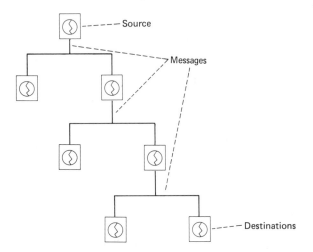

at different times. Because of differences in awareness of information, problems in coordination may develop. Time lags in the dissemination of information may make it difficult to make decisions because people are just not informed. When large numbers of people are to be informed, serial processes may require a longer period of time to get the information to them. Of course, as we shall discuss later, the fidelity, or accuracy, of the information may suffer as a result of the frequent interpretations and reproductions involved in the serial dissemination of messages.

Of great significance to organizational communication is the fact that hierarchically structured organizations—bureaucracies, for example—make most of their decisions on the basis of information and other decisions resulting from this serial communication process. Messages are received at each level in the organization, interpreted, and integrated into a body of information to be transmitted to the next level. Information tends to be tailored to fit the needs of the person or group to whom it is being sent. Ference (1970) explains that "the tailoring may require only a shift in emphasis and an underplaying of undesirable matters" (p. 84), not the transmission of false information. He also suggests that the integration of information at each level and position in the organization in preparation for sending it to the next position may include "interpretation, reconciling conflicting reports, discarding information, and applying weights to information from different sources" (pp. 85–86).

Because the serial dissemination and gathering of information are inevitably related to the functioning of hierarchically structured, bureaucratic organizations, it is especially urgent that we understand some of the usual, even natural, consequences of the serial reproduction of information on the content of organizational communication messages. We shall focus on this issue in Chapter 14. Since organizational structures and the serial dissemination of messages are intimately related, we shall now discuss the effects of various patterns of communication flow on key organization features.

PATTERNS OF INFORMATION FLOW

Although formal organizations rely heavily on general serial processes for gathering and disseminating information, specific patterns of information flow evolve out of regular interpersonal contacts and routine ways of sending and receiving messages. Katz and Kahn (1966) point out that a pattern or organized state of affairs requires that communication among the members of the system be restricted. The very nature of an organization implies limitations on who can talk to whom. Burgess (1969) observed that the peculiar characteristic of communication within organizations is that "message flows become so regularized that we actually may speak of communication networks or structures" (p.138). He also noted that formal organizations exert control over the communication structure by such means as the designation of authority and work relations, assignment of offices, and special communication functions.

The experimental analysis of communication patterns suggests that certain arrangements of "who talks to whom" have fairly prominent consequences on organizational functioning. We shall compare two contrasting patterns—the wheel and the circle—to illustrate the effects of restricted information flow on organizations (Figure 13.3). The wheel is a pattern in which all information is directed toward the individual occupying the central position. The person in the central position receives contacts and information provided by other organization members and solves the problem with the advice and consent of the other members. The circle allows all members to communicate with one another only through some sort of relayor system. No one member has direct contact with all other members, nor does any one member have direct access to all the necessary information to solve the problem. Several different combinations of contacts are possible: A may communicate with B and E, but not C and D; B may communicate with A and C but not D and E; C may communicate with B and D but not A and E; D may communicate with C and E, but not A and B; and E may communicate with D and A, but not B and C. For D to communicate with A, information must be relayed through E or C and B.

Results of research on the wheel and circle patterns suggest that they produce quite different consequences (Bavelas, 1950; Bavelas & Barrett, 1951; Burgess, 1969;

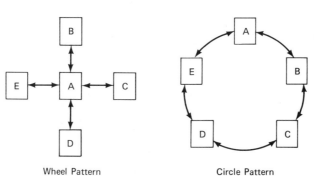

FIGURE 13.3
Two Basic Communication Patterns

Wheel Pattern   Circle Pattern

TABLE 13.1
Effects of Two Patterns
on Ten Organizational Communication Processes

ORGANIZATIONAL COMMUNICATION VARIABLE	WHEEL PATTERN	CIRCLE PATTERN
Accessibility of members to one another	Low	High
Control of message flow	High	Low
Morale or satisfaction	Very low	High
Emergence of leader	High	Very low
Accuracy of solutions	Good	Poor
Speed of performance	Fast	Slow
Number of messages sent	Low	High
Emergence of stable organization	Fast	Very slow
Adaptability to job changes	Slow	Fast
Propensity to overload	High	Low

Leavitt, 1951; Shaw, 1956, 1958). Table 13.1 summarizes the effects of the wheel and the circle patterns on ten organizational communication variables.

The circle pattern, involving combinations of relayors, tends to be superior to the wheel pattern, involving highly centralized communication flow, in overall accessibility of members to one another, morale or satisfaction with the process, number of messages sent, and adaptability to changes in tasks; on the other hand, the wheel pattern allows for more control over message flow, experiences rapid leader emergence and a stable organization, demonstrates high accuracy in solving problems, is fast in solving problems, but seems prone to message and work overload.

Burgess (1969) observed that in order to solve problems in experiments, group members had to "learn how to properly and efficiently manipulate the experimental apparatus; and to efficiently transfer messages to the position or positions with which they are linked" (p. 150). This implies that certain complex role behaviors may need to be learned in order to make the communication patterns function in any optimal way. Some recent research on communication networks in large organizations suggests that a distribution of network roles is important to the efficient functioning of an organization. We shall summarize some of the concepts on network roles in order to highlight these new developments.

COMMUNICATION NETWORK ROLES

An organization consists of people in positions. As individuals in those positions begin to communicate with one another, regularities in contacts and "who talks to whom" develop. The location of any given individual in the patterns and networks that emerge impose a role upon that person. Some individuals occupy more central positions, such as Person A in the wheel pattern, that require them to receive and process more information than do other members of the network. Individuals who occupy central positions need to have skills for handling information since they

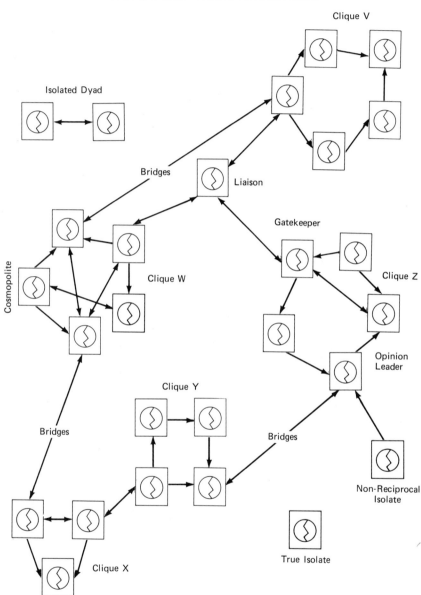

FIGURE 13.4
Hypothetical Network Diagram
Showing Communication Network Roles

will have to receive, integrate, and see that the appropriate information gets disseminated to the right people in a timely, accurate, and complete manner. Network analysis has revealed the characteristics of a number of communication network roles (Figure 13.4). We shall identify and briefly describe seven roles (Danowski,

1976; Farace, 1980; Farace, Monge, & Russell, 1977; Farace, Taylor, & Stewart, 1978; Richards, 1974; Roberts & O'Reilly, 1978; Rogers & Agarwala-Rogers, 1976).

Clique Member

A *clique* is a group of individuals who have at least half of their contacts with each other. Farace et al. (1977) indicate that a clique is identified when "more than half of their communication is with each other, when each member is linked to all other members, and when no single link nor member can be eliminated and have the group break apart" (p. 186). You might wonder whether members of a clique are or need to be in close physical proximity to one another, such as occupying adjoining offices or working in the same department. Research on small group ecology (Sommer, 1969) suggests that individuals were more likely to "interact with people whom they could see" (p. 61). The environment also has an impact on the development of contacts. Smith (1973) summarized research on constraints of the environment on behavior in organizations and concluded that the environment "may prevent certain patterns of communication. If it permits them, this still does not ensure that those patterns will arise, but the prevented patterns are definitely ruled out" (p. 55). Thus it seems consistent with experience to have Rogers and Agarwala-Rogers (1976) conclude that "most clique members are relatively close to each other in the formal hierarchy of the organization, suggesting the similarity of the formal and informal communication systems" (p. 130).

One requirement of clique membership is that individuals must be able to make contact with one another, even by indirect means. Baird (1977) analyzed the impact of a person's attitudes on the choice of media used in making contacts. He postulated that we might be more attracted to some people than to others and observed that "in communicating with those we like, we usually use the most immediate channel available: face-to-face, even though it may necessitate traveling relatively long distances; telephone calls become too expensive. On the other hand face-to-face contact with those we dislike usually is avoided; we resort to written communication or to sending messages through intermediaries" (p. 260). His concept of *immediate* was derived from Mehrabian (1971) and refers to situations involving "an increase in the sensory stimulation between two persons" (p. 3). Thus face-to-face contact is the most immediate, whereas letters and relayors are less immediate.

It is likely that cliques will consist of individuals whose environmental circumstances (offices, work assignments) permit contact, who like one another, and who find contacts of high immediacy satisfying. These three conditions do suggest that cliques may frequently consist of individuals who have both formal, positional reasons for making contacts as well as informal, interpersonal reasons.

Isolate

The first task of network analysis is to identify those who are members of cliques and those who are not. Since clique members are individuals who have more than half of their contacts with other members of the clique, *isolates* are those who have less frequent contact or no contact at all with other group members. The concept of isolate is relative and must be defined for each analysis of communication networks. Networks are usually defined in terms of the content of messages. Thus it is possible for an organization member to be an isolate in a network whose messages concern governmental relations with the organization but to be a central clique member when messages concern the internal administration of a division of the organization. Some organization members are isolates when it comes to the personal lives of other employees but are clearly clique members when messages concern changes in organization policies and procedures.

Goldhaber (1979) has summarized the characteristics of isolates. He suggests that isolates differ from clique members by being

1. Less secure in their self-concepts;
2. Less motivated by achievement;
3. Less willing to interact with others;
4. Younger and less experienced with the system;
5. Less often in positions of power in the organization;
6. More inclined to withhold information than facilitate its flow;
7. Relatively more dissatisfied with the system; and
8. Concerned that the communication system is closed to them.

Bridge

A *bridge* is a member of a clique who has a predominant number of intragroup contacts and who also has contact with a member of another clique. A bridge serves as a direct contact between two groups of employees. Farace et al. (1977) estimate that the distortion of messages will increase when contacts between and linkages among cliques is handled primarily by bridges. As a relayor of messages and a central figure in the communication system of a clique, a bridge is susceptible to all of the conditions that produce information forfeiture, message decay, and distortion. We shall look more closely at some of those conditions in Chapter 14.

Liaison

The relayor relationship discussed in an earlier chapter is illustrated most clearly by the liaison communication network role. A *liaison* is a person who links or connects two or more cliques but who is *not* a member of any of the groups connected. Liaisons have been the subject of research longer than any other role because they were recognized early as critical to the functioning of an organization or social system (Coleman, 1964; Davis, 1953; Jacobsen & Seashore, 1951; Schwartz, 1977; Schwartz & Jacobsen, 1977; Weiss & Jacobsen, 1955). Liaisons tie units of the organization together and represent people through whom much of the information of the organization is funneled. Ross and Harary (1955) noted that "if a liaison person is a bottleneck, the organization suffers badly, while if he is efficient, he tends to expedite the flow of the entire organization" (p. 1).

Most of the evidence suggests that liaisons are important roles for the effective functioning of an organization. They can facilitate the flow of information or block it. Rogers and Agarwala-Rogers (1976) suggest that "liaison roles may have to be formally created in an organization if they do not exist informally" (p. 138).

The major differences between liaisons and nonliaison members of an organizational communication system have been summarized by Farace et al. (1977). Figure 13.5 shows the major differences between liaisons and nonliaisons in terms of their actual communication behaviors, how they perceive themselves, and how others perceive them.

The distinctiveness of the liaison role stems not so much from any special personal characteristic as from the unique relayor function they hold in the communication network (Rogers & Agarwala-Rogers, 1976).

Gatekeeper

Gatekeeping, report Katz and Lazarsfeld (1955), means "controlling a strategic portion of a channel . . . so as to have the power of decision over whether whatever is flowing through the channel will enter the group or not" (p. 119). In an organizational communication network a *gatekeeper* is a person who is strategically located in the network so as to exercise control over what messages will be disseminated through the system. The gatekeeper is most noticeable in serial communication networks, since information and messages can be controlled at just about every link. Every relayor in a serial chain can be a gatekeeper. Thus our discussion of the functions of a relayor—linking, storing, stretching, and controlling—represents a description of the activities of a gatekeeper.

In a university, the chair of a department is a fairly clear example of a gatekeeper at work. Faculty are asked to funnel their requests through the chair. The dean, the superior of a chair, in turn funnels information for the faculty back through the chair. The chair controls what information the faculty will receive about the budget, directives and requests from the dean, and information about hiring, firing, and retiring. Figure 13.6 portrays a typical gatekeeper which many of you will recognize. In order for a faculty member to have access to the chair, he or she must negotiate past the gatekeeper—the department secretary. The secretary provides the chair with information about people who want appointments and provides selected information to assist the chair in deciding how the appointment will proceed. One positive consequence of having an efficient secretary-gatekeeper is the reduction in communication load. The secretary-gatekeeper may screen out or handle a great many contacts that may considerably relieve the load on an administrator. A secretary-gatekeeper may also keep a manager from knowing important information and reduce the manager's effectiveness. One interesting research question concerns what guidelines a gatekeeper, such as a secretary, uses in deciding what information should get into the system or to the manager.

Opinion Leader

In contrast to official leaders who exercise authority in organizations by virtue of the positions they hold, there are individuals without a formal position within all social systems who guide opinions and influence people in their decisions. These

FIGURE 13.5
Characteristics of Liaisons

Objective Characteristics of Liaisons

1. Liaisons have higher agreement (between themselves and others with whom they talk) about the identity of their contacts than do nonliaisons.
2. Liaisons are more likely to serve as first sources of information than are others in the organization.
3. Liaisons have higher formal status in the organization than do nonliaisons.
4. Liaisons have been organizational members for longer periods of time than have nonliaisons.
5. The levels of formal education and the ages of liaisons are similar to those of nonliaisons.

Liaisons Perceive Themselves as

6. having greater numbers of communication contacts in the organization;
7. having greater amounts of information with respect to the content dimensions upon which their role is defined;
8. participating in a communication system that is more "open"—information is seen as more timely, more believable, and more useful;
9. having greater influence in the organization.

Liaisons Are Perceived by Others as

10. having greater numbers of communication contacts in the organization;
11. having a wider range throughout the organizational structure;
12. having more information on the content dimensions on which the network is defined;
13. having more control over the flow of information in the organization;
14. having more influence over the "power structure" of the organization;
15. more competent at their organizational activities.

FIGURE 13.6
Example of a Gatekeeper Role

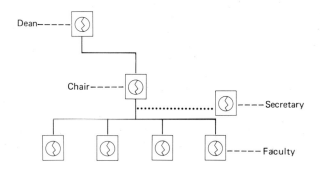

individuals, called *opinion leaders,* are sought out for their opinions and influence. They are the people who keep up on things and whom others trust to let them know what is really going on. Katz and Lazarsfeld (1955) describe the opinion leader as an "almost invisible, certainly inconspicuous, form of leadership at the person-to-person level of ordinary, intimate, informal, everyday contact" (p. 138).

The characteristics of opinion leaders identified in studies of communities, as opposed to businesses and agencies, were summarized by Pace (1969) and indicate the following:

1. Opinion leadership is more common during the middle years of life rather then during either youth or seniority, although a few senior opinion leaders have been recognized as the most powerful in public affairs.
2. Women have rarely been mentioned as opinion leaders.
3. Opinion leaders are usually long-term, permanent residents in the community and belong to a number of community organizations.
4. Opinion leaders in the United States are usually white, native-born and Protestants, although members of racial and ethnic minority groups assume opinion leadership within their respective minority populations.
5. No social stratum appears to have a monopoly on opinion leadership, with individuals in all walks of life exercising personal influence on other members of the community.

Formal organizations, as well as communities, have opinion leaders who influence what people believe and do. They serve a key communication function by influencing opinion formation and attitude change. They are asked for their opinions, and members of the organization listen to them (Peterson, 1973).

Cosmopolite

A cosmopolitan person is one who belongs to all the world or one who is free from local, provincial, or national ideas, prejudices, or attachments. A *cosmopolite* is an individual who has contact with the outside world, with individuals beyond the organization. Cosmopolites link organization members with people and events beyond the confines of the organization structure. Organization members who travel a lot, are active in professional associations, and read regional, national, and international publications tend to be more cosmopolitan. They have more frequent contact with sources outside the organization and serve as conduits or channels for new ideas to enter the organization.

SUMMARY

We have discussed seven communication network roles:

Clique Member
Isolate

Bridge
Liaison
Gatekeeper
Opinion Leader
Cosmopolite

Each role plays a special part in communication networks. The clique member is the heart of the system and serves as the final destination for most messages. The isolate challenges the system and creates a degree of uncertainty in the effectiveness of the message dissemination program. The bridge is a central information-processor who provides direct connections between different cliques. The liaison integrates and interconnects cliques. The opinion leader facilitates the formation and change of attitudes and aids in informal decision making. The gatekeeper controls the movement of messages and contacts in order to minimize overload and increase effectiveness. The cosmopolite connects the organization with people and ideas in the larger environment.

REFERENCES

BAIRD, JOHN E., JR., *The Dynamics of Organizational Communication.* New York: Harper & Row, Pub., 1977.

BAVELAS, ALEX, "Communication Patterns in Task-Oriented Groups," *Journal of the Acoustical Society of America,* 22 (1950), 725–730.

BAVELAS, ALEX, and DERMOT BARRETT, "An Experimental Approach to Organizational Communication," *Personnel,* 27 (March 1951), 38–50.

BURGESS, R. L., "Communication Networks and Behavioral Consequences," *Human Relations,* 22 (1969), 137–160.

COLEMAN, J. S., "Relational Analysis: The Study of Social Organizations with Survey Methods," *Complex Organizations: A Sociological Reader,* ed. A. A. Etzioni, pp. 441–453. New York: Holt, Rinehart & Winston, 1964.

DANOWSKI, JAMES A., "Communication Network Analysis and Social Change," in *Communication for Group Transformation in Development,* ed. Goodwin C. Chu, Syed A. Rahim, and D. Lawrence Kincaid, pp. 277–306. Honolulu: East-West Communication Institute, Communication Monograph, No. 2, September 1976.

DAVIS, KEITH A., "A Method of Studying Communication Patterns in Organizations," *Personnel Psychology,* 6 (1953), 301–312.

FARACE, RICHARD V., "Organizational Communication," in *Human Communication: Principles, Contexts, and Skills,* ed. Cassandra L. Book, pp. 166–193. New York: St. Martin's Press, 1980.

FARACE, RICHARD V., PETER R. MONGE, and HAMISH M. RUSSELL, *Communicating and Organizing.* Reading, Mass.: Addison-Wesley, 1977.

FARACE, RICHARD V., JAMES A. TAYLOR, and JOHN P. STEWART, "Criteria for Evaluation of Organizational Communication Effectiveness: Review and Synthesis," in *Communication Yearbook 2,* ed. Brent D. Ruben, pp. 271–292. New Brunswick, N.J.: Transaction Books–International Communication Association, 1978.

FERENCE, T. P., "Organizational Communication Systems and The Decision Process," *Management Science,* 17 (1970), 83–96.

GOLDHABER, GERALD M., *Organizational Communication.* Dubuque, Iowa: Wm. C. Brown, 1979.

GUETZKOW, HAROLD, "Communications in Organizations," in *Handbook of Organizations,* ed. James G. March, p. 537. Skokie, Ill.: Rand McNally, 1965.

GUETZKOW, HAROLD, "Differentiation of Roles in Task-Oriented Groups," in *Group Dynamics: Research and Theory,* ed. Dorwin Cartwright and Alvin Zander, pp. 512–526. New York: Harper & Row, Pub., 1968.

HANEY, WILLIAM V., "Serial Communication of Information in Organizations," in *Concepts and Issues in Administrative Behavior,* ed. Sidney Mailick and Edward H. Van Ness, pp. 150–165. Englewood Cliffs, N.J.: Prentice-Hall, 1962.

JACOBSEN, EUGENE, and STANLEY SEASHORE, "Communication Practices in Complex Organizations," *Journal of Social Issues,* 7 (1951), 28–40.

KATZ, DANIEL, and ROBERT KAHN, *The Social Psychology of Organizations.* New York: John Wiley, 1966.

KATZ, ELIHU, and PAUL F. LAZARSFELD, *Personal Influence.* New York: The Free Press, 1955.

LEAVITT, HAROLD J., "Some Effects of Certain Communication Patterns on Group Performance," *Journal of Abnormal and Social Psychology,* 46 (1951), 38–50.

MEHRABIAN, ALBERT, *Silent Messages.* Belmont, Calif.: Wadsworth, 1971.

PACE, RONALD F., "A Study of Opinion Leaders in Summit County and Their Attitudes toward Federal Aid Programs Affecting Local Education and Highway Systems." Unpublished master's thesis, Institute of Government Service, Brigham Young University, May 1969.

PETERSON, BRENT D., "Differences between Managers and Subordinates in Their Perception of Opinion Leaders," *Journal of Business Communication,* 10 (1973), 27–37.

RICHARDS, WILLIAM D., "Network Analysis in Large Complex Systems: Techniques and Methods—Tools." Paper presented at the Annual Meeting of the International Communication Association, New Orleans, 1974.

ROBERTS, KARLENE, and CHARLES A. O'REILLY III, "Organizations as Communication Structures," *Human Communication Research,* 4 (Summer 1978), 283–293.

ROGERS, EVERETT M., and REKHA AGARWALA-ROGERS, *Communication in Organizations.* New York: The Free Press, 1976.

ROGERS, EVERETT M., with F. FLOYD SHOEMAKER, *Communication of Innovations: A Cross-Cultural Approach.* New York: The Free Press, 1971.

ROSS, I. C., and F. HARARY, "Identification of the Liaison Persons of an Organization Using the Structure Matrix, *Management Science,* 1 (April–May 1955), 251–258.

SCHWARTZ, DONALD F., "Liaison Roles in the Communication of a Formal Organization," in *Communication in Organizations,* ed. Lyman W. Porter and Karlene H. Roberts, pp. 255–271. Middlesex, England: Penguin Books, Ltd., 1977.

SCHWARTZ, DONALD F., and EUGENE JACOBSEN, "Organizational Communication Network Analysis—The Liaison Communication Role," *Organizational Behavior and Human Performance,* 18 (1977), 158–174.

SHAW, M. E., "Random Versus Systematic Distribution of Information in Communication Nets," *Journal of Personality,* 25 (1956), 59–69.

SHAW, M. E., "Some Effects of Irrelevant Information upon Problem Solving by Small Groups," *Journal of Social Psychology,* 47 (1958), 33–37.

SMITH, PETER B., *Groups within Organizations.* London: Harper & Row, Pub., 1973.

SOMMER, ROBERT, *Personal Space.* Englewood Cliffs, N.J.: Prentice-Hall, 1969.

WEISS, R. S., and EUGENE JACOBSEN, "A Method for the Analysis of the Structure of Complex Organizations," *American Sociological Review,* 20 (1955), 661–668.

14

MESSAGE FIDELITY
AND DISTORTION
IN
ORGANIZATIONAL
COMMUNICATION

*the effects of communication systems
on message content*

"Why can't people get things straight?" How frequently has this question been asked silently or out loud in an organization? Probably as often as employees get together to discuss problems with the boss, or bosses talk about misunderstandings with employees. Routine person-to-person communication is subject to a multitude of pitfalls and processes that have detrimental effects on understanding. Many of the problems stem from the way in which human beings process information. Other sources of misunderstanding are a function of the system by which messages are distributed throughout an organization. Organizational communication is subject to not only the maladies of interpersonal interaction but also to the anomalies of relaying messages through human links in a communication system.

DEFINITION OF FIDELITY AND DISTORTION

Communication fidelity refers to the ability of a person to reproduce or re-create a message accurately. In human communication the term *fidelity* is used to describe the degree of correspondence between an initiated message and an individual's reproduction of that message. As we mentioned in Chapter 4, a message has at least two dimensions: a display and an interpretation. A *display* consists of verbal or language symbols, nonverbal behavior (including vocal and physical actions), appearances, and spatial relations. In communicating, a person simply creates and presents a display of sounds, movements, and emblems that can be taken to symbolize or represent something else. The display dimension of a message is a pattern of symbols that can be perceived by someone. Individuals have the capacity to interpret aspects of a display. An *interpretation* is the act and process of assigning meaning to and making sense out of a display.

The measurement of message fidelity or its opposite, message distortion, is complicated by the two dimensions of display and interpretation. If fidelity is the degree of correspondence between an initiated message and a reproduced message, than we must be prepared to measure the correspondence between an initiated display and some form of reproduced display, *plus* the correspondence between some form of intended meaning or interpretation and the reproduced or imputed interpretation or meaning associated with the display. A lack of fidelity is usually demonstrated by some type of distortion resulting from changes between the initial display and the reproduced message-display or some differences between an intended meaning and the meaning imputed to the display as part of the reproduction.

Serial reproduction studies illustrate most clearly how distortion is identified by comparing the correspondence between message-displays. A message, usually verbal but often pictorial, is prepared in advance so as to be consistent in length, content, and style. The message is presented to a person who listens to it and, after a specified period of time, reproduces the message. The reproduction may be accomplished by writing, by orally repeating the message, or by recording the message on audio or video tapes. The fidelity of the message-display is determined by comparing the original message with the reproduced message. Verbal messages can be compared directly by (1) counting the number of words that are exactly the same in both messages and/or by (2) counting the number of predetermined themes occurring in both displays.

The correspondence between the intended meaning of a message-source and an imputed meaning of the reproducer of the messages is more difficult to compare than are message-displays. However, differences in meanings and distortions in the meanings of messages may be the most critical aspect of organizational communication. Authorities on communication have forcefully argued that the only message upon which a person can act is the message (interpretation or meaning) that the person creates, regardless of the display (Redding, 1972). Two people may read the same memo and impute quite different meanings to it. The only meaning that counts is the one created by the receiver of the message. Since it is not possible to measure meanings directly, research on communication fidelity has used attitude instruments and associative group analysis (Szalay, Windle, & Lysne, 1970) procedures to get as close as possible to meanings.

In the real organization world the measure of message fidelity may be more related to how a person completes his or her work than it is to how precisely the message-display or the meaning of the message are reproduced. A popular laboratory exercise on message reproduction involves having one person give another person instructions on how to reproduce a drawing. Haney (1964) reported research using figures that appeared to be drawings of domino blocks. The criteria for accuracy were the orientation of the rectangles to one another and the arrangement of the circles within the rectangles. To be considered accurate, the reproduced drawings had to meet both criteria. Brissey (1964) devised a procedure for measuring fidelity by having subjects complete a task described by a message rather than by analyzing the reproduced message directly. Subjects were given instructions concerning how to complete a prearranged display on a pegboard. Fidelity was measured by the extent to which pegs were placed in the correct holes. Any holes not filled and all pegs outside the design were considered to be inaccuracies. He reasoned that as the adequacy of the message decreased, a receiver's uncertainty about where to place pegs correctly in the display would increase. Higher message fidelity would result in fewer errors. Alkire, Collum, Kaswan, and Love (1968) had subjects select the correct design from among several, based on instructions received from another person. The person giving the instructions had a copy of the design and created his or her own initial descriptions. Such a procedure seems to simulate actual organizational communication situations, since the initiator of the message had to create the original message.

In this chapter we are concerned with what happens to the content of a message as it flows throughout an organization. Personal experience and communication research have confirmed the idea that information and the meaning of messages change from what was intended as they are passed from individual to individual in an organization. The processes of upward, downward, horizontal, and cross-channel communication all occur by contacts that are *simultaneous* (one person contacting other members of the organization directly) or *serial* (one person serving as a relayor between two other members of the organization). Messages that are distributed by simultaneous contacts are susceptible to changes and distortions associated with interpersonal communication. We shall review some personal communication factors that affect the interpretation of messages. The serial reproduction of a message is compounded by systematic errors or biases that stem from the information-processing activities of human links in communication systems. Distortions in messages are accelerated when a series of human relayors interpret and display their versions of what was meant. Thus we shall also look at how messages are affected by the serial process of information distribution.

PERSONAL FACTORS THAT DISTORT MESSAGES

We shall discuss a number of principles that reflect personal factors that contribute to the distortion of messages. These factors issue naturally from our concept of communication as the act and process of assigning meaning to displays. A display is anything that activates one of our senses—seeing, hearing, tasting, smelling, feeling. At any moment we are bombarded by a limitless variety of displays originating from inside ourselves as well as from outside. Hence the first factor that contributes to the distortion of messages is related to our perception of displays.

Principle 1:
People Perceive Things Selectively

Our sensory receptors—eyes, ears, fingers, noses, tongues—are physically limited so that they can respond to only a few of the stimuli impinging upon them. Each of us responds to those sensations that get past our natural barriers or limitations, that seem most pertinent to our situation, and that are consistent with our own personal preferences and perspectives. The fidelity, or accuracy, of information is limited by the selective perceptions we make.

Selectivity means that a person is able to focus on some sensations while excluding others. In fact, in order to focus on one aspect of a situation you must ignore other aspects of it. Look out the window and concentrate on an activity across the street. Can you also look at what is happening on the table in front of you? Visually you can look through the bugs on a windshield, or you can focus on the bugs and actually be unable to see the hood of the car. The same process occurs with our minds. Try this experiment: Think very hard about a problem you are having. Mentally analyze the problem. Do you block out what other people in the room are doing and saying? If you concentrate on what is happening inside you, you will ignore what is happening outside you. If you are worried about what your supervisor will think about the report you have just finished, you may very well not hear some of the things he or she says.

Principle 2:
People See Things Consistent with What They Believe

Our perceptions are affected by the way we talk about people, things, and events. What we believe changes our perceptions. If we expect to see a friend react in a negative way to a suggestion, we shall no doubt perceive him or her react negatively. This is sometimes called the *Pygmalion Effect*. If we believe that people are very smart and intelligent, we will tend to see their behavior as consistent with our belief. On the other hand, if other people see that we expect great things from them, they will try to behave consistently with our expectations.

Such characteristics as friendliness, attractiveness, loyalty, and supportiveness are judgments that we project on other people. I may see you as trusting whereas the person working right next to me may see you as untrusting. Part of the judgment of trust may be related to selectively focusing on some reactions while selectively ignoring other reactions; it may also be a function of a preconception or belief that you are untrusting, which may encourage you to selectively perceive certain acts that you feel are untrusting. Beauty is in the eye of the beholder. Trust, supportiveness, warmth, and kindness are also perceptions.

Believe and ye shall see. A person will probably expect quite different patterns of behavior from another individual if he or she believes that the person is

Able to cope	vs.	Unable to deal with events
Friendly and well-intentioned	vs.	Unfriendly and evil-intentioned
Worthy and important	vs.	Worthless and unimportant
Trustworthy and dependable	vs.	Untrustworthy and unpredictable
Helpful and enhancing	vs.	Frustrating and impeding

Principle 3:
Language Itself Is Inaccurate

Our perceptions of people, things, and events never correspond exactly with their reality because we selectively see them and because we tend to see what we believe about people, things, and events. In communicating we use language to represent our perceptions. Our talking involves language that is supposed to portray or describe that about which we are talking. It is through language that we make our private perceptions somewhat public so that others may get some idea of what we mean. Language does not diminish the importance of nonlanguage. Nonverbal signals clue others in to what we mean. In fact, we shall talk more about them later. Nevertheless, we must not lose sight of the basic principle that language symbols do not accurately represent what a person means. Why is that?

First, words are not the things they represent. The word *tree* is not the object *tree.* The word *manager* is not the person *manager.* Words can only refer to or represent events, happenings, activities, and people.

Second, in order for language to refer to a constantly changing world, we develop generalizations about a group of activities and relationships and apply words and terms to describe the characteristics they have in common. We call these generalizations *abstractions.* The larger the number of activities, relationships, or people referred to by a word, the more abstract the word is. The fewer activities to which a word refers, the more specific it is. Technical language tends to be less abstract and more specific. The term *phoneme* is more specific than the term *symbol;* the term *symbol,* however, is more specific than the term *display.* Even our most specific language is still abstract. We actually have a somewhat limited number of words to refer to an almost unlimited number of atoms, movements, feelings, reactions, stars, planets, and even universes. Because of the constantly changing multitude of things and events in the world, our language just cannot be too accurate in what it represents.

Third, when we use language to talk about differences, one of our basic tendencies is to allow only two alternatives—good or bad, for example.

The way we use language in our everyday work tends to be fairly bipolar, or at least to give the impression that our choices fall into either-or categories. Language itself encourages this tendency. To see for yourself how strong this tendency is, try this exercise:

On the right side of this page, list the *opposites* of the following words.

calm	_____
exciting	_____
intelligent	_____
fast	_____
kind	_____

Now in the space between the two lists, write in one or more words that refer to or describe the in-between positions. For example, if a person was neither calm nor agitated, what word would describe him or her? Most people are neither intelligent nor stupid. What word describes them?

Truly accurate language represents people and things as they actually exist. With so many gradations in feelings, reactions, and existences, there is little wonder that our language is limited in its ability to represent the world and the things that happen in it (Haney, 1967).

Principle 4:
The Meaning of a Message Occurs at Both Content and Relational Levels

A message consists of both verbal or language (oral and written) and nonverbal or nonlanguage (aural and pictorial) symbols. What a person says and how a person behaves combine to make a message-display. Each message can be analyzed at a *content* or denotative level and at a *relational* or interpretive level (Watzlawick, Beavin, & Jackson, 1967).

The content, or denotative, level of meaning concerns the ideas, things, people, events, and happenings to which the message literally refers. You are functioning at the content level when you respond to the information of the message—that is, when you respond to the ideas, attitudes, opinions, and facts referred to by the message, you are dealing with the message at the content level.

The relational, or interpretive, level of meaning concerns how the message is to be taken, for example, lightly or seriously, When you say, "Smile when you say that," you are dealing at the relational level because your comment tells the other person how to interpret the message and what kind of relationship you are to have. The relational level indicates how the information and the relationship is to be understood. Your attitudes toward other people are expressions at the relational level.

Lack of fidelity, distortions, and misunderstandings often result from our failure to recognize relational information and distinguish it from content, or denotative, information.

Principle 5:
Distortions Are Encouraged by Inconsistencies
between Verbal and Nonverbal Aspects of a Message

A basic axiom of communication theory is that *a person cannot not behave.* Thus as Redding (1964) has concluded, "Communication is always going on, then, whether one desires it or not—so long as there is someone to interpret what we say, or fail to say, or do, or fail to do" (p. 31). It has been estimated that in a conversation involving two people, verbal aspects of a message account for less than 35 percent of the social meaning whereas nonverbal aspects of a message account for 65 percent of the social meaning (Knapp, 1972). On the other hand, Mehrabian (1971) states that "a person's nonverbal behavior has more bearing than his words on communicating feelings or attitudes to others" (p. 44). He estimates that 7 percent of the total feeling is derived from verbal aspects, 38 percent from vocal aspects, and 55 percent from facial aspects, resulting in 93 percent of the feeling communicated being based on nonverbal features.

Since the dominant source of meaning and feeling derived from a message comes from the nonverbal dimensions, it is not surprising to discover that inconsistencies between nonverbal behaviors and the verbal aspects of a message reduce its fidelity. When some inconsistency occurs between words and actions, we tend to believe what we infer from the nonverbal behaviors. Our messages may be misunderstood, be distorted, or lack fidelity if our nonverbal behaviors fail to support what we say. Knapp (1972) has identified six ways in which nonverbal behaviors support our verbal comments:

1. *Nonverbal behaviors may repeat what is expressed verbally.* Since nonverbal behaviors, like gestures, usually precede what is said, it might be more accurate to say that verbal statements repeat nonverbal behaviors. In any case when you agree with a person, notice that you tend to nod your head in agreement just prior to saying, "I think maybe you are right." The verbal and nonverbal behaviors tend to repeat or confirm each other.

2. *Nonverbal behaviors may contradict what is expressed verbally.* You may have experienced a nonverbal behavior contradicting a verbal statement when being told, "I'd really like to go with you," but said in a tone of voice that you knew meant something else. You might have rushed through the house slamming doors and dropping your coat, only to remark to someone, "I don't care. I'm not in a hurry." A more common experience is when a close friend stands looking longingly at a new suit of clothes, but comments," Oh, It's nothing; I'm not interested." Nonverbal behaviors may very well clearly contradict verbal statements made in organizations.

3. *Nonverbal behaviors may substitute for what could be expressed verbally.* When you go back to your apartment or room, don't say anything. Just open the door and leap into the air, smile, and clench your fists. Your roommate or spouse may not need verbal confirmation of the nonverbal display. With a little practice you may be able to identify a great many substitute nonverbal displays.

4. *Nonverbal behaviors may modify or elaborate on verbal messages.* You may indicate a change in attitude through nonverbal behaviors before the verbal expression of such a change occurs. You might, for example, say that you aren't all that sure about going to a movie tonight and let your nonverbal behaviors elaborate the statement into a definite "no." A supervisor may tell a subordinate that things seem a little slow, but the squint of the supervisor's eye and the turned-down mouth more clearly fill out the verbal message so that the subordinate understands that things are at a standstill.

5. *Nonverbal behaviors may emphasize parts of a verbal message.* If you have ever greeted someone you haven't seen for a long time, you may recall the special emphasis given to the greeting: "Oh, hi." As you uttered those very short verbal expressions, you may have hugged the other person, shook his or her hand firmly and warmly, and smiled broadly. A supervisor may speak to a subordinate about finishing a piece of work with some clearly nonverbal emphases, such as raising eyebrows, speaking more slowly, and gesturing firmly.

6. *Nonverbal behaviors may regulate the flow of messages between people.* If you are having a conversation with someone and you have another appointment, you may try to signal nonverbally by moving your eyes or shifting from leg to leg or smiling tensely that the other person should stop speaking and terminate the conversation. If you want the other person to continue talking, you may nod your head and say, "Uh huh," or look at the other intently and attentively. In these ways you control who talks, how long, how often, and about what.

Misunderstandings, distortions, and nonfidelity in communication may result from our failures to recognize or respond to the nonverbal cues that accompany what people say verbally. Since a great deal of the meaning involved in a communicative exchange comes from nonverbal behaviors, lack of fidelity and distortion may frequently be traced to failures to recognize and understand nonverbal signals.

Principle 6:
Message Ambiguity Often Leads to Distortions

Ambiguity may be defined as some degree of uncertainty associated with information or actions. If a statement you make seems ambiguous to me, that means that I am uncertain how to take what you say. There are three types of ambiguity that may occur in communication: ambiguity of meaning, ambiguity of intent, and ambiguity of effect (Thayer, 1968).

Ambiguity of meaning concerns the uncertainty of predicting what the originator of a message means. To the extent that you cannot readily and efficiently determine what a person meant when he or she said or wrote a message, the message will have a degree of ambiguity for you. The greater the ambiguity of meaning, the greater the difficulty you will have in comprehending the message.

Ambiguity of intent concerns the uncertainty of predicting why the originator of a message said or wrote this particular message to you at this particular time in this particular way and under these particular conditions. To the extent that you cannot figure out why the person is communicating with you, the message will be ambiguous to you. For example, suppose you go home and find a note pinned to your bedroom curtain with this message on it: "The president of the university called and wants to talk to you tomorrow morning." Why would the president want to talk to you? What does he or she want? The degree to which you are unable to answer such questions indicates how ambiguous the intent of the message is to you.

Ambiguity of effect concerns the uncertainty of predicting what the consequences of responding to a message might be. You may accurately interpret the meaning of the note about the president's request for a meeting—the president wants you to arrive at his or her office in the morning; you may even predict his or her intent fairly accurately—to talk to you about your standing in the university; however, what will be the effect or consequence of understanding the message, arriving at the president's office, and engaging in a conversation about your standing in the university? Of course, nothing may come of it; on the other hand, what might be some possible consequences? The extent to which some of these questions have unclear answers is the extent to which the message involves ambiguity of effect.

A person may fail to comprehend a message or distort its meaning because of an inability to determine what the originator of the message means, why the message was sent, or what the consequences are of comprehending the message in a particular way.

Principle 7:
Memory Propensities toward Sharpening and Leveling Details
Encourage Distortion to Occur

Some evidence suggests that people may have some patterns associated with their memory systems that lead to distortions in verbal communication. Holzman and Gardner (1960) developed a schematizing test that differentiated between *levelers* and *sharpeners.* Individuals who are levelers had fewer correct memories of an incident or story and tended to show more loss and modification of the overall structure of the story than did those who were sharpeners. Gardner and Lohrenz (1960) demonstrated that the serial reproduction of a story underwent different fates when transmitted through separate chains of levelers and sharpeners. Levelers lost more themes, lost more of the overall story, and showed increasingly more fragmented messages than did sharpeners. A person may be structured toward leveling information or toward sharpening information. A propensity toward stripping away the details in a verbal message is called *skeletonizing* (Paul, 1959), and a propensity toward the invention of details is called *importing*. Each of us may have a memory propensity that leads toward leveling, stripping away, or skeletonizing details in messages or a memory propensity that leads toward sharpening, inventing, or importing details into messages. In either case a memory propensity may contribute to distortions and lack of fidelity in communication.

Principle 8:
Motivational Factors May Encourage Message Distortions

Three basic motivational factors tend to produce changes in messages that result in lack of fidelity: attitudes toward the message content; desires, self-interest, and motives of communicators; and attitudes of intended receivers.

1. *Attitudes toward the message content.* A study by Johnson and Wood (1944) demonstrated that subjects who held positive attitudes toward a racial minority tended to "abstract" the positive information about them from a passage containing both positive and negative information; on the other hand, a subject who had negative attitudes tended to abstract negative information from the same passage. The tendency for communicators to distort information in a message according to their attitudes seems to be well supported by other research (Alper & Korchin, 1952; Bouillut & Moscovici, 1967; Higham, 1951; Manis, Cornell & Moore, 1974).

2. *Desires, self-interest, and motives of communicators.* Jackson (1959) suggested that people in organizations communicate or fail to communicate with others in order to accomplish some goal, satisfy a personal need, or improve their immediate situation. Downs (1967) identified four major biases that produce distortions in the communication of officials in bureaucracies: (1) They tend to distort information by exaggerating data that reflect favorably on themselves and to minimize data that reveal their shortcomings. (2) They tend to prefer policies that advance their own interests and the programs they advocate and to reject those that injure or fail to advance their interests. (3) They tend to comply with directives from superiors that favor their own interests and drag their feet or ignore those that do not. (4) They tend to take on additional work if it is directly beneficial to their own goals and avoid work that weakens their ability to achieve their own goals.

Haney (1962) described three motives that encourage distortions to develop in messages: (1) The desire to convey simple messages. The communication of complex information is difficult and psychologically taxing on the individual; thus organization members tend to simplify messages before or as they pass the information along. (2) The desire to convey a "sensible" message. When a person receives a message that doesn't seem to make sense, the desire is to make sense out of it before passing it along. Most of us tend to avoid sending along messages that seem illogical, incomplete, or incoherent. (3) The desire to make message sending as pleasant (or at least as painless) as possible for the sender. Organization members tend to avoid conveying messages that are painful for them. Instead they make changes that soften the message and make it less painful.

3. *Attitudes of intended receivers.* There is evidence to support the idea that the initiator of a message will tend to distort it in the direction of the announced attitude of whoever is to receive the message. This may be a subcategory of motivational factors, since expressing ideas contrary to those held by an intended receiver may be viewed as potentially painful.

So far we have discussed eight principles that represent personal factors that contribute to the distortion of messages in communication. In summary, the principles appear as follows:

1. People perceive things selectively.
2. People see things consistent with what they believe.
3. Language itself is inaccurate.
4. The meaning of a message occurs at both content and relational levels.
5. Distortions are encouraged by inconsistencies between verbal and nonverbal aspects of a message.
6. Message ambiguity often leads to distortions.
7. Memory propensities toward sharpening and leveling details encourage distortions to occur.
8. Motivational factors may encourage message distortions.

We shall now review some of the organizational factors that contribute to the distortion of messages.

ORGANIZATIONAL FACTORS THAT DISTORT MESSAGES

Characteristics of organizations themselves tend to encourage distortions to occur in messages. We shall briefly review a number of organizational factors that contribute to message distortion in organizational communication.

1. *Occupying a position in an organization influences the way a person communicates.* By becoming a functioning member of an organization who occupies a position with duties and authority assigned to it, an individual acquires a point of view, a value system, and develops expectations and limitations that are different from a person who holds a different position or is a member of a different organization entirely. A supervisor, for example, is compelled at times to look at the functioning of the organization differently from subordinates. The supervisor must react to production problems somewhat differently from the way a particular subordinate might react to them. In fact, a supervisor must think about the organization in a different way. The person within the organization sees its operations differently from an outsider. Each position in an organization demands that the person who occupies it must perceive and communicate about things from the perspective of the position. Occupying a position tends to contribute to distortions in organizational communication messages (Katz & Kahn, 1966).

2. *Hierarchical—superior-subordinate—relationships influence the way in which a person communicates.* The arrangement of positions in hierarchical fashion sug-

gests to those who occupy the positions that one set of individuals is "superior" and another set is "subordinate." The fundamental difference is one of perceived status. People and positions located higher in the hierarchy have greater control over the lives of those who are located lower in the organization. Lower-downs find it desirable to be cautious in communicating with higher-ups. Information may be distorted because a subordinate is careful to talk about things that his or her superior is interested in hearing and to avoid topics and ways of saying things that are sensitive to the boss. The superior, on the other hand, would not wish to discuss things that tend to undermine his or her position in the organization by reflecting negatively on his or her competence and decision-making abilities. Even between friends, hierarchical relationships affect what can be discussed and the way in which things can be discussed (Strauss & Sayles, 1960).

3. *Restrictions in who may communicate with whom and who may make decisions influence the way in which a person communicates.* Coordination of activities and the flow of information in an organization require some centralization of decision making. To avoid having members of the organization going in too many different directions, making contradictory decisions, and having imbalances in work loads, an organization is structured so that certain decisions are made by a limited number of individuals. We have referred to them in different ways—as liaisons, gatekeepers, people in authority, decision makers, or superiors—but in nearly all cases those individuals get information from a variety of others within and without the organization. When central decision makers receive too much information too fast or have too many decisions to make too quickly, distortions are likely to occur as a result of *overload.*

When too many messages or contacts enter a system or the messages or contacts come too fast to be handled properly, one or more of the individuals or units in the organization will experience overload. Networks, organizations, and individuals create ways of adjusting to and avoiding messages when an overload appears to be developing. To maintain an uninterrupted sequence in processing information, individuals may do some of the following:

1. Ignore some messages.
2. Delay responding to unimportant messages.
3. Answer or respond to only parts of some messages.
4. Respond inaccurately to certain messages.
5. Take less time with each message.
6. React to messages at only superficial levels.
7. Block messages before they can enter the system.
8. Shift the burden of responding to some messages to others.
9. Create a new position or unit to handle specialized kinds of messages.
10. Reduce standards to allow for more errors in responding to messages.

Each of these adjustments encourages distortion to develop in messages.

4. *Impersonalization of organizational relationships influences the way in which a person communicates.* One fundamental characteristic of formal organizations is that relationships are to be formal and impersonal. The impersonalization

of relationships leads to the suppression of emotional messages. In order to hide or disown emotional expressions, individuals develop ways of keeping others from expressing their emotions. Eventually organization members avoid or refuse to consider ideas that might allow or encourage the release of feelings. The consequence, in the long run at least, is a lessened awareness of the impact of a person's feelings on others and an inability to predict accurately the emotional reactions of others. Ultimately the organization is comprised of individuals who cannot communicate their feelings and who substitute rules for solving problems.

5. *The system of rules, policies, and regulations governing thoughts and actions influences the way in which a person communicates.* As a philosophy of impersonal relationships encourages the development of a system of rules that substitutes for authentic problem solving, so the characteristic of having general but definite policies for guiding decisions leads to impersonal relationships. A rigid application of rules and policies to behavior and decisions leads to an inability to make compromises and fosters impersonality and lack of emotional communication. Rules encourage the evolution of rigid, routine, and traditional patterns of communicating. Institutionalization of behavior is the consequence, with remote and distant, rather than face-to-face, interpersonal communication. Positional relationships are reinforced, and interpersonal relationships are discouraged. Information and messages may be distorted to accommodate the rules and maintain impersonality.

6. *Task specialization narrows a person's perceptions and influences the way in which a person communicates.* Although specialization has contributed immensely to national productivity by increasing efficiency, it is also the source of many communication problems. Individuals identify with their own areas of expertise, learn entire vocabularies unknown to other employees, and often fail to integrate their efforts with other departments. The result is often a bottleneck in the flow of information or a great deal of "buck passing" from one person to another because the client's problem is not in the employee's area of specialization. To some extent specialization fosters conflicts through competition for resources to accomplish narrow objectives. Although competition may help keep employees functioning with alertness, it may lead very quickly to destructive relationships and dysfunctional communication. Specialization may be the source of much of the message distortion that occurs in organizations. Task specialization leads to what some call *trained incapacity,* or a limited ability to perform general organizational functions. Accompanying an incapacity to do varied tasks is the inability to perceive the total picture and act for the good of colleagues and the organization. Such limited perspectives reduce a person's ability to comprehend other's problems, resulting in lower levels of empathy. Without empathy, understanding may be diminished and distortion increased.

We have identified six general organizational characteristics that encourage the distortion of messages in communication. Since organizational communication is affected by personal and organizational factors, it is a small wonder that communication proceeds as well as it does. Some of the reasons why organizational communication has as much fidelity and facilitates the work of organizations as it seems to have done lies in what Downs (1967) calls "antidistortion factors in the communication system" (p. 118).

ANTIDISTORTION FACTORS
IN ORGANIZATIONAL COMMUNICATION SYSTEMS

Messages in every organization are subject to a degree of distortion, but formal organizations also have forces that limit the amount of distortion that occurs in communication. Although the antidistortion forces may reduce the level of distortion below that implied by the lengthy list of personal and organizational factors contributing to distortion, they do not entirely eliminate distortion. Downs (1967) lists four general ways in which organization members attempt to increase the fidelity of information communicated in an organization.

1. *Establish more than one channel of communication.* When an employee (manager or operative) believes that information he or she is receiving may be distorted, one way to counter the distortion is to verify the information through multiple sources of messages. This can be done in several ways:

   a. Use sources of information outside the organization, including publications, friends in other organizations, clients of the organization, suppliers of the organization, social acquaintances, political contacts, and the grapevine.

   b. Create overlapping areas of responsibility among employees so that an element of competition is introduced into the communication process. Each person learns that any distortions in his or her reports may be revealed by the reports of other employees. For example, a manager who receives three conflicting reports and is unable to determine which has the greatest fidelity may be led to search for accuracies and distortions with greater care.

2. *Develop procedures for counterbalancing distortions.* If we assume that those who work in organizations realize that personal and organizational factors produce distortions, then those who receive information can routinely adjust reports to counteract the distortions contained in them. To the extent that a manager, for example, has accurately identified the distortions, he or she can adjust the information more closely to the original design. When counterbalancing procedures are used throughout the organization, as they tend to be, much of the cumulative effect of personal and organizational distortion factors tends to be reduced. The main distorting effect will be the inaccurate estimate of the source and degree of distortion in the information.

   If a person does not know what kinds of distortions are included in a report, he or she will have difficulty making adjustments. The only alternative is to discount or possibly not use the information in making decisions. There is a tendency, of course, for managers, as well as other employees, to adjust potential distortions in a direction that tends to benefit them most rather than in terms of objective estimates of real fidelity. Superiors and subordinates tend to resolve those kinds of questions in their own favor, of course. The weakness of using counterbalancing procedures is that organization decision makers may distort decisions in the very process of attempting to reduce distortions.

3. *Eliminate the intermediary between the decision maker and those who provide information.* This can be done by maintaining a basically flat organization structure or by using various bypassing strategies.

   By reducing the number of links in the communication network, the number of relayors through which information may be filtered and distorted is reduced. Flat organizations require a wide span of control. Subordinates have a larger degree of discretion because supervisors spend less time with each subordinate. The number of messages passed between levels in the organization is lower than in tall structures, since supervisors need to approve fewer actions. The tendency in flat structures is toward less vertical communication distortion.

All organizations have ways in which employees can circumvent the usual chain of command and communicate directly with officers or managers two or more levels higher in the organization. Although bypassing may have some detrimental consequences for other aspects of the organization, it does help reduce distortion that occurs when messages must pass through a large number of relayors at different levels in the organization. The major types of bypassing seem to be the following.

  a. *The straight scoop.* Higher-level managers make direct contact with individuals below them in the hierarchy in order to get the "straight scoop" from the "horse's mouth."

  b. *The check-out.* A manager seeks to test ideas before putting them on record through official channels; thus the manager checks out a proposal informally before announcing it formally by making contact with employees at other levels in the organization.

  c. *The end run.* A supervisor has a manager who distorts information passed up the line, so the supervisor makes an end run around the manager to a higher-level official.

  d. *The speed-up.* A supervisor wants to get information to a higher-level executive for some urgent purpose; hence the supervisor speeds up the information-flow process by contacting the higher-up executive directly.

  e. *The co-option.* A manager wants to provide lower-level supervisors with an opportunity to be involved in the decision-making process, so he or she conducts oral briefings or has meetings involving individuals of different levels in the organization or of entire units. By involving supervisors of lower levels with their immediate supervisors, the middle-line supervisor is effectively bypassed.

4. *Develop distortion-proof messages.* One way to reduce distortion is to create message systems that cannot be altered in meaning during transmission, except through direct falsification. To be distortion-proof, a message must be able to be transmitted without condensation or expansion (skeletonizing or importing) between the source and the terminating point. Obviously only a very small proportion of all messages directed to any individual in an organization can be distortion-proof. Nevertheless, carefully prepared codes and easily quantifiable information may represent messages that are less subject to distortion through selective omission of qualifiers, shifts in emphasis, ambiguous terminology, and other perceptual and language factors that affect many messages.

So far we have discussed personal tendencies and organizational characteristics that permit, facilitate, and encourage messages to be distorted. We have also noted some antidistortion forces that limit the amount of distortion that actually occurs in organizations. As a final section in this chapter, we would like to identify six kinds of modifications that occur in messages that lead to distortions and that reduce the fidelity. These modifications are based on a review of the work of Bartlett (1932), Paul (1959), Allport and Postman (1947), and others, but follow the outline of Lee and Lee (1957).

TYPES OF MODIFICATIONS IN MESSAGES THAT LEAD TO DISTORTIONS

Six kinds of modifications take place during the reproduction of messages in organizations:

1. *Omissions.* Details that are not mentioned at all in later transmissions but which were included in the original message and seemed to be overlooked by the relayor.
2. *Losses.* Details that are mentioned by an early relayor but that are dropped in part or completely later in the chain.
3. *Changes.* Details that are moved to a different location in the message, roles made to appear different, events reported in different order, and ideas that have different interpretations.
4. *Additions.* Details that are not mentioned in the original message but that appear as new information in later reproductions.
5. *Elaborations.* Details that are part of the original message but that are highlighted and amplified.
6. *Adjustments toward definiteness.* Details that are included in the original message as qualified statements but are later made to appear more definite by dropping phrases such as, "I think," "It may have been," or "It looked like."

THE EFFECT OF DISTORTIONS ON MEMBERS OF THE ORGANIZATION

There has been little effort devoted to evaluating the effect of distortions on organization members and processes; nevertheless, everyday organizational living suggests that constantly distorted messages have a detrimental effect on people and results in some, if not all, of the following consequences:

1. Reduced morale
2. Lowered motivation
3. Diminished status
4. Alienation
5. Anxiety
6. Monotony
7. Rejection of authority
8. Confusion

SUMMARY

In this chapter we defined message fidelity and distortion in terms of the correspondence of a reproduced message with that of an original message. It was suggested that messages have two dimensions: a display of verbal symbols and nonverbal behaviors and an interpretation or intended and imputed meaning. Eight principles relating to perception, language, nonverbal behaviors, ambiguity, memory, and motivation were discussed as factors that contribute to the distortion of messages. Six characteristics of formal organization were discussed in terms of how they influence the distortion of messages. Four general antidistortion forces that function in organizations were also discussed. Finally, six types of modifications that lead to distortions were identified and characterized, and eight effects that distorted messages have on people in an organization were listed.

REFERENCES

ALKIRE, A., M. COLLUM, J. KASWAN, and L. LOVE, "Information Exchange and Accuracy of Verbal Behavior under Social Power Conditions," *Journal of Personality and Social Psychology,* 9 (1968), 301–308.

ALLPORT, G. W., and L. J. POSTMAN, *The Psychology of Rumor.* New York: Holt, Rinehart & Winston, 1947.

ALPER, T. G., and S. J. KORCHIN, "Memory for Socially Relevant Material," *Journal of Abnormal and Social Psychology,* 47 (1952), 25–37.

BARTLETT, F. C., *Remembering.* London: Cambridge University Press, 1932.

BOUILLUT, J., and S. MOSCOVICI, "Transformation des messages transmis en fonction de l'interest des sujets et de l'image du destinatiare," *Bulletin du C.E.R.P.,* 16 (1967), 305–322.

BRISSEY, F. L., "An Experimental Technique for the Study of Human Communication," Technical Report, Communication Research Laboratory, University of Montana, 1964.

DOWNS, ANTHONY, *Inside Bureaucracy.* Boston: Little, Brown, 1967.

GARDNER, R. W., and L. J. LOHRENZ, "Leveling-Sharpening and Serial Reproduction of a Story," *Bulletin of the Menninger Clinic,* 24 (November 1960), 295–304.

HANEY, WILLIAM V., "Serial Communication of Information in Organizations," in *Concepts and Issues in Administrative Behavior,* ed. Sidney Mailick and Edward H. Van Ness, pp. 150–165. Englewood Cliffs, N.J.: Prentice-Hall, 1962.

HANEY, WILLIAM V., "A Comparative Study of Unilateral and Bilateral Communication," *Academy of Management Journal,* 7 (June 1964), 128–136.

HANEY, WILLIAM V., *Communication and Organizational Behavior.* Homewood, Ill.: Richard D. Erwin, Inc., 1967.

HIGHAM, T. M., "The Experimental Study of the Transmission of Rumor," *British Journal of Psychology,* 42 (1951), 42–55.

HOLZMAN, P. S., and R. W. GARDNER, "Leveling-Sharpening and Memory Organization," *Journal of Abnormal and Social Psychology,* 61 (1960), 176–180.

JACKSON, JAY M., "The Organization and Its Communications Problem," *Advanced Management,* February 1959, pp. 17–20.

JOHNSON, W., and C. B. WOOD, "John Told Him What Joe Told Him: A Study of the Process of Abstracting," *Etc.,* 2 (1944), 10–28.

KATZ, DANIEL, and ROBERT L. KAHN, *The Social Psychology of Organizations.* New York: John Wiley, 1966.

KNAPP, MARK L., *Nonverbal Communication in Human Interaction.* New York: Holt, Rinehart & Winston, 1972.

LEE, I. J., and L. L. LEE, *Handling Barriers in Communication.* New York: Harper & Row, Pub., 1957.

MANIS, M., S. C. CORNELL, and J. C. MOORE, "Transmission of Attitude-Relevant Information through a Communication Chain," *Journal of Personality and Social Psychology,* 30 (1974), 81–94.

MEHRABIAN, ALBERT, *Silent Messages.* Belmont, Calif.: Wadsworth, 1971.

PAUL, T. H., "Studies in Remembering: The Reproduction of Connected and Extended Verbal Materials," *Psychological Bulletin,* 1 (1959), Monograph 2.

REDDING, W. CHARLES, *Communication within the Organization.* New York: Industrial Communication Council, Inc., 1972.

REDDING, W. CHARLES, and GEORGE A. SANBORN, *Business and Industrial Communication: A Source Book.* New York: Harper & Row, Pub., 1964.

STRAUSS, GEORGE, and LEONARD R. SAYLES, *Personnel: The Human Problem of Management.* Englewood Cliffs, N.J.: Prentice-Hall, 1960.

SZALAY, L. G., C. WINDLE, and D. A. LYSNE, "Attitude Measurement by Free Verbal Associations," *Journal of Social Psychology,* 82 (1970), 46.

THAYER, LEE, *Communication and Communication Systems.* Homewood, Ill.: Richard D. Irwin, 1968.

WATZLAWICK, PAUL, JANET HELMICH BEAVIN, and DON D. JACKSON, *Pragmatics of Human Communication.* New York: W. W. Norton & Co., Inc., 1967.

15

ORGANIZATIONAL COMMUNICATION POLICIES

Most organizations have a manual of policies that cover a wide variety of activities, including the duties, responsibilities, and authority of employees; human resource planning; employee records; compensation; benefits; safety; equipment mainte-nance; training; market selection and expansion; and growth plans. The policies provide general but definite guidelines for all employees in carrying out their assign-ments. Policies give direction to and provide standards for making decisions. Policies are some of the most important statements an organization can have for maintain-ing efficient operations. They standardize ways of thinking about and doing things. They provide for uniform treatment of problems and people.

Policies are also statements by which the effectiveness of communication in the organization can be judged. Deviations from a policy should lead to less efficient communication—they should cost more and be less effective. Farace, Taylor, and Stewart (1978) point out that the overall effectiveness of organizational com-munication is limited by the resources that can be devoted to communicating and, conversely, that the degree of effectiveness depends upon the amount of resources expended on communicating. Thus, they conclude, "the critical decision topic for managers is the selection of those effectiveness criteria which need to be maximized in order to achieve the greatest overall efficiency of communication in the organi-zation" (p. 274). They discuss six categories of criteria for the evaluation of organi-zational communication effectiveness: (1) communication rules, (2) communication structure, (3) message characteristics, (4) communicator characteristics, (5) cost and relative efficiency, and (6) media characteristics. Melcher and Beller (1967) present criteria for the selection of channels and methods of communicating when a choice between the formal and informal channels or some combination would make an administrator more effective or when a choice of oral, written, or some combination of those methods might increase an administrator's effectiveness. A comprehensive organizational communication policy should probably include state-ments on all the areas of effectiveness.

Although communication is one of the most pervasive activities occurring in most organizations, a policy statement on organizational communication is usually the most frequently missing section in the policy manual. The purpose of this chapter is to outline the general features of some communication policies for use in organizations. To accomplish this purpose, the concept of policies is defined, some basic requirements for stating policies are reviewed, a list of communication activities and how policies might be phrased to cover them, and an example of an organizational communication policy are presented.

DEFINITION OF POLICY

A *policy* is a general statement that is designed to guide a person's thinking about decision making in an organization. A policy specifies a definite course of action to be followed under certain circumstances. Often policies are merely implied rather than stated directly. For example, incoming correspondence may be placed in a manila folder and filed in a drawer for several days, after which it is sorted and distributed to appropriate individuals for reading and replies. A new employee may observe this practice and ask why correspondence is handled in that manner. The secretary who does the filing may not be entirely clear on the reasons for such a procedure, but the explanation will surely be grounded in the expression, *"It's policy."*

What the secretary means is that there is some understanding that correspondence will be placed in a manila folder and filed in a drawer for two to four days, depending on how full the folder gets, after which the mail is separated according to employee and placed in the employees' mail boxes. In reality an employee, long parted from the organization, may have been rushed one day and simply used the manila folder device as a means to reduce work overload. Over time the practice was followed rather strictly, allowing it to be interpreted as a policy. Thus what began as a temporary activity in a limited area developed into an organization-wide course of action to be adhered to rigorously and, at times, needlessly.

Policies, in any case, consist of general statements, or *understandings* when not stated, that tell what kinds of actions should be taken in a given circumstance. For example, a policy statement of PACECO, Inc., on the issue of discrimination in employment might be stated as follows:

> PACECO shall provide employment, training, compensation, promotion, and other conditions of employment without regard to race, color, religion, national origin, sex, or age, except where age or sex are essential, bona fide occupational qualifications.

This policy statement clearly asserts that PACECO, Inc., employees are to take actions that provide employment without discrimination.

IMPORTANT FEATURES OF POLICIES

Effective policies are guided by five basic requirements:

1. *Policies should reflect the goals of the organization.* Policies should translate the plans and objectives of the organization into statements that guide the thinking

of managers and operators. Policies should emerge out of the basic philosophy and overall directions of the organization. Thus by studying the policies of the organization, you ought to have a fairly clear idea of what the organization is about and what it values.

2. *Policies should be internally consistent.* This guideline asks that policies be developed logically and appropriately from one another. Policies should neither contradict one another nor countermand policies of higher and lower orders within the organization. This means that policies in one part of the organization must be phrased so that they do not conflict with policies in another part.

3. *Policies should allow for discretionary decision making.* Policies represent general statements that *guide the thinking* of members of the organization. Policies should avoid dictating specifically how a person is to behave. Rules and procedures, on the other hand, are designed to channel action, and they allow for little or no discretion. Policies are often implemented by means of a set of rules and procedures directing employees to act in specific ways. Policies have a degree of ambiguity and uncertainty associated with them. Policies must be interpreted.

4. *Policies should be written down.* Writing a policy down, of course, does not make it a clear and concise statement, but a policy that cannot be written down is usually, at minimum, ambiguous and, at most, fuzzy, inconsistent, and potentially irrelevant. The issuance of a written policy does not ensure that it will be understood, either. If the policy is written, however, it can be reviewed and updated. Even at that, a great deal of interpersonal communication is usually necessary to make the application of policies consistent and fair.

5. *Policies should be communicated to members of the organization.* Although policies may reflect the goals of the organization, may be stated carefully so as to be fully consistent with one another, may allow for the proper discretionary decision making, and may be written down, they will be ineffective unless they are adequately distributed to members of the organization. Since policies are written with some ambiguity involved, they must be interpreted for those who are to apply the policies. Continued application of a policy to specific situations, unfortunately, tends to gradually evolve into a procedure that eventually becomes a regulation which is often applied as a rule, with no discretion. The process of communicating policies is a continuing activity. Policies ought to be discussed on a regular basis to make certain that they are being applied with discretion as guides to thinking rather than as rules for action.

COMMUNICATION POLICIES

Communication policies represent a set of objectives that the organization wishes to achieve with regard to communication. As with policies guiding manufacturing, sales, and finance, communication policies express the philosophy of the organization so as to achieve some consistency in attitude and practice throughout the organization. In an organization where there are no formal communication policies, each individual manager, supervisor, section head, and employee may have his or her own communication policies that may conflict with those of other members of the organization with whom he or she interacts. Sigband (1969) observed that "when firms have no philosophy of communications we almost invariably have as a result:

1. Little or no discussion on controversial issues (labor problems, salaries, promotion, layoffs, etc.),
2. Different ways of handling similar issues throughout the organization,
3. Continued discussion on superficial and surface topics to the exclusion of items of real importance to individuals in and outside the firm." (p. 63)

Seybold (1966) reported an analysis of the formal written communication policy statements of 80 large companies, which revealed a wide range of philosophies regarding why managers or supervisors should communicate with employees. Some policies, for example, indicated that managers should keep employees informed because the *employees want information;* others stated that *employees have a right to know things;* others expressed the philosophy that managers should communicate with employees in order to give the *employees a feeling of participating in decisions.*

Burhans (1971) observed that even though organizations may differ in their formally stated policies, communication difficulties in an organization may arise frequently because *employees* of a firm or work group may have preferences for certain communication policies and practices that differ from that of their supervisors, without the supervisors being aware that the differences exist. Burhans developed a *Communication Policy Preference Scale* of 35 items that appeared to be sensitive to both the communication preferences of employees and their supervisor's misassumptions about those preferences. The items represented a fairly full range of answers to five basic questions:

1. Why communicate?
2. What should be communicated?
3. When should it be communicated?
4. Who should communicate to whom?
5. How should an organization's management communicate with its employees?

Within certain limitations those five questions (Why, What, When, Who, and How) establish a framework for thinking about the content of a communication policy. Sigband (1969), however, suggested that an adequate communication philosophy might include the following points:

1. Employees should be informed about ongoing activities of the company.
2. Employees should be informed about company goals, objectives, plans, and directions.
3. Employees should be informed about negative, sensitive, and controversial issues.
4. Employees should be encouraged to participate in a steady flow of two-way communications.
5. Employees should meet periodically with their supervisors for discussions of job performance aand appraisal.

6. Meetings should be held to explore important areas and to encourage free expression.

7. Employees should have important events and situations communicated to them as quickly as possible.

Sigband concluded that "when a philosophy such as this is established, a policy will evolve. This then permits *all* managers *in all* of the company's plants to recognize their boundaries. They know what, when, and how completely they may communicate with their subordinates" (p. 65).

Sigband offers two key reservations concerning implementing a communication policy. He suggests that there are constraints, boundaries, and limits. Judgment must be used. A corporate philosophy of communication, he asserts, is not "a license to communicate everything to everyone" (p. 65). On the other hand, an effective philosophy of communication, he argues, commits the organization to a long-range plan of informing others, opening channels of communication, and developing a freer flow of ideas.

It is within this general framework and philosophy that the tentative set of communication policies is offered for analysis and discussion, something for consideration and improvement. These policies are presented as some tentative principles to guide the thinking of organization members about the philosophy and practice of communication in organizations. In addition to the sample set of communication policies, a communication policy statement representing a government agency is presented for comparison.

SAMPLE SET
OF ORGANIZATIONAL COMMUNICATION POLICIES

The sample set of communication policies will focus more specifically on the communication climate and the flow of information in the organization. Forms, relationships, practices, and skills of communication are referred to in the policies and should rightfully reflect the policies.

Policies on Message or Information Flow
in Organizations

Policies to guide our thinking about the most desirable approaches to message or information dissemination in organizations are derived from ideas appearing in the literature over a 30-year period (Barnard, 1938; Baker, Ballantine, & True, 1949; Greenbaum, 1973). Message or information-flow policies guide our thinking in ten areas. Each policy area is named and described briefly.

1. *Establishment of networks.* Communication networks should be established and maintained to ensure that information related to the major objectives of the organization is shared among personnel of the organization.

The primary function of top management is to establish and maintain a system of communication in the organization. The major system of communication is referred to as the *lines of authority.* Other networks, however, may develop and be important to maintain in order to ensure the flow of information to encourage productivity, to promote flexibility and adaptiveness, to improve morale, and to improve the technical know-how of personnel.

2. *Knowledge of networks.* A clearly defined network of lines of authority should be known by all personnel. All personnel should know whom to contact for information related to efficient and effective job performance. Insofar as possible, specific channels within networks should be known by all organization personnel.

3. *Size and use of networks.* Lines or channels of communication within the organization should be as direct and as short as possible. The complete line of communication, in any given instance, should be used; however, where efficiency can be achieved by shortening networks, the individual abbreviating a channel must inform both his or her own superior and the superior of the person contacted.

4. *Authentication of messages.* All official messages should clearly but simply show official authorization. Methods and procedures should be established for indicating officially authorized messages.

5. *Timing.* Messages should be disseminated so that a supervisor always hears information before his or her subordinates. When personnel are to be informed about an event or decision, informing procedures should take place well in advance of rumors, gossip, and conjectures. Such information should be released soon enough to be useful to the individuals whom it was intended to benefit.

6. *Transmittal.* All personnel on any level who receive information for passing on should share responsibility for and take specific steps to pass the information on as nearly simultaneously and uniformly as possible. Every effort should be made to ensure that accurate, nondistorted messages are transmitted throughout the organization.

7. *Who is to be told.* If one person in a unit is to be told some information, all personnel who are equally in need of the information should also be told.

8. *Who is to tell.* Information should be transmitted to subordinates by their immediate superiors; however, occasionally all personnel should have the opportunity to hear information directly from managers at all levels in the organization. When matters arise that employees would like to discuss directly with top management, they should feel free to go directly to the manager's or executive's office.

9. *How telling is to be done.* Managers and employees should have frequent face-to-face, oral (interpersonal) communication. Nevertheless, both oral and written communication techniques should be employed in transmitting information throughout the organization. The following subpoints are part of this policy:

a. Managers should make frequent visits to the field, plant, offices, and work areas to make personal contacts with workers. Both line and staff groups should hold regular and frequent meetings at various levels during which full discussion of group work takes place.

b. Reports of discussions at management levels should be disseminated regularly for ideas and reactions at other levels; a serious and systematic effort should be maintained for getting *a return flow* of information, ideas, and suggestions from all levels and from all personnel in the organization.

c. Agreements and understandings reached during face-to-face meetings should be confirmed in writing.

d. Information being sent outside the unit by correspondence that may be of interest to the unit should be circulated promptly, regularly, and freely to members of the unit.

e. Incoming printed matter of general interest should be made available promptly and regularly to individuals who should have access to it.

f. A simple, fast, and neat system for getting written and pictorial materials before individuals by means of a bulletin board system should be maintained.

g. An organized program of employee and employee-family social activities should be maintained; the program should permit spouses and children of employees to occasionally visit plants, offices, and work areas.

h. A variety of devices and techniques for keeping personnel fully informed should be used regularly.

10. *Evaluation.* A regular system for evaluating the effectiveness of internal communication should be initiated and maintained; information derived from a continuing analysis should be reviewed, studied, and used in making desirable changes in modes, techniques, and forms of communication.

Although policies about the flow of information in an organization can aid immensely the effectiveness of organizational communication, research and personal experience strongly suggests that a primary determinant of how messages are transmitted, how they are interpreted, and what is communicated are the climate of communication and the employee's satisfaction with communication.

Policies on Communication Climate and Satisfaction

Policies to guide our thinking about communication climate and satisfaction have developed much more recently than have policies on information flow (Beckstrom, 1980; Downs, 1977; Redding, 1972). Policies on climate and satisfaction reflect the attitudes that managers and employees hold toward communication flow, toward how the organization should be managed, and toward the people working in the organization. Policies on information flow, communication climate, and communication satisfaction are all important in guiding people to think about organizational communication and human resource development.

ORGANIZATIONAL COMMUNICATION CLIMATE

1. *Trust.* Personnel at all levels should make every effort to develop and maintain relationships where trust, confidence, and credibility are sustained by statement and act.

2. *Participative decision making.* Employees at all levels in the organization should be communicated with and consulted in a meaningful way on issues in all areas of organization policy relevant to their positions. Personnel at all levels in the organization should be provided with avenues of communication and consulta-

tion with management levels above theirs for the purpose of participating in decision-making and goal-setting processes.

3. *Supportiveness.* A general atmosphere of candor and frankness should pervade relationships in the organization, with employees being able to say *what's on their minds* regardless of whether they are talking to peers, subordinates, or superiors.

4. *Openness in downward communication.* Except for necessary security information, members of the organization should have relatively easy access to information that relates directly to their immediate jobs, that affects their abilities to coordinate their work with that of other people or departments, and that deals broadly with the company, its structure, leaders, and plans.

5. *Listening in upward communication.* Personnel at each level in the organization should listen continuously and with open minds to suggestions or reports of problems made by individuals at each subordinate level in the organization. Information from subordinates should be viewed as important enough to be acted upon until demonstrated otherwise.

6. *Concern for high performance goals.* Employees at all levels in the organization should demonstrate a commitment to high performance goals—high productivity, high quality, low cost—as well as a high concern for other members of the organization.

ORGANIZATIONAL SATISFACTION

1. *The work itself.* The management of this company should do everything possible to ensure that the work itself will be satisfying for employees through an opportunity to turn out quality products or services, desirable working conditions, an interesting and challenging assignment, and an opportunity to feel a sense of accomplishment in what they are doing.

2. *Supervision.* Employees should feel that they have freedom to work on their own, that their supervisors will discipline with tact, give positive criticism as well as negative comments, and let them know how they stand in the organization. The relationship between the supervisor and the supervised should be viewed as satisfying.

3. *Pay and benefits.* Employees should feel that they are well paid for what they do. Pay benefits include such things as competitive salaries, fair vacation arrangements, pensions and other forms of security, and rest breaks.

4. *Promotion.* Employees should feel that they have opportunities to be promoted and a chance to grow with the organization. The organization should have a quality performance review system, a consistent promotion policy, and demonstrate that an employee can progress in the company.

5. *Coworkers.* Employees should feel that their fellow workers are stimulating and fun to be with, easy to get along with, and supportive of them and their work.

ORGANIZATIONAL COMMUNICATION SATISFACTION

Satisfaction with the organization is most often a function of the kind of information that a person receives about each of the key areas. Policies on communication satisfaction involve the quality and adequacy of information received from the organization.

1. *Communication climate.* All members of the organization should be satisfied with the communication climate.

2. *Superiors.* All members of the organization should be satisfied with the degree to which superiors in the organization are open to ideas, listen and pay attention to subordinates, and offer guidance for solving job-related problems.

3. *Organizational integration.* All employees should be satisfied with the information they receive about their immediate work environment, including departmental plans, requirements of their jobs, and personnel matters.

4. *Media quality.* All members of the organization should be satisfied with the extent to which meetings are organized, the length and clarity of written directives, and the number of messages disseminated in the organization.

5. *Horizontal and informal communication.* All employees should be satisfied with the degree to which the grapevine is active and the extent to which horizontal and informal communication is accurate and free flowing.

6. *Organizational perspective.* All employees should be satisfied with the kind of information they receive about the organization as a whole, including notification of changes, financial status, and the overall policies and goals of the organization.

7. *Subordinates.* All employees should be satisfied with the degree to which they are responsive to downward communication and the degree to which they anticipate the supervisor's needs and initiate upward communication that will be helpful to them.

8. *Personal feedback.* All employees should be satisfied with the information they have about how they are being judged and how their performance is being appraised.

COMMUNICATION POLICIES OF A GOVERNMENT AGENCY

To illustrate the way in which communication policies may be phrased, we have included the draft statement of intramanagement communication and consultation policies of a large federal agency (see Figure 15.1). Although the policy statements are offered for analysis, they should not be construed as the final statement.

FIGURE 15.1
Draft Statement of Intramanagement Communication and Consultation Policies
of a Large Federal Agency

INTRAMANAGEMENT COMMUNICATION AND CONSULTATION

Intramanagement Communication Policy

The _____ is committed to seeking employee involvement in its decision-making–goal-setting process.

A significant part of this involvement includes management and supervisors at all levels of the organization.

Executive Order 111491 established a basis for communicating with management and supervisors when it specified that

Figure 15.1 (cont.)

An agency shall establish a system for Intramanagement Communication and consultation with its supervisors or Association of Supervisors. The communications and consultation shall have as its purposes the improvement of Agency operations, the improvement of working conditions of supervisor, the exchange of information, the improvement of managerial effectiveness, and the establishment of policies that serve the public interest in accomplishing the mission of the Agency.

It is, therefore, policy that supervisors at all levels must be communicated with and consulted in a meaningful way on issues in all areas of Agency policy, especially those concerning the many facets of work for which supervisors have significant responsibility and concern. In furtherance of this policy, supervisors at all levels must be provided with effective avenues of communications and consultation with their top management for the purpose of participating in both the decision-making–goal-setting process and program development. Supervisors are to be encouraged to assume responsibility for participating in and contributing to the formulation of policies and procedures.

Definition

A manager or supervisor is anyone who has responsibility to control, direct, and plan programs or work generally involving supervision of others. Specific duties and responsibilities include most of the following:

1. Planning work to be accomplished by subordinates; setting priorities and preparing schedules for completion of work.
2. Assigning work to subordinates based on priorities, selective consideration of the difficulty and the requirements of the assignments, and the capabilities of employees.
3. Evaluating performance of subordinates.
4. Giving advice, counsel, or instruction to individual employees on both work and administrative matters.
5. Interviewing candidates for positions in the unit; making recommendations for appointment, promotion, or reassignment involving these positions.
6. Hearing and resolving complaints from employees; referring group grievances and the more serious complaints not resolved to higher-level supervisors.
7. Effecting minor disciplinary measures such as warnings and reprimands; recommending action in more serious cases.
8. Identifying developmental and training needs of employees; providing or making provision for this development and training.

Responsibilities

Each regional director, and deputy chief is responsible for implementing this policy within his or her organization and program areas and establishing systems and means of intramanagement communications and consultation. The division of personnel is responsible for providing advice, assistance, and guidance in the establishment and development of Intramanagement communications systems, including the establishment of an association of supervisors.

Figure 15.1 (cont.)

Minimum Characteristics
of Intramanagement Communications Systems

Systems or means established to communicate and consult with managers and supervisors must have the following characteristics:

1. Supervisors should be reached in the normal course of work, and each supervisor should be aware that he or she is included.
2. Systems of communication and consultation should include the supervisor in the decision-making process and assure that he or she is notified of the final decision on a timely basis. The supervisor should never be the last to know about the decision that involves work and employee.
3. Supervisors should be assured that they will be able to express their views and recommendations to other members of management in a candid and forthright manner without fear of reprisal or discrimination.
4. The systems should be designed so that individual supervisors as well as the association of supervisors are able to participate.
5. The system(s) should stress that supervisors are viewed as an integral part of the management team.
6. The system(s) established should avoid overly formal or rigid standards or techniques for relationships with supervisors.
7. The system(s) developed need to reflect differences among organizations and programs, and therefore the system(s) will necessarily reflect different situations and needs.

Practices and Techniques
for Intramanagement Communication and Consultation

The _____ has a long history of positive efforts in communicating with supervisor and manager. Many of the current efforts and techniques are still valid and should be recognized in developing system(s) in intramanagement communications.

CURRENT PRACTICES AND TECHNIQUES

The techniques and practices currently used for intramanagement communication and consultation can be divided into six categories: written communications, meetings and conferences, training, organizational techniques, special programs, and informal techniques and practices. The following list is grouped by these categories. The listing of these techniques is not a suggestion that every technique is appropriate for use by every unit, or is all inclusive, but rather is a checklist of procedures that have proved beneficial in the past.

Written Communications

1. Supervisor's handbooks, reference manuals. These manuals usually contain agency policies and procedures plus guidelines on supervisory practices. Some examples of subjects included are rules of conduct, attendance, discipline, safety, training, smoke-jumping, log-scaling, fiscal, and wildlife.

Figure 15.1 (cont.)

2. Regulatory and guidance issuances in areas such as budget, personnel management, operations, fiscal, timber management, and research.
3. Informational memoranda, bulletins, letters, notices, and circulars.
4. House organs.
5. Reports and studies from upper management to supervisors and from supervisors to upper management, such as *Personnel Program Review, Framework for the Future.*
6. Special supervisory publications mailed to the supervisor's home.
7. Questionnaires.
8. Fact sheets on land management alternatives.
9. Request for comment on implementations of new policies or practice such as in promotion plan, classification standards, pay policies, land management, organizational changes.
10. Minutes of labor relations meetings.

Meetings and Conferences

1. Supervisor's meetings, sometimes attended by representatives of higher management.
2. Cross-functional supervisory meetings conducted to discuss projects of mutual concern.
3. Staff meetings and conferences in general.
4. Consultation meetings with supervisory associations.
5. Telephone conferences (selected supervisors attend the conferences that are recorded and played back to other supervisors who discuss them).
6. Annual management conferences.

Training

1. Supervisory seminars conducted to increase supervisory knowledge and to emphasize the supervisor's authorities, responsibilities, and importance in relation to overall agency operation.
2. Basic supervisory training courses providing the basics of good supervisory practices plus familiarization with administrative information and management philosophy.
3. Special orientation.
4. Workshops to teach and develop the skills of supervision.
5. Prenegotiations training of local management negotiating teams.
6. Participation in commission and other interagency training courses for supervisors.

Organizational Techniques

1. Special task forces, composed of selected supervisors, to study, for example, leave and promotion policies and procedures, safety, training, and agency organization, recreation practice and policies, fiscal practices, organization goals and objectives.

Figure 15.1 (cont.)

2. Special assignments for supervisors to work with management staff on projects involving safety, equipment acquisition, planning-programming-budget system, and so on.
3. Inspection and program evaluation such as GII, GFI, functional assistance.

Special Programs

1. Incentive awards programs with supervisors given an active role, including participating in public award ceremonies held for their employees.
2. Suggestion program.
3. Equal Employment Opportunity committees. These committees serve as an effective means of communicating at all levels.
4. Zero defects and management improvement programs and other special cost reduction, quality control, and safety programs requiring supervisory understanding of, and commitment to, management goals for success.
5. Personnel management and position classification reviews involving in-depth interviews with supervisors.
6. Use of supervisors on promotion advisory boards.
7. Attitude surveys.

Informal Techniques and Practices

1. Normal person-to-person contact between executive management and supervisors.
2. Advance notice to supervisors of all new policies and significant changes.
3. Feedback from executive management on status of ongoing studies on staffing, budget, training, and so on.
4. Management luncheons.
5. Visits by higher management.
6. Brainstorming sessions.
7. Discussion groups.

When to Communicate and Consult

Determining when and which decisions require communication and consultation with supervisors and the extent of involvement are essential factors to be considered in carrying out this intramanagement communication-consultation policy. There are instances when consultation is required by law or regulation such as in making changes in the promotion plan. Generally, the decision to communicate and consult will rest with a manager within guidelines established by the director or deputy chief. No clearcut guide can be established for these broad areas of decision making. Most decisions on communication and consultation will be based on an awareness by the unit manager or program specialist that supervisors are a key linkage in the management process. The involvement and participation of supervisors are an important element for effective decision making and implementation of management goals, objectives, policies and programs.

Figure 15.1 (cont.)

The key to involving others is (a) the establishment of attitudes conducive to successful supervisor involvement and (b) an awareness that an effective organization depends on an effective communication and decision-making process.

EFFECTIVE COMMUNICATION AND DECISION MAKING

Effective communication and decision making is achieved when

1. The amount of interaction and communication aimed at achieving organization goals is extensive with individuals and groups.
2. The direction of information flow is down, up, and with peer.
3. Subordinates are free to openly and candidly question downward communication.
4. Accuracy of upward communication through the line is high.
5. Supervisor and decision maker understand and know problems of subordinates.
6. There is friendly interaction with high degree of trust.
7. Decision making is widely done throughout the organization but well integrated through linking communication and consultation.
8. What knowledge, information, or skills available anywhere in the organization is used.
9. Subordinates are involved in decisions related to their work.
10. Decisions are made at the best level in the organization.

ATTITUDES CONDUCIVE
TO SUCCESSFUL SUPERVISOR-MANAGEMENT INVOLVEMENT

To be successful in obtaining the maximum value out of the intramanagement communication process, one must enter into it with the free interchange of facts and opinions and in an atmosphere of cooperation and concern.

1. Recognize that supervisor involvement is an essential part of decision making since it can enable the decision maker to render a better decision.
2. Discard any notion that actions affecting land resources, personnel practices, or the public interest can be judged only by top management professionals. Although a proposed action may be professionally correct, those who must implement policies may have considerations to justify modification.
3. Be willing to accept criticism of yourself or the organization with a positive rather than a defensive attitude. If the criticism is clearly unjustified, do not glorify it by an overdefensive reaction. Meet such criticism with well-substantiated facts that set the record straight. Wherever criticism has any validity, show a willingness to accept it in considering possible changes.
4. Give as much consideration to the opinion of those who oppose or question policies as you would to those who have supported them. All points of view should be considered. Recognize that success in achieving support for a decision may well depend on whether the opinions of all interested individuals have been considered.

Figure 15.1 (cont.)

5. Do not feel that you, as an officer, are in any way abdicating responsibilities in making management decisions because you have involved others as a factor in reaching these decisions. The final decision is still up to you.

6. Research workers should recognize that at some point it is desirable to seek comment on the design and operation of research projects that may arouse the concern of the scientist or project leader.

7. Once a decision has been reached by an officer, the supervisor should be immediately informed of the decision. Since it may not be possible to incorporate all contributions in a decision, it is imperative that publication of the decision or policy include an explanation of how it was reached.

SUMMARY

This chapter introduced the concept of communication policies. A policy was defined as a general statement designed to guide a person's thinking about decision making in an organization. Policy statements indicate what kinds of actions should be taken in a given circumstance. Five basic requirements of effective policies were discussed. Communication policies were defined as a set of objectives that the organization wishes to achieve with regard to organizational communication. A very tentative set of organizational communication policies was presented. They included guidelines on information flow, organizational communication climate, organizational satisfaction, and communication satisfaction. Finally, a draft statement of some communication policies of a government agency was presented to illustrate how an organization might proceed to develop its own organizational communication policies.

REFERENCES

BAKER, HELEN, JOHN W. BALLANTINE, and JOHN M. TRUE, "Transmitting Information through Management and Union Channels: Two Case Studies." Princeton: Industrial Relations Section, Department of Economics and Social Institutions, 1949.

BARNARD, CHESTER I., *The Functions of the Executive.* Cambridge, Mass.: Harvard University Press, 1938.

BECKSTROM, MARK R., "Measuring Communication Satisfaction." Unpublished master's thesis, Brigham Young University, Provo, Utah, August 1980.

BURHANS, DAVID T., JR., "The Development and Field Testing of Two Internal Communication Measuring Instruments." Unpublished paper, California State College, Los Angeles, December 1971.

DOWNS, CAL W., "The Relationship between Communication and Job Satisfaction," in *Readings in Interpersonal and Organizational Communication* (3rd ed.), ed. Richard C. Huseman, Cal M. Logue, and Dwight L. Freshley, pp. 363–376. Boston: Holbrook Press, Inc., 1977.

FARACE, RICHARD V., JAMES A. TAYLOR, and JOHN P. STEWART, "Criteria for Evaluation of Organizational Effectiveness: Review and Synthesis," *Communication Yearbook 2,* ed. Brent D. Ruben, pp. 271–292. New Brunswick, N.J.: Transaction Books, 1978.

GREENBAUM, HOWARD H., "The Appraisal and Management of Organizational Communication." Unpublished paper, Fordham University at Lincoln Center, New York City, May 1973.

MELCHER, A. J., and R. BELLER, "Toward a Theory of Organizational Communication," *Academy of Management Journal,* 10 (March 1967), 39–52.

REDDING, W. CHARLES, *Communication within the Organization.* New York: Industrial Communication Council, 1972.

SEYBOLD, GENEVA, *Employee Communication: Policy and Tools.* New York: National Industrial Conference Board, Inc., 1966.

SIGBAND, NORMAN B., "Needed: Corporate Policies on Communications," *S.A.M. Advanced Management Journal* (April 1969), pp. 61–67.

16

ANALYSIS IN ORGANIZATIONAL COMMUNICATION*

*the analytical role
in human resource development*

Organizations use human, physical, and technological resources to accomplish their goals. To use these resources, organization members must make decisions and share information. The process by which individuals interact, share, and cooperate is called *communication*. Although effective communication does not guarantee an efficiently operating organization, ineffective communication creates a condition that virtually precludes organizational efficiency from occurring. Organizations owe their very existence to communication; it is through communication that efforts are coordinated and resources used to accomplish goals. Communication and the effective functioning of human resources are intimately interrelated.

Communication has long been recognized as the very means of survival for both people and organizations. The information system of an organization influences the way in which the organization copes with its problems. Since organizations consist of people, the information-processing problems of individuals are part of the problems of the larger organization. The individual confronted with those unique and peculiar problems finds his or her personal problems compounded.

Changes in the ways in which people process information for themselves, in which people distribute information through the organization, in which people relate to one another, in which people present information, and in which people make their needs and preferences known are changes in communication. Developments in a person's capacity to handle communication are developments in a person's capacity to cooperate with others, to solve problems, to engage in organized activities, and to acquire the skills and attitudes necessary to prepare for advancement along career lines. An understanding of individual, group, and institutional communication may be the most crucial of all understandings for success in a human resource development career.

DEFINITION OF ANALYSIS

Analysis is the process of studying the nature of something, determining its constituent elements, or determining its essential features and their relations. An analyst in human resource development is a person who learns about the status of communication and other activities of members of an organization.

Analysis is used extensively in organizations to determine the current status of its functions, programs, and activities. Analyses are used to find out what is happening and to decide what is preferred at a given time. Like a medical diagnosis or an automotive diagnosis, organizational diagnosis provides a picture of how the system is functioning. From the description derived from the analysis, it is possible to recognize strengths and weaknesses and establish procedures for taking corrective action.

DEFINITION OF A PROBLEM

Analysis is grounded in the philosophy of problem solving. Before a decision is made, a problem should be identified. A *problem* is defined as the difference between what is and what ought to be. The nature and location of differences between what is happening and what we would like to have happen usually determine the strategies for making changes.

An *organizational problem* is the difference between what we think is taking place in the organization and what we would like to have taking place. Thus the way to determine whether something should be changed is to compare the current way of doing things against some measures of organizational effectiveness. For example, you may feel that turnover, absenteeism, indifference, low performance goals, lack of cooperation, complaints, grievances, work errors, accidents, profits, morale, net operating costs, work units produced, or other consequences of working in the organization are different from what you would like. The question is, "What is happening in the organization that results in consequences that are different from what we would like?" In other words, those observable consequences may be reflections of an inadequate or unhealthy communication system and indicate human resource weaknesses.

RESULTS OF ANALYSIS

Analysis provides the basis for selecting, designing, and implementing strategies for making changes in and developing human beings and organizations. Through the process of analysis, difficulties can be recognized and classified so as to make them amenable to improvement. Analysis can provide information on three important issues related to human resource development: employee task performance, information, and skills deficiencies. Analysis can often go beyond the identification of deficiencies in individual performance and reveal a great deal about the organization itself. The organization's managerial and operational philosophies and assumptions, leadership, decision-making and reward systems, interpersonal communication, organizational influence, group dynamics, conflict, information flow, and the other elements of organizational communication can be understood through analysis.

THE PROCESS OF ANALYSIS

Figure 16.1 portrays the process of analysis in human resource development and organizational communication. We shall discuss this general model as the prelude for dealing with specific issues of analysis.

Historical Performance: Point of Concern

All organization performance has some type of history. A drop in productivity represents a movement in time from one position of production to another, lower one. It is usually very difficult for a newcomer to understand an organization as the old-timers do, since the two groups have different histories with the organization. Information about what has happened in the past may be highly revealing about what organization members perceive as the problem and some of its causes (Leach, 1979).

Analysis is usually provoked by a sense that something seems wrong, that what has been done historically is now producing consequences that appear different and undesirable. If what has been happening in the past seems to have positive results, it is unlikely that much analysis will occur, even simple and informal analysis, much less complex, in-depth, and scientifically based analysis. Some point of concern nearly always triggers interest in analysis. In a fictitious but impelling description of one company's problems and the efforts of a consultant to assist in resolving them, Perry and Straus (1952) recount points of concern when union contract negotiations faltered and a strike was threatened:

> Productivity went down and down. Foremen tried to step up the pace but found themselves without followers. Figures on rejected work were alarming. . . . Several customers expressed their sympathy—but bought from other manufacturers when Acme could not deliver. Two salesmen quit. A deputation of local merchants urged him to avoid a strike at all costs: "The town can't afford it." A publicity-conscious minister offered to mediate. (p. 53)
> The president, Braden, "found himself worrying, spending too much time plugging gaps, wasting time he should be spending on Acme's market expansion. And he wasn't getting anywhere. He needed help." (p. 54)[1]

This is a dramatic demonstration of the point of concern—the point at which someone in the organization realizes that something seems to be wrong. Usually

---

[1] Reprinted by permission of the *Harvard Business Review*. Copyright © 1952 by the President and Fellows of Harvard College; all rights reserved.

FIGURE 16.1
*Process of Analysis
in Human Resource Development
and Organizational Communication*

Historical Performance	Current Performance	Future Performance	Problem Identification	Problem Classification
What has happened in the past? (something seems wrong?)	What is happening now?	What ought to be happening tomorrow?	Are there differences between what is happening and what ought to be happening? Are the differences important enough to do something about?	Are the performance deficiencies training needs or are they development needs?
Point of Concern	Documentation of Concern	Development of Guidelines	Point of Comparison	Point of Determination

the point of concern is more subtle; things just seem to feel a bit different from what they have historically. At that point, however, concern should seem strong enough to move to the next phase—documentation.

Current Performance: Documentation of Concern

Once a concern has been sensed, the next step is to provide some documentation for the concern, which is often the most critical activity of researchers and consultants. However, the human resource development and the organization development departments find that concerns must be documented if they are to be believed and accepted as the basis for training and development programs.

The methods, procedures, and instruments for conducting a task analysis, performance appraisal, and needs analysis will be explained later in this chapter.

Future Performance: Development of Guidelines

The third stage in an analysis involves the discovery or development of guidelines to decide what kind of performance, behavior, activity, skill, knowledge, or organizational change is expected or desired. After documenting concerns and establishing somewhat clearly what appears to be happening with employees and within the organization, the next step is to create a picture of what ought to be taking place. This necessitates having or developing a set of guidelines to assist in thinking about future performance. Guidelines can be located in three places: (1) job and position descriptions, (2) performance standards statements, and (3) policies.

We have described and illustrated different ways of stating organizational communication policies in Chapter 15. Policies about information flow, communication climate, and communication satisfaction, for example, provide guidelines for thinking about how communication should occur in an organization. An organization that has a communication system consistent with those guidelines has created ways for new ideas to be initiated and implemented so as to be competitive in its markets. Employees find that the organization is a pleasant place to work. An organization that has a communication system that is inconsistent with the policies has a need to improve.

Performance standards indicate the level of competence and proficiency with which employees should work. Performance standards that are met represent an organization in which the employees put in the effort to make the organization successful. Managerial and supervisory employees take their duties seriously and compare their assumptions with what actually happens in the organization. An effective communication system and clear performance standards lead to competent employees who know what to do and how to improve their performances. A pool of promotable employees is ready to assume responsibility in the organization. The entire organization encourages productivity and rewards employees who perform well.

Job and position descriptions allow the best people to be selected for the work and good of the organization. Employees can develop with the organization because they have the physical and mental capabilities to handle the job requirements. Future staffing needs can be identified and employees prepared because the organization knows where it is going, why it wants to go there, and how it is going to get there. If those goals do not exist, the organization may have a problem, or at least the organization may have difficulty recognizing that it has a problem.

Problem Identification: Point of Comparison

Stage four in analysis involves identifying the problems. "In its simplest terms the process of problem analysis consists of determining the *difference* between what you have and what you would like to have" (Patton & Giffin, 1973, p. 141). The point of comparison attempts to answer the questions, "Are there differences between what is happening and what ought to be happening?" and "Are the differences important enough to do something?" If both the documentation of concern and the guidelines are clear, differences may be easy to recognize. In other instances the existence of differences may be a matter of interpretation. This stage is critical in evolving a commitment to action. If few people recognize the problem, little support may be given to solving it. Hence the point of comparison may need to be worked out very carefully, with the best data available and the clearest guidelines you can create.

Problem Classification: Point of Determination

The fifth and final stage in analysis is the point of determination. The question to be answered here is, "Are the performance deficiencies training needs, or are they development needs?" A *need* is defined as a demand, a lack of something that is required by the circumstances. In human resource development and organizational communication, a needs analysis consists of an effort to document those things that the employees of an organization feel are lacking or are required to perform their work efficiently (that is, cost-effectively). The emphasis in a needs analysis is on what the employee perceives as the lack of, want for, or circumstances that require a change.

Deficiencies in knowledge and skill that interfere with the competent performance of an employee's job or knowledge and skills that can aid the employee in doing his or her job better are called *training needs*.

Knowledge and skills, on the other hand, that help an employee prepare for a different position in the organization or to move into jobs, positions, and careers that have not been defined clearly as yet are called *development needs*.

The task at stage five is to decide whether the problems identified are training or development needs or whether they are problems of management or organization development. Training and development needs are met through the methods and strategies of human resource development. Management problems are resolved through changes in management practices. Organization development needs are alleviated through systems intervention procedures. The careful classification of the types of problems or needs confronting the organization can lead to more powerful methods and strategies for solving the problems.

APPROACHES TO DOCUMENTING
NEEDS AND DEFICIENCIES

We shall now turn our attention to the ways in which concerns can be documented. Several general approaches may be used to document a concern. Deficiencies in individual employee task performance may be documented through *task analysis* or through *performance appraisal methods.*

Task Analysis

Task analysis is a method for determining the specific performance requirements for a job in order to identify what an employee must know and do to complete a job. "Task analysis is a method for specifying in precise detail and in measurable terms the human performance required to achieve specific management objectives, the tools and conditions needed to perform the job, and the skills and knowledge required of the employee" (Michalak & Yager, 1979, p. 43). A task analysis includes approximately ten steps to complete:

1. *Make a list of all major tasks and subtasks necessary to perform the job.* The idea is to identify what is to be done and what the steps are to get the job done. The tasks are usually listed in chronological order, or in the time sequence in which they are done. Jobs that require quite a bit of physical activity usually have the steps in the job listed chronologically. For example, a good practice exercise involves listing the steps required to change a flat tire. Assume that you are driving down the freeway and hear air escaping from a rear tire. List the tasks you need to do in order to stop, change the tire, and get back on the road. List them in the order that they should be done.

Jobs that involve less systematic tasks may be analyzed more efficiently by completing a highly detailed job description. Some jobs have tasks to do but not in any particular order. For example, an executive secretary may answer the telephone, make appointments, schedule travel arrangements, brief the boss, supervise typists and clerks, and maintain surveillance over certain budget items. A task analysis of the executive secretary's job might be accomplished by preparing a list of the different types of tasks that are done from time to time, although not necessarily in any particular order. Of course, each of the tasks, such as answering the telephone, could be analyzed by listing the steps chronologically.

2. *Record when and how often each task is to be done.* The frequency with which tasks are completed should be noted. If a task is done each Tuesday, it may be treated differently from one that is done only every six months. The kinds of problems that may develop and the discrepancies that surface may imply quite different approaches for making changes, designing training sessions, and reinforcing learning.

3. *State the levels of acceptable performance associated with each major task.* Whenever possible, a specific quantifiable measure of acceptable performance should be noted. The best standards refer to such measures as time, distance, and number

of errors. Scores of 90 percent may be acceptable, within three seconds, with a tolerance of .005 of an inch, or with a minimum of three typing errors. Some jobs are less amenable to objective measures and require a consensus of judgments. "With the concurrence of three of the five team members" might be an acceptable level of performance. "Written consistent with the guidelines provided by the manual" might also be an acceptable standard of performance.

4. *Note the perceived importance of each task to accomplishing the overall objectives of the job.* In performing the job of a student, there may be a difference in the importance assigned to attending class every period and completing the final examination. Missing the final exam may have considerably greater consequences on a positive evaluation of the student's performance than missing a day of discussion in class. The importance of the task may reveal quite a bit about the kinds of problems that may develop if the task is not done well.

5. *List the skills and knowledge required to do the job.* At this stage in the task analysis, we are interested in what the employee needs to know and what skills the employee needs to have in order to complete the tasks. In order to construct a sidewalk, knowing what cement to use and how to mix it might be helpful.

6. *Note the type of learning activity involved.* Some tasks require the employee to tell the difference between two or more items, others require remembering names for tools, a third may require determining whether something is correct, a fourth may require executing some physical movements, whereas a fifth may require special uses of speech.

7. *Record the conditions under which the task is to be performed.* Some tasks must be performed under a great deal of pressure with people watching whereas others are done in relative solitude where corrections can be made in private. Some tasks are done with other people whereas others are done alone.

8. *Make an estimate of how difficult it seems to learn to perform the task.* On a scale from one to ten, some tasks are ones and others are nines in terms of figuring out how to do them. More time and effort may have to be expended in alleviating problems with difficult-to-learn tasks.

9. *Itemize the equipment, tools, and materials needed to do the task.* Difficulties in the performance of some tasks may be related to the number and quality of tools and other equipment to be used. Complicated pieces of equipment may create more problems than they solve.

10. *Note where the skills seem to be acquired best.* Some skills, such as operating a terminal on a sales floor, may be introduced in a simulated situation, but the actual learning and skill acquisition may take place more effectively on the floor.

Task analysis is frequently the basis for identifying and solving problems in industrial settings. The development of an industrial or technical training program, for example, is usually grounded in a task analysis of each task and piece of equipment. A training manual, leader's guide, and tests are all part of a technical training package. They nearly always evolve from a sound task analysis (Dowling & Drolet, 1979).

Once the task analysis has been completed, it must be validated or compared to the way in which the task is performed in the actual work location. Observation and on-site interviews with those who do the work is essential.

Performance Appraisal Methods

The way in which the task is done is clearly an important component in documenting a concern about what is happening in the organization. The ability of employees to do tasks and the motivation with which they do the tasks are important considerations in achieving high productivity. Documentation that employees are unable to do particular tasks or are unable to do them with peak efficiency would clearly reveal evidence that something is wrong in the organization.

How well employees are doing their jobs is frequently determined by a performance appraisal process. Appraisals are performed not only to help maintain control over the organization's resources but also, especially, to measure the efficiency with which the human resources are being utilized and to identify places where improvement needs to take place (Cummings & Schwab, 1973). Appraisals can be an important factor in increasing both employee performance and satisfaction. Areas of deficiency in employee abilities can be identified and relationships between performance and on-the-job goals and rewards can be clarified, thus leading to increased motivation. With the ability to perform tasks efficiently and with high-intensity motivation, employees have the potential for increased productivity.

Cummings and Schwab (1973) describe four major appraisal methods: (1) comparative procedures, (2) absolute standards, (3) management by objectives, and (4) direct indexes. *Comparative procedures* focus on employee-to-employee evaluations; *absolute standards* focus on employee-to-common-standards assessments; *management by objectives* focuses on employee-to-specific-objective appraisals; and *direct indexes* focus on objective measures of behavior.

COMPARATIVE PROCEDURES

These procedures usually involve comparing one employee with another on one or more global or general criteria that attempt to assess the employee's overall effectiveness in the organization. The question to be answered is something like, "Which one of the employees is the most successful, competent, effective, and valuable?" Two general types of comparative procedures are used: ranking and forced distribution.

Ranking

Three types of ranking procedures are the most common: straight ranking, alternative ranking, and paired comparisons.

Straight ranking. This procedure involves arranging the employees being appraised in the order of excellence on the criterion being used, assigning the very best performer a ranking of one, the next best a ranking of two, and so on through all employees being evaluated.

Alternative ranking. This procedure is a little more complex and begins with an alphabetical list of employees being appraised. The evaluator is asked to identify the very best employee and the very weakest employee from the list. The best employee is ranked number one, and the weakest employee is ranked last. Their names are removed from the list, and the best employee and the weakest employee

TABLE 16.1
Paired Comparison Matrix for Five Employees

	Sara	Don	Jim	Jo	Mel	Times Chosen	Rank
Sara		Sara	Jim	Jo	Mel	1	4
Don	Sara		Jim	Jo	Mel	0	5
Jim	Jim	Jim		Jo	Mel	2	3
Jo	Jo	Jo	Jo		Mel	3	2
Mel	Mel	Mel	Mel	Mel		4	1

are again identified from among the remaining employees on the list. Each time the best and weakest employees are removed from the list and added to the separate rankings. In this way the evaluation alternates between selecting the best and the poorest employee from an ever-reducing list.

Paired comparison. This procedure has each evaluator compare each employee being appraised with every other employee, one at a time. A matrix listing every employee along both the X and Y axes, as illustrated in Table 16.1, is used. The evaluator simply picks the one employee from the pair who ranks highest. The employee's final evaluation and ranking is determined by how many times he or she is chosen.

Forced Distribution

This system requires the evaluator to assign a percentage of the employees being appraised to each of several categories based on several performance factors. Typically a forced distribution assigns 10 percent of the employees to a superior category, 20 percent to an excellent category, 40 percent to an average category, 20 percent to a below-average category, and 10 percent to a poorest category. Table 16.2 illustrates the forced distribution system of appraising employees. The forced distribution system minimizes leniency in ratings, but the employees as a group may not fit the distribution all that well in terms of actual performance.

TABLE 16.2
Forced Distribution System for Appraising Employees

EMPLOYEES BEING EVALUATED	POOREST	BELOW AVERAGE	AVERAGE	ABOVE AVERAGE	SUPERIOR
20	2	4	8	4	2
9	1	2	3	2	1

ABSOLUTE STANDARDS

Systems that evaluate employees using absolute standards compare individuals with an authoritative model or measure rather than with other employees. A *standard* is a statement that describes what is expected in terms of behavior, value, suitability, and other characteristics. There are two basic ways of applying absolute standards: qualitative and quantitative.

Qualitative Methods

We shall comment on three qualitative methods, all of which ask the evaluator to determine whether a particular standard applies to a specific employee. In general the appraiser makes an either-or judgment—the employee does what is asked or the employee does not do what is asked.

The critical-incident method. The steps involved in using critical incidents begin with the collection of examples of when any employee is considered very effective or very ineffective—the middle ground is usually not included—from supervisors and others who are familiar with employees who do a particular job. The examples, illustrations, or incidents are analyzed for similarities and grouped under a number of general categories. The International Communication Association (ICA), Organizational Communication Audit Project, researchers collected hundreds of critical incidents reflecting highly effective and highly ineffective communication in organizations. Eight general categories of issues emerged from the analysis of incidents: (1) clarity of role, (2) adequacy of information, (3) syntactic disparity, (4) adequacy of feedback, (5) channel usage, (6) participation in decision making, (7) perception of interpersonal relationships, and (8) personal communication competencies.

After the categories are identified and defined, each evaluator is given a list to use in recording positive and negative incidents involving the employee being appraised. The incidents secured are used as the basis for determining whether the employee does what is expected of effective employees.

Weighted checklists. Checklists are developed by collecting a comprehensive list of statements about employee performance when they are doing the job to be rated. Each statement is evaluated by a group of supervisors or people familiar with the job in terms of how favorable or unfavorable the statement is for successful performance on the job. On a seven-point scale, unfavorable values have low scores, and favorable values have high scores. Statements on which the judges cannot agree are eliminated from the list. The items retained are weighted by the average score obtained from the group of evaluators.

Each evaluator is given a copy of the checklist, without the weightings, and indicates whether the employee performs the behavior mentioned in each item in the checklist. The final evaluation is determined by summing the scores of the items that have been checked.

The forced-choice method. This method involves gathering statements about the performance of a job from individuals familiar with the job. Judges evaluate very effective and very ineffective employees using the statements. Items that distinguish between the best and the worst employees are given weights. Judges also classify each statement according to whether it is favorable or unfavorable to job effectiveness. Items are then clustered so that several are capable of discriminating between effective and ineffective employees and at the same time determining favorability of unfavorability.

A forced-choice instrument, for example, might have four items. The evaluator would choose between A and B and between C and D. Items A and B would both be favorable to the job, but only B would discriminate between effective and ineffective employees. Items C and D would both be unfavorable to the job, but only C would discriminate between effective and ineffective employees. The person doing the appraisal would have the items without knowing which ones were favorable or unfavorable or which ones distinguish between effective and ineffective employees. The evaluator would check the item among the four that was most descriptive of the employee and the item least descriptive of the employee. The employee's score consists of the sum of the indexes for the items checked. High scores represent more desirable performance; low scores indicate less desirable performance.

Quantitative Methods

Two general types of quantitative methods are used: conventional rating scales and behaviorally anchored rating scales. Unfortunately conventional rating scales permit a *halo effect* to occur which may consistently bias evaluations for or against an employee. They also tend to focus on personality characteristics rather than on performance. Nevertheless, conventional rating scales are widely used. Behaviorally anchored rating scales are designed to reduce bias and error while providing useful information for employees during a development program.

Conventional rating scales. This method generally consists of a series of statements about employee characteristics. A scale is established for each characteristic, usually ranging from unsatisfactory to outstanding on a five-point scale. The evaluator places a check along the scale to represent his or her evaluation of the employee. From 5 to 25 characteristics may be evaluated. Figure 16.2 illustrates a typical conventional rating form for appraising employee performance.

Behaviorally anchored rating scales. These scales are developed by using critical-incident procedures. Supervisors and others familiar with the persons being evaluated describe incidents in which the employees have been highly effective or highly ineffective. The incidents are grouped under a small number of categories based on similarities in behaviors. Judges, supervisors, and others then rate each incident on the basis of how well it represents extremely good performance or extremely poor performance. The incidents are ordered according to the average value assigned by the judges, and the incidents are placed along a scale from extremely poor performance to extremely good performance. The evaluator is given the scale with the critical incidents describing specific behaviors at each point on the scale. The employee is evaluated on each general category; the sum of the assigned scores across all categories is the employee's rating. A specific development program can be devised on the basis of weaknesses as revealed by the ratings.

FIGURE 16.2
Conventional Rating Scale Form

RATING SCALE

PERFORMANCE CATEGORIES	Unsatisfactory	Meets minimum	Average	Above average	Outstanding
		Satisfactory			
1. Accuracy, thoroughness, and completeness of work					
2. Presentability of work					
3. Care and maintenance of property and space					
4. Judgment					
5. Communication (oral and written expression)					
6. Leadership					
7. Public relations					
8. Safety of self and others					
9. Productiveness					

MANAGEMENT BY OBJECTIVES

In addition to the use of comparative procedures and absolute standards, a third type of appraisal method is that of management by objectives. MBO, as it is called, is based on the assumptions that goals can be accomplished better if a person knows what is to be accomplished and progress toward a goal should be measured in terms of the goal to be accomplished. These seem like simple-minded premises, but they call our attention to the fact that clearly understood goals are easier to accomplish than are unclear ones.

Another assumption of MBO is that both the subordinate and the supervisor are to be involved in defining and clarifying the goals to be accomplished. A well-stated goal, also, is one that is as quantitative as possible, with specific figures and dates. The process of involvement continues through the period of MBO, with the employee doing what is necessary to accomplish the goals. Finally, periodically the supervisor and the employee compare the employee's performance against the goals that were set. During the meeting the level of goal accomplishment is discussed, and the reasons why shortcomings occurred and how performance can be improved are reviewed. MBO is clearly a human resource development procedure that can be used to upgrade below-standard performance, to maintain acceptable levels of performance, and to strengthen high levels of performance that may lead to advancement, unique contributions to personal growth, and organization accomplishment.

The four basic phases in MBO may be summarized as follows (Cummings & Schwab, 1973):

1. Planning the objectives.
   a. The manager and employee meet and discuss the goals to be accomplished during the next review period—4, 6, or 12 months.
   b. The goals, stated in written form, identify (1) the specific tasks to be accomplished and (2) the measures of satisfactory performance.
   c. During the meeting the manager and the employee discuss and resolve any differences between their perceptions of the size of the goals to be accomplished and where accomplishment of the goals will lead.
   d. The meeting to establish objectives should also include the identification of specific operational and measurable targets against which a performance program can be compared.
2. Working toward accomplishment of objectives.
   a. The employee implements a plan leading to the accomplishment of the objectives.
   b. The observable checkpoints are used to measure progress.
3. The manager and the employee meet later at some specified time to review jointly what has happened during the performance period. This usually begins with a self-appraisal by the employee which is submitted to the manager in writing. The self-appraisal is reviewed jointly by the manager and the employee. An analysis of why some goals were not met and others were and the successes experienced is made.
4. New objectives are set and continuing objectives reinforced.

Both the strength and weakness of the MBO system lies in its ability to provide unique objectives and standards for each employee. Individual differences and personal contributions can be considered. Regretfully the identification and allocation of rewards on an equitable basis is much more difficult to achieve. Because the employee plays a fairly direct role in identifying, setting, and evaluating goal accomplishment, employee performances may vary considerably, or the entire system may be subverted to the interests of employees.

DIRECT INDEXES OF PERFORMANCE

Cummings and Schwab (1973) refer to two direct indicators of performance: (1) units of output and (2) turnover and absenteeism. Number of items made, number of items sold, number of students taught, number of majors in a program, number of clients interviewed, and number of cartons shipped are all units of production. The frequency of absences and tardiness and the number of permanent terminations and resignations are special measures of employee productivity, especially the performance of supervisors. Complaints, grievances, and reprimands may also be indicators of supervisory performance.

So far we have discussed methods associated with two forms of documenting individual employee task performance: task analysis and employee performance appraisal. Straight ranking, alternative ranking, paired comparison, forced distribution, critical incident, weighted checklists, forced choice, conventional rating scales, behaviorally anchored rating scales, and management by objective have been discussed as measures of individual employee task performance. We shall continue our discussion of methods for documenting the concern by examining needs analysis procedures.

Needs Analysis

A needs analysis looks at those things that are keeping employees from making their strongest contribution to the organization. Procedures for conducting a needs analysis consist mainly of talking to employees about their work and having employees respond to feelings about their work in writing. Two other basic approaches also provide information about what is keeping employees from making the best of their resources: files analysis and clinical observation. We shall discuss the methods of conducting a needs analysis by looking at files analysis, clinical observations, interviewing, and the use of questionnaires.

FILES ANALYSIS

Files analysis consists of a study of (1) organization policies, plans, organization charts, and position descriptions; (2) employee grievance, turnover, absenteeism, and accident reports; (3) records of meetings and program evaluation studies; (4) past performance appraisals and attitude surveys; and (5) audits and budget reports. The files and documents are examined for indications of deficiencies and circumstances that appear to interfere with optimal performance of employees.

CLINICAL OBSERVATIONS

Clinical observation refers to making a set of observations that are extremely objective and realistic, in contrast to highly subjective observations in artificial settings. Objectivity is achieved by observing behaviors that can be counted and verified. Realism is achieved by observing employees working at their jobs. The purpose of clinical observations is to identify and record the frequency with which critical behaviors occur. Clinical observations represent a system for discriminating between very high and very low performing individuals or groups. Clinical observations are most useful when differences between employees concern frequency or quantity of performance rather than quality of performance.

Clinical observations help to verify critical incidents and represent an application of Vilfredo Pareto's principle of the unequal distribution of wealth. Pareto discovered that about 80 percent of the wealth of Italy was controlled by 20 percent of the population. This principle has been demonstrated in other ways, such as 20 percent of a company's sales force makes 80 percent of its sales; that 20 percent of the sales generates 80 percent of the profits; and 20 percent of a person's effort results in 80 percent of his or her productivity. Clinical observations seek to identify those behaviors in the 20 percent category that differentiate between high and low producers and result in 80 percent of the organization's effectiveness.

Three general steps are involved in making clinical observations: (1) Determine the behaviors to be observed. Tentative decisions about specific behaviors to be observed could be derived from interviews and, possibly, experience. Eventually a clearly stated description of some clusters of behaviors to be observed should be used. (Four types of behaviors might be observed in public contact situations: *Rude behaviors* that are curt, short, and argumentative; *Indifferent behaviors,* such as speaking to a customer only when addressed, making few eye contacts, speaking in an impersonal tone; *Pleasant behaviors,* such as smiling and greeting the customer warmly, making definite eye contact and ending the contact with a personal comment; and *value-added behaviors,* such as smiling at, greeting, and chatting with customers during the transaction, offering information, and making statements that are adapted to the customer, with a personal salutation at the end. (2) Observe some highly effective employees and some highly ineffective ones and keep the observations on separate record forms. (3) Make observations of each group of employees for a specified period of time, such as 30 minutes at a time in the morning and in the afternoon for five days.

Portray the data in Pareto-type diagrams. The procedures for creating a Pareto diagram include summarizing the data from the record form to show the number of times (frequency) each employee observed engaged in the types of behaviors described. Arrange the data in order from the largest to the smallest numbers and total them. Compute the percentage of behaviors exhibited by each person observed. Plot the percentages on a graph. Construct a bar chart putting the longest bar (highest frequency) on the far left. The vertical scale (up the left-hand side) shows the percentage, usually in multiples of 10 percent, and the horizontal scale (along the bottom) shows the type of behaviors. Separate charts should be constructed for high performers and for low performers. Figure 16.3 illustrates a Pareto diagram. The arrangement of the bar graphs from highest frequencies on the left to lowest frequencies on the right provides a quick visual picture of where the problems are occurring. By developing a behavioral frequency Pareto-type diagram before and after training and development, the effectiveness of certain strategies can be determined.

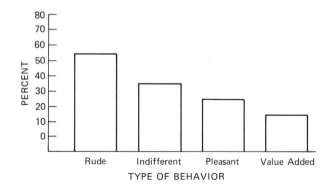

FIGURE 16.3

Pareto Diagram of Behaviors of Ineffective Public-Contact Employees

INTERVIEWING

Interviewing or talking to people about their work is one of the most commonly used methods for conducting a needs analysis. Interviews are also a basic method for gathering information for task analyses, performance appraisals, and organizational communication systems analysis. Interviews in needs analysis are often referred to as *gap interviews* and are designed to gather information about opinions and attitudes, values, thoughts and ideas, and expectations. Interviewing allows employees to talk about their perceptions of a problem or need and their proposed solutions.

Interviews are frequently used at different stages of documenting a concern, but they are especially helpful early in a needs analysis to get an idea of the general feelings of select organization members. An early interview is usually called *exploratory* since it seeks to get a sense of what is happening in order to select other procedures and develop instruments.

Interviews may be conducted with one person or with a group, often employing brainstorming or nominal group processes, and can be either face to face or over the telephone. Interviews can be formal or casual, structured or unstructured, lengthy or brief. Interviews are probably most effective in revealing employee feelings, causes of problems, and expectations and anticipated difficulties. Because they are usually personal and involve predominantly oral communication, they help establish and strengthen relationships between parties involved in the needs analysis.

Interviews have their disadvantages also. They may be somewhat costly when one interviewer works with one employee. They may seem quite slow when only four or five individuals are interviewed in a day. Employee responses are almost entirely qualitative, making them difficult to analyze and interpret. The quality of an interview may depend heavily upon the interpersonal skills of the interviewer, particularly in face-to-face interviews. Employees can feel very uneasy and self-conscious with an unskilled interviewer. If employees doubt that their comments will be held in confidence, they may be reluctant to answer questions openly, fully, and candidly. Interviewers must have the sensitivity to nonverbal behaviors to tell when the employee wants to say more, to talk in greater confidence, or to discuss something controversial.

Individual Interviews

One-on-one interviews are conducted near the employee's place of work and cover certain basic questions while allowing the employee to comment on what topics he or she prefers. Procedures for conducting a needs analysis interview follow closely its use in other types of analyses and involve arranging for a private location in which to conduct the interview, such as an office or secluded work area.

Put the interviewee at ease and assure him or her that what is being discussed will be handled so as to maintain confidences and the anonymity of information and the interviewee.

Ask each question in the order presented on the interview schedule. Record the interviewee's answers to the questions as accurately as possible. The responsibility of the interviewer is to secure and record precise and accurate answers to each question asked. If possible, note the exact, verbatim wording of answers, especially when the answers respond directly to questions. You may find, however, that interviewees provide information relevant to some other question; record answers as unobtrusively as possible, but under the question for which they are the answers, then guide the interview back to the original question and continue with the sequence. When you arrive at the later question and discover that you have already recorded answers, simply pose the question to verify that the responses are accurate and to allow the interviewee to elaborate on answers. Record the answers to each question on a *separate* sheet of paper. This will facilitate the analysis later.

The interview schedule for a supervisory needs analysis might include the following questions (Kirkpatrick, 1971):

1. What problems exist in your department?
2. What problems do you expect to develop in the future?
3. What ought to be included in a training program to resolve the problems?
4. What information would help you to do your job better?
5. When would be a good time to hold a training session?
6. What is the best time for you to attend a training session?

The interview should be opened with some comments to establish rapport and goodwill with the interviewee, then reveal the purpose of the interview. Give some assurances that confidences will be maintained and that no names or personal identification will be associated with any response. Mention that only general needs and group concerns will be included in any reports. Request permission to take notes. Make a transition to the first question.

Analysis of Interview Responses

Interview responses are analyzed in an eight-step procedure:

1. Assign a code number to each interview schedule; put the code on all pages.
2. Place the answers to Question One from all schedules together.
3. Sort the answers to Question One according to some prearranged category system—position, years in service, level of authority.
4. Bring all answers to a single question together on one or more pages—cut, paste, and Xerox or type the answers.
5. Identify themes occurring in the answers of the respondents to each question.
6. State each theme and excerpt some typical responses from the lists, appropriately disguised to protect the anonymity of interviewees, to illustrate how you arrived at the theme.
7. After all responses to all questions of all interviewees have been reviewed for themes, compare and contrast—look for similarities and differences among and between the themes—individual and group responses of different categories of employees.
8. Write an analysis of the interview response to indicate what the needs are.

Group Interviews

Group interviews are often held to get the ideas and needs of a work group or team. In addition to following the procedures for personal interviews, including having a set of clear questions in the form of an interview schedule which are adapted to the group, two techniques can be used to get the maximum benefit from group interaction and to reduce the pressures toward conformity implicit in face-to-face interaction. Brainstorming, force-field analysis, and nominal group process are three techniques that can be used effectively to identify needs in groups (Pace, Peterson, & Burnett, 1979).

Brainstorming. This is a group session in which members think up ideas without being critical or giving judgmental reactions. A question such as "What do we need to do our jobs better?" could be used in brainstorming. A brainstorming session is most effective when some simple guidelines and rules are adhered to; the leader should call the meeting to order and review the following:

1. No questions should be asked during the brainstorming period; all questions should be answered before the start of the session.
2. To maintain order, the leader recognizes each person, as quickly as possible, who has an idea; if you are not called upon immediately, jot down your idea for use later.
3. Avoid elaborating on, defending, or editorializing on any suggestion; merely state the idea without personal reservations, as quickly and concisely as possible.
4. Suggest even the obvious, since some apparent need may trigger some ideas in others; don't be guilty of self-criticism.
5. Don't be afraid to restate an idea in a different way.
6. Strive for the workable but allow the ridiculous to occur.
7. Follow all brainstorming rules faithfully. Four rules must not be violated; the leader may ring a bell or slam a gong if even one is:
   a. Criticism is not allowed.
   b. Freewheeling is encouraged.
   c. Quantity is wanted.
   d. Combination and improvement are sought.

The person doing the needs analysis is usually the leader. After the session is over, the ideas and needs are processed and grouped in much the same way that ideas from an interview are handled.

Force-field analysis. This is the special application of group interviews and brainstorming (Michalak & Yager, 1979). Its basic objective is to provide a way of systematically identifying factors that produce and deter action in the organization. The idea of a force-field is one of balance. In an organization, the current way of doing things is a result of counterbalancing factors, some producing and some deterring. As shown in Figure 16.4, the technique is relatively simple and involves a flip chart with newsprint, a felt pen, and a brainstorming group. The leader/ interviewer draws a force-field diagram on the flip chart, with the issue stated at the top of the page. A vertical line running down the page represents the way things are being done now. The arrows represent the producing and deterring factors.

As group members call out forces that produce or deter the current status, the leader/interviewer should record each item as close to verbatim as possible in order to avoid interrupting the group with questions of interpretation and meaning.

FIGURE 16.4
Sample Force-Field Analysis

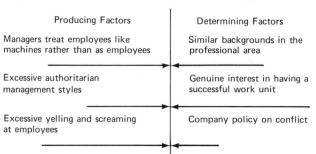

POOR INTERPERSONAL RELATIONSHIPS

Producing Factors	Determining Factors
Managers treat employees like machines rather than as employees	Similar backgrounds in the professional area
Excessive authoritarian management styles	Genuine interest in having a successful work unit
Excessive yelling and screaming at employees	Company policy on conflict

Along with each force, the leader/interviewer draws a horizontal line toward the vertical line to represent the strength of the producing or deterring force. Each line will be a different length depending upon the strength of the force. The current circumstances are a balance between the forces. To make a change, a force-field analysis suggests, remove or strengthen the forces that produce or deter the kind of action that you want.

Nominal group process. This is a structured group meeting in which participants alternate ideas silently, listing ideas in serial order orally for posting on a flip chart, offering pro and con and clarifying comments, and voting on ideas.

Nominal group process balances the influence of high-status, highly expressive, strong personalities, allowing equality of participation and consideration of ideas. NGP facilitates more open discussion and the contribution of unusual and controversial ideas while applying simple mathematics to reduce errors when individual judgments are combined into group decisions.

Nominal group process involves a number of stages plus some preparation. Since NGP relies heavily on the posting of ideas in front of the group, it is essential to have a flip chart and newsprint to be mounted on an easel or attached to the wall. A roll of masking tape, 3 X 5 cards, felt pen, and paper and pencil for each participant are important also. The NGP develops as follows:

1. Welcome participants, and explain the process. Place the question before the group: "What kinds of problems are you experiencing in your work?"
2. Each member writes ideas in response to the question, working silently and independently.
3. The leader-recorder asks for one idea from each group member, going around the table one at a time; the recorder writes the ideas on the flip chart without comment about the ideas until all are posted.
4. Each idea in the list is taken in the order listed, and comments of clarification are made about each one; the purpose of this period is to clarify, not to argue, the merits of any idea.
5. From the list of ideas on the flip chart, the group selects a specific number that seem to be the most important—from five to ten items. Each group mem-

ber writes the priority items on separate 3 X 5 cards and rank-orders the items from one to ten. The cards are collected, shuffled, and recorded on newsprint in front of the group. The sum of the rankings across all group members is the final order of items. Group members may discuss the final rankings and rate the importance to them of each need. The results represent the needs analysis.

Consensus ranking. This is a two-stage group activity in which employees (1) individually rank a list of potential needs and (2) as a group arrive at consensus on a ranking of the same items. A sample ranking form is illustrated in Figure 16.5. Instructions for the group consensus step should read something like those in Figure 16.6.

Card sort. Another approach to interviewing employees about needs is to use a card-sort activity (Bellman, 1975). Use of the card-sort technique involves (1) preparing the cards and (2) conducting the survey interview. Pick a target population, such as supervisors, and develop a long list of responsibilities. Translate the responsibilities into questions. Group the questions into common areas, such as motivation, delegation, training, planning, time use, teamwork, or communication. Transfer the questions to cards. Put only one question per card. Number each card on the

FIGURE 16.5
Sample Consensus Ranking Form for Needs Analysis

INDIVIDUAL TRAINING NEEDS RANKING FORM

Instructions: Below are listed 15 training needs identified by typical employees. Your task is to rank-order them in terms of their importance to your personal needs. Place a 1 in front of the type of training that you feel to be your greatest need, and so on, to 15, your lowest training need.

____ Coping with stress
____ Fulfilling management functions
____ Maintaining interpersonal communication
____ Writing memos and reports
____ Inducting new employees
____ Appraising employee performance
____ Listening
____ Planning
____ Interviewing
____ Training new employees
____ Problem solving and decision making
____ Developing self
____ Supervising ethnic minorities
____ Motivating employees
____ Handling complaints and grievances

FIGURE 16.6
Sample Instructions for Group Consensus Exercise

GROUP RANKING FOR TRAINING NEEDS

Instructions: This phase of the needs analysis is designed to discover the most important *group* needs. Your group is to reach consensus on rankings for the 15 employee needs. This means that the final rankings for each of the needs must be agreed upon by each group member before it becomes part of the group decision. Consensus may be difficult to achieve; therefore, not every item will meet with everyone's complete approval. Try, as a group, to make each ranking one with which all group members can at least partially agree. Here are some guidelines in reaching consensus:

1. Avoid arguing for your own individual judgments; approach the task on the basis of logic.
2. Avoid changing your mind only in order to reach agreement and avoid conflict; support only needs with which you are able to agree somewhat, at least.
3. View differences of opinion as helpful rather than as a hindrance to reaching agreement.

reverse side so that each group of questions is represented by a sequence of numbers, such as 1, 2, 3, 4. With the questions on cards, a supervisor can quickly compare one question with another and physically separate the cards into stacks and sequences. You are now prepared to conduct the survey interview.

Begin the interview by explaining the purpose of the interview, how the employee can help, and the card deck. Give the cards to the employee while asking, "If you could have the answers to ten of these questions, which ten would be most helpful to you in doing your job?" Ask the employee to select the ten most important questions and to place them in order from most important to least important. Explain that after the cards have been selected and ordered, you will return and discuss them. Leave the room until the employee has finished, about 10 to 15 minutes.

When you return, have the employee read the number of each question (on the reverse side) while you record the rank order of the ten questions for later analysis. Assign the most important question ten points, the second most important nine points, down to the least important question which is given one point. Review the sheet on which you recorded the rankings and the weightings, answering questions for the employee. Ask the employee to respond to the question, "What is happening in your job that caused you to select this question?" Ask the question in a variety of ways for each of the ten questions selected. Elicit specific job performance comments. Record the employee's comments on index cards, putting one to a card for easier sorting later. Code the index cards and the cards with questions in the same way so they can be sorted according to location, work group, position, and demographic characteristics such as experience or age, depending on what might be important.

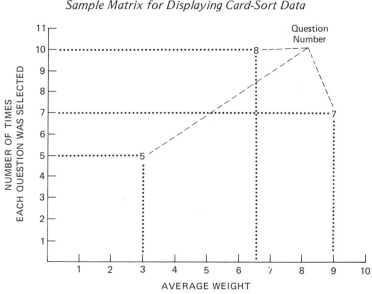

FIGURE 16.7
Sample Matrix for Displaying Card-Sort Data

At the end of the interview, review the cards with the employee to make certain they are accurate. Assure the employee that the comments are for your use only and no identities will be revealed. Conclude by explaining when the analysis is to be finished, how the employees will learn about the results, and how the data will be used to determine needs.

Analyze the card sorts by portraying the results in a matrix as illustrated in Figure 16.7 with the horizontal axis reading from 1 to 10 and the vertical axis running from 1 to the number of times any question was selected most frequently. Using the matrix the more important questions are located in the upper-right-hand quadrant.

Telephone Interview

A final interviewing procedure is to use telephone interviews. Interviewing over the telephone is a common market-research technique (Downs, Smeyak, & Martin, 1980). Calls are usually made to a random sample of individuals using an interview guide or schedule. The schedule must be developed carefully. Downs et al. suggest that the schedule should be as simple as possible in order to reduce fatigue, that respondents should not be asked questions they cannot answer, that the questions should be restricted to essential information, and that the smallest sample size consistent with the objectives of the study should be used.

The telephone interviewer should ask questions exactly as they are worded in order to have comparable information from all respondents. Interviewers should probe answers when necessary to avoid incomplete or unclear responses. The interviewer should not be drawn into giving answers. Finally, some answer should be recorded for every question. Avoid leaving blank spaces by probing or writing in "don't know." Telephone interviewing requires a great deal of skill and patience, but few survey techniques are as quick and economical.

QUESTIONNAIRES

Questionnaires and other written instruments and procedures are probably the most widely used methods for conducting a needs analysis. Questionnaires can provide fairly precise information from large and small groups of employees. A variety of questions can be used and combined with other written instruments, such as rating scales, rankings, and free-response questions. Questionnaires can be administered individually, in groups, or mailed to employees. They are relatively inexpensive to use and can reach a large group of people in a fairly short time. The responses to a questionnaire are about as easy to summarize, analyze, and report as any needs analysis procedure. Questionnaires can be simple or complex. The major problem associated with questionnaires is that they may require a great deal of time and expertise to develop effective instruments.

An effective questionnaire for use in needs analysis should be as simple as possible to achieve the purpose of the survey (Zemke & Walonick, 1980). Questionnaires of two or three pages may appear unnecessarily complex and may intimidate employees. Longer questionnaires can be used, of course, but they require special expertise to construct. Wilson (1980) argues that needs analysis can profitably use "demonstrably valid surveys" developed by professionals. Although well-constructed questionnaires are important to getting accurate information, some simple instruments can be very effective.

Figure 16.8 illustrates a needs assessment questionnaire that covers four general areas and includes 24 items about specific abilities. The items are fairly specific and the response categories ask for indications of importance to the job as well as the need for training or organizational changes.

From an analysis of the differences between what is required and what the employee possesses in areas of importance, some critical needs can be identified.

SUMMARY

This chapter has discussed the process of analysis in human resource development and organizational communication. A point of concern is the first stage in the process of analysis and involves recognizing that something seems wrong. The second stage is documentation of the concern by answering the question, "What is happening now?" The third stage involves the development of guidelines in response to inquiry, "What ought to be happening tomorrow?" The fourth stage is a point of comparison that involves identifying a problem or problems by answering the questions, "Are there differences between what is happening and what ought to be happening?" and "Are the differences important enough to do something?" The final and fifth stage is the point of determination where the problem is classified as a training need or a development need.

Three general approaches to documenting a concern were explained and illustrated: (1) task analysis, (2) performance appraisal, and (3) needs analysis.

FIGURE 16.8
Sample Needs Analysis Questionnaire

SURVEY OF TRAINING AND DEVELOPMENT NEEDS

	THIS ABILITY IS IMPORTANT TO MY JOB					I COULD DO MY JOB BETTER IF	
	Not Important		*Very Important* (circle a number)			*I Had More Training*	*Some Conditions Were Changed in the Organization*

Planning Abilities

1. Set objectives or develop projects	1	2	3	4	5	_____	_____
2. Develop plans	1	2	3	4	5	_____	_____
3. Set priorities for work	1	2	3	4	5	_____	_____
4. Use program budgeting procedures	1	2	3	4	5	_____	_____
5. Use special budgeting systems	1	2	3	4	5	_____	_____
6. Use time effectively	1	2	3	4	5	_____	_____

Managing Abilities

7. Assign work to people	1	2	3	4	5	_____	_____
8. Delegate	1	2	3	4	5	_____	_____
9. Motivate people	1	2	3	4	5	_____	_____
10. Understand people of different ages, races, backgrounds	1	2	3	4	5	_____	_____

Problem-Solving Abilities

11. Recognize and analyze the problems	1	2	3	4	5	_____	_____
12. Identify solutions to problems	1	2	3	4	5	_____	_____
13. Decide which solution is best	1	2	3	4	5	_____	_____
14. Make decisions in emergencies	1	2	3	4	5	_____	_____

Communication

15. Inform supervisor	1	2	3	4	5	_____	_____
16. Inform subordinates	1	2	3	4	5	_____	_____
17. Answer questions about programs	1	2	3	4	5	_____	_____
18. Answer questions about merit, production, EEO, and classification	1	2	3	4	5	_____	_____
19. Conduct formal briefings	1	2	3	4	5	_____	_____
20. Lead meetings	1	2	3	4	5	_____	_____
21. Listen and accept views of others	1	2	3	4	5	_____	_____
22. Provide negative information	1	2	3	4	5	_____	_____
23. Complete reports and forms	1	2	3	4	5	_____	_____
24. Write formal letters	1	2	3	4	5	_____	_____

Specific techniques and methods explained were chronological listing of tasks and job description; comparative procedures such as straight ranking, alternative ranking, paired comparison, and forced distribution; absolute standard methods such as critical incidents, weighted checklists, and forced choice, as well as conventional rating scales and behaviorally anchored rating scales; management by objectives; direct indexes of performance; file analysis; clinical observation; interviewing, including individual and group interviewing methods such as brainstorming, force-field analysis, nominal group process, consensus ranking groups, a card-sort technique, telephone interviews; and questionnaires.

REFERENCES

BELLMAN, GEOFFREY, "Surveying Your Supervisory Training Needs," *Training and Development Journal* (February 1975), pp. 25–33.

CUMMINGS, L. L., and DONALD P. SCHWAB, *Performance in Organizations: Determinants and Appraisal.* Glenview, Ill.: Scott, Foresman, 1973.

DOWLING, JOHN R., and ROBERT P. DROLET, *Developing and Administering an Industrial Training Program.* Boston: CBI Publishing Company, Inc., 1979.

DOWNS, CAL W., G. PAUL SMEYAK, and ERNEST MARTIN, *Professional Interviewing.* New York: Harper & Row, Pub., 1980.

GOLDHABER, GERALD M., "The ICA Communication Audit: Rationale and Development." Paper presented at the Academy of Management Convention, Kansas City, Kansas, August 1976.

GOLDHABER, GERALD M., "Evaluating Internal Communication: The ICA Communication Audit," *New Directions for Institutional Advancement,* No. 2 (1978), 37–54.

KIRKPATRICK, DONALD L., *A Practical Guide for Supervisory Training and Development.* Reading, Mass.: Addison-Wesley, 1971.

LEACH, JOHN L., "Organization Needs Analysis: A New Methodology," *Training and Development Journal,* 33 (September 1979), 66–69.

MICHALAK, DONALD F., and EDWIN G. YAGER, *Making the Training Process Work.* New York: Harper & Row, Pub., 1979.

PACE, R. WAYNE, BRENT D. PETERSON, and M. DALLAS BURNETT, *Techniques for Effective Communication.* Reading, Mass.: Addison-Wesley, 1979.

PATTON, BOBBY R., and KIM GIFFIN, *Problem-Solving Group Interaction.* New York: Harper & Row, Pub., 1973.

PERRY, JOHN, and ROBERT WARE STRAUS, "A Story of Executive Relationships," *Harvard Business Review,* 30 (March–April 1952), 53–72.

WILSON, CLARK, "Identifying Needs with Costs in Mind," *Training and Development Journal,* 34 (July 1980).

ZEMKE, RON, and DAVE WALONICK, "The Non-Statistician's Approach to Conducting and Analyzing Surveys," *Training/HRD* (September 1980), pp. 89–99.

17

STRATEGIES OF ORGANIZATIONAL COMMUNICATION

*the strategic role
in human resource development*

A *strategy* is a method, plan, or series of movements or activities used for accomplishing a specific goal or result. A *strategist* is an expert in the use of strategy. In the field of human resource development, strategies for improving human performance and organizational functioning are usually selected following an analysis of personnel and organizational processes. Strategies that are based on solid analyses are usually more effective. When a need or deficiency (the difference between what we have and what we would like) is identified, the challenge becomes one of locating or devising the strategies for minimizing or eliminating the need.

CATEGORIES OF STRATEGIES

Four broad categories of strategies for strengthening human performance and the organization cover the range of activities:

1. *Training* strategies that provide knowledge and skills that aid an employee to do his or her job better.

2. *Individual development* strategies that provide knowledge and skills that help an employee prepare for a different position in the organization or for jobs, positions, and careers that have not as yet been clearly defined.

3. *Organization development* strategies that produce changes at the organizational systems level, resulting in restructured work rules, norms, and power, and that affect intergroup relations, planning, rewards, climate, and managerial activities.

4. *Technical resource development* strategies that produce changes in work methods and technology and involve the restructuring and design of jobs and organization operations.

UNDERLYING PHILOSOPHIES AND THEORIES

Within each category of strategies, specific choices of training and development methods are based on one or more of three different philosophies or theories of producing change in human beings. They are often referred to as three basic approaches to behavior modification (Bandura, 1969): *rational, behavioral,* and *experiential.*

The Rational Approach

The rational approach is grounded in the assumption that what we believe determines how we behave. *Beliefs* are those statements that we make to ourselves as well as to others that represent what we accept as true. This approach suggests that what we believe or accept as true about a situation determines the strategies that we select and use in performing a task and in dealing with others—that is, if you believe that you can supervise others and hold certain beliefs about those whom you are to supervise, you will behave in ways that will make you an effective supervisor.

In terms of training and development, a human resource developer using rational theory would select strategies that focus on changing beliefs. The change in beliefs would then affect how the employee behaves. In discussing the training of professional workers, Combs, Avila, and Purkey (1971) argue that the trainees should be provided with "opportunities for discovering personal meanings" (p. 9) which are the guides for the day-to-day behaviors they will use in carrying out their professional duties. *Personal meanings* are the images that you hold about people, events, and objects. Personal meanings are expressed in the ways that we talk about things.

The place of language in affecting behavior has long been recognized in communication and other social sciences. Craighead, Kazdin, and Mahoney (1976) note that "individuals respond to language in the form of instructions, commands, and rules that govern behavior. However, there are more subtle means, such as in self-verbalizations, through which language influences behavior" (p. 145). A rational approach to training and development builds on the powerful effect that beliefs, personal meanings, language, and self-verbalization have on behavior.

The foundational premise of rational-emotive training (RET), a rational approach, is expressed by Ellis and Harper (1975) as follows: " . . . unlike lower animals, people tell themselves various sane and crazy things. Their beliefs, attitudes, opinions, and philosophies largely . . . take the form of internalized sentences or self-talk. Consequently, one of the most powerful and elegant modalities they can use to change themselves . . . consists of their clearly seeing, understanding, disputing, altering, and acting against their internal verbalizations" (p. x).

RATIONAL EMOTIVE TRAINING

A rational approach to training and development deals clearly with the verbal-communicative aspects of behavior and is belief-oriented. Rational emotive training (Ellis & Harper, 1975) is typical of most rational approaches. It assumes that problems are the result of irrational thinking and verbalizing; thus the emphasis is on the cultivation of rationality. Rational thinking assumes that people feel the way they think. Consequently change occurs when a person decides (thinks) to do things differently. By obtaining the help of others, such as a trainer or personnel development specialist, a person can more clearly see optional ways of talking about things and deciding what to do.

Rational emotive training has been called a form of *semantic therapy.* Ellis and Harper (1975) acknowledge that they appear to have developed a way of applying the teachings of general semantics, which Bois (1978) says is the "world of happenings-meanings . . . ; it is the world of self-awareness and self-management. . . . General semantics deals with the meaning we find or put in whatever we do and whatever happens to us" (pp. 43-44). Rational emotive training argues that our desires and emotions have deep biological and social foundations, directly related to our thinking processes and are consequently largely under our control when approached as personal meanings and beliefs.

Rational emotive training brings about individual development by presenting problems and discussing their implications as a reexamination of reality and an individual's personal meanings. Perceptions and meanings are revised by obtaining the analysis of others about problems. One's perceptions of reality are tested for accuracy by comparing them with external sources. Rationality is cultivated by confronting so-called nonrational concerns and by implementing specific ways of thinking and talking.

TRANSACTIONAL ANALYSIS TRAINING

James and Jongeward (1971) describe transactional analysis (TA) as a "rational approach to understanding behavior" which is based on the assumption that people can learn to trust themselves, think for themselves, make their own decisions, and express their feelings accurately. A person who participates in a transactional analysis training session gains both emotional and intellectual or rational insight, but the emphasis is on the thinking processes.

Morrison and O'Hearne (1977) argue that "transactional analysis is the simplest way we know to understand and modify, if necessary, human behavior. It is the study of moves people make in their dealings with each other and is based on the idea that people's interactions resemble moves in a game" (p. 7). If an employee understands TA, he or she can predict how another person will feel and react. TA also helps a person become aware of his or her transactions and to predict their consequences. The focus of TA is on understanding and controlling interactions and their consequences; this characterizes the rational approach.

The Behavioral Approach

The behavioral approach is firmly rooted in the assumption that changes in human beings can be produced more efficiently by focusing on observable behaviors rather than on ways of thinking. In fact, both attitudes and thought processes (internal) are understood by observing and measuring overt behaviors. This is not to say that behaviors are unaffected by internal processes and thinking; it simply means that *observable behaviors* are the focus of attention. The behavioral philosophy also assumes that changes in behaviors typically produce corresponding changes in thoughts and attitudes. Bartlett (1967) argued that " it is easier to change behavior than attitudes! Why launch a direct onslaught upon the latter when they will follow if the former is changed?" (p. 39).

The basic premise underlying the behavioral approach to training and development is that behaviors occur as a consequence of reinforcements—any event that rewards the behavior immediately preceding it. Williams and Long (1975) apply the principles of behaviorism in a program for developing self-management and argue that "effective self-management primarily involves the rearrangement of behavioral consequences so that desired behavior is *immediately* reinforced" (p. 22).

THREE BEHAVIORAL STRATEGIES

Three general strategies represent the applications of behaviorism in training and development: (1) structuring contingencies, (2) simulations, and (3) modeling.

Structuring Contingencies

Contingencies are consequences that positively reinforce desirable behaviors or punish undesirable behaviors. Contingencies may be a natural part of the work environment, such as assignments to work shifts, use of old versus new equipment, reporting procedures, arrangements of offices, and communication contacts and channels. They may all involve positive or negative consequences that serve as contingencies. Organization development strategies frequently involve structural changes in the organization that serve to reduce negative consequences and increase positive consequences. Changes in behavior are often a direct result of structural changes in both task and nontask situations in organizations. Since most training and human resource development departments do not have the power to create structural changes in the organization, training and development programs tend to focus on making behavioral changes in organization members.

Communication behaviors are frequently the focus of training and development programs, especially when a behavioral approach is used. This is understandable if we accept Schein's (1969) observation that "one of the most important processes in organizations, and one of the easiest to observe, is how the members communicate with each other, particularly in face-to-face situations" (p. 15). Communicative behaviors can be changed by the external management of reinforcement contingencies, by self-directed efforts in which individuals regulate their own behavior by arranging appropriate contingencies for themselves, or by both methods.

Williams and Long (1975) describe an approach to self-management of a person's life that is based on behavioral principles. They suggest that "effective self management primarily involves the rearrangement of behavioral consequences so that desired behavior is *immediately* reinforced" (p. 22). The principle of immediate reinforcement of desired behaviors is fundamental to a behavioral approach. Frequently the unwanted behaviors are rewarded naturally; thus the program of self-management requires the individual to administer his or her own punishment for unwanted behaviors and to reward the desired behaviors more vigorously.

How to structure contingencies: an example

Five steps epitomize the implementation of a behavioral training program involving the structuring of contingencies.

1. *Select a goal.* Identify a single goal so that you work on one change at a time. There are four considerations involved in selecting an appropriate goal:

   a. *Select a goal that is important to you.* If you experience some form of pain, such as embarrassment or anxiety, any positive improvement will be noticeable and reinforcing. You should be somewhat cautious in trying to change well-entrenched behaviors at the beginning. It may be better to take a goal that seems important but that involves behaviors that might be changed more easily.

   b. *Define the goal in measurable behavioral terms.* In this context *behavioral* means some type of overt action that can be seen and recognized by others. Nodding, smiling, speaking up, stepping back, and holding hands are overt behaviors. Feeling better, being more confident, and doing what's right must be translated into some type of behavior before we understand what is actually happening. For example, being more confident is expressed in some overt behavior. What do you do? How about looking right into the eyes of a person who disagrees with you? At least you can tell when you are being more confident with that kind of goal. By identifying the overt behaviors clearly, you can carefully select contingencies that help strengthen new and desirable ones. By changing overt behaviors, the behavioral approach contends, you change the internal feelings associated with them.

   c. *Set a goal that is readily attainable.* One mistake often made in behavioral modification programs is to set goals too high. It is important to set goals that are only a little bit higher than your present level of behaving. When you can regularly perform a new behavior, then raise your standards and set a higher goal. Behaviorally we change in small increments.

   d. *State the goal positively.* The end results of the behavior-change program is to develop the presence of positive behaviors. You might eliminate a great many negative behaviors and still not produce much improvement in what you do. It is also easier and more motivating to recognize and experience the presence of positive behaviors than to notice the absence of negative ones.

2. *Record the quantity and the context of behaviors.* This step allows you to recognize the extent to which offending behaviors occur and the circumstances in which they take place. You might discover that you say, "Oh Yea!" more frequently when someone disagrees with you in a group than at any other time. Keeping a record of the behavior to be changed will sensitize you to the progress you are making. Three major types of records of behavior can be used in behavior modification.

   a. *Frequency counting.* This involves tabulating the number of times a particular behavior occurs. To be counted, a behavior must be defined in terms of discrete cases. The behavior must occur over a short period of time and have an identifiable beginning and ending.

   b. *Duration of behavior.* Staring, crying, dozing, and other types of behaviors do not occur in discrete instances all of the time and are best recorded in terms of the amount of time devoted to the behavior. The simplest approach to recording the duration of behavior is to indicate when it starts, (with a stopwatch or by recording the time) and when it stops.

c. *Results of behavior.* Rather than recording the behavior directly, occasionally you can monitor the behaviors by keeping track of what happens as a result of the behavior. By recording the amount of waste in a manufacturing plant, it is often possible to tell a great deal about the behaviors occurring in the plant. Weighing yourself can give you information about your eating habits. Nevertheless, to make changes, you will need to identify the specific behaviors that lead to waste or to overweight.

The very act of making a recording may lead to changes in behavior. When a person is able to see an objective report of a behavior, he or she may be motivated to change. Identifying the behavior and maintaining a record of how frequently it occurs may be all that some people need to do to implement a behavior modification program. Some, on the other hand, may need to proceed to the next step.

3. *Change the situation in which the behavior occurs.* Some behaviors are triggered by the situation in which they occur. One way to modify behavior is to change the situation that encourages it. This can be done in two different ways:

a. *Avoid the situation.* Although staying away from someone because he or she tends to provoke an angry response in you will not eliminate your undesirable behavior entirely, it will do much to limit the situations in which it does occur. Ultimately you will need to deal with the behavior directly; nevertheless, at the beginning, avoidance may help you get control of and start to modify the behavior.

b. *Alter the situation.* If you tend to get sleepy sitting in a lounge chair, modify the behavior by sitting in a chair that seems less conducive to sleeping. On the other hand, if you tend to eat snacks at your desk, you might put the snacks in a sealed container and place the container in a file drawer so that you have to think about what you are doing before engaging in the behavior. You might even put a mirror on the desk so that you have to watch yourself eating.

By altering the situation you are providing yourself with supportive settings in which to control behavior. These are ways of applying contingencies to modify behavior. The direct application of contingencies, however, is important in a behavioral approach to change.

4. *Arrange reinforcing or punishing consequences.* A behavioral approach assumes that a person's behaviors are controlled by the consequences that result from them. If you unnecessarily argue with other people, but in the end you receive a lot of praise and encouraging comments, you will tend to be reinforced in your arguing. A difficulty in arranging consequences is that most of us have not thought about how things affect us. We are not sure how a particular event will affect our behavior. Thus we nearly always need to broaden the list of consequences that might be used as reinforcers or punishers.

a. *Require yourself to exhibit the preferred behavior before participating in the reinforcing activity.* This means that you earn certain privileges by behaving in certain ways. If speaking in a negative manner to others is the behavior you wish to change, a highly satisfying or reinforcing privilege should be made contingent to or conditional upon speaking in a positive way to others. The reinforcers will be most effective if they are applied immediately after the desired behaviors are exhibited and if the new behaviors are not too hard to perform. Because it is not entirely feasible to give direct rewards immediately, a system of credits may be used. When you earn five or ten credits, they apply toward the direct reward, such as going to a movie or having some quiet time.

b. *Use punishers as well as reinforcers.* Although the idea may not seem very appealing, the idea of flipping yourself with a rubber band or administering pain in some other way when you fail to carry out the new behavior is clearly a procedure consistent with a behavioral approach to changing behavior. Pain can be administered through social disapproval also. You can arrange a punishing contingency by telling those with whom you work about what you are trying to accomplish and asking them to administer the contingency or to simply remind you to administer the punishment.

5. *Focus on and verbalize the contingencies.* The strongest program for managing behavior change through contingencies keeps the person aware of and focusing on the consequences of his or her behavior. One of the main problems in behavior change is impulsive responses. We often react before we have had a chance to think about the consequences. Behavior modification seeks to heighten a person's awareness so he or she thinks about the consequences of his or her behavior before acting. One way to do this is to talk about the consequences to yourself before behaving. The verbalizations must be said aloud, at least in the beginning. It appears that the sound, as well as the statements, heighten awareness more than just the thought or silent verbalization of behavior.

Craighead et al. (1976) describe procedures for modifying marital problems by using contingencies. Couples are taught how to "pinpoint" the behaviors they wish to change, how to discriminate between positive and negative responses, how to improve their listening skills, how to share communication equally, how to reduce aversive behaviors, how to solve problems as a unit, and how to contract for the application of contingencies—consequences that positively reinforce compliance with agreed-upon changes and punish failures to comply. The entire process represents a training program based on a behavioral approach.

Simulations

A second strategy for applying the principles and philosophy of behaviorism to training and development is called *simulation*. The term *simulation* refers to some type of vicarious experience. The behaviors in which a person participates have the characteristics of or are similar to those that occur on the job. The term *simulator* is frequently used to refer to machines that have the appearance of the real thing but that are mounted in a laboratory rather than in the field. In a simulation the trainee gets to engage in the behavior that is desired back on the job without taking all of the risks associated with authentic work conditions.

Odiorne (1970) has referred to the use of simulations in training as *action training* and explains that "the specific forms of action training break down into different kinds of simulations. The common element is that all of them simulate the situation in which the trainee must operate in the real world and require him to behave in a way that he might behave back in that environment if he were to apply the new behavioral skills desired" (p. 264). In simulation the important requirement is to have a plausible resemblance to the main task.

Through a task analysis the specific behaviors to be acquired are identified and defined. Behavior is changed by having the trainee engage in the desired behaviors in a progression of small steps. At each step in the training the trainee obtains information on how well he or she is performing the behaviors.

Bartlett (1967) has suggested that simulation is "one unconventional method for changing behavior, strong enough to pierce the 'attitudinal' sound barriers" (p. 40). Consistent with the behavioral theory on which it is based, he notes that "this involves, under the guise of skill training, having subjects (Ss) practice doing differently (in a laboratory situation). As they are given rewards for doing differently, their attitudes will (absent pressure) tend to soften." Bartlett proposes that a training program to improve communication should be the primary vehicle to use when attempting to improve interpersonal competence on the job.

Communication training is a more or less neutral subject that focuses on processes and behaviors rather than on company policies and procedures. Skill training in communication provides employees with practice in listening and telling and lends itself naturally to broadening their perspectives with regard to perceptions of human behavior. Interpersonal competencies develop by doing things differently, by behaving as a communicatively competent person. To bring about changes in a person's communication skills and to enhance the transference of the new patterns of behavior from classroom simulations to the real world of the job, Bartlett argues that the training should be conducted in a company conference room that is used exclusively for the program.

There are two basic strategies for conducting simulations: role playing and games. We shall look at each of these briefly to illustrate how a behavioral philosophy can be implemented through simulations.

Role playing

As a simulation method role playing involves acting out a situation that parallels real-life experiences (Pace, Peterson, & Burnett, 1979). Role playing can be carried out in two different ways: structured and spontaneous (Wohlking & Weiner, 1981). Wohlking and Weiner compared structured and spontaneous role playing on four stages involved in the use of role playing: (1) objectives, (2) warm-up, (3) enactment, and (4) post-role-playing techniques. We shall briefly review their analysis to highlight the training applications of role playing.

Structured role playing is accomplished by having a series of written role descriptions with guidelines for the facilitator that structures the situation and sets the scene. Spontaneous role playing evolves somewhat naturally from the discussion of a problem, during which a potential solution is identified and tested through role playing.

Objectives. Structured role playing is designed to develop skills in areas such as problem solving, interpersonal communication, and interviewing; to teach procedures and instruct in how to do tasks, and to modify attitudes involved in superior-subordinate relationships. (Spontaneous) role playing, on the other hand, is designed to provide insight into a person's own behavior and the behavior of others, to modify attitudes and perceptions, and to develop ways of diagnosing problem situations.

Warm-up. Regardless of how the role playing is conducted, time should be spent preparing participants to engage in the role playing activity. They should be ready to participate by understanding the relevance of the problem and by wanting to be involved physically in role playing. The warm-up for structured role playing can be accomplished by presenting a lecture on a principle related to some aspect of effective organizational communication, for example, or by showing a film on the topic, which includes principles that can be translated into skills in role playing. In addition the written case itself can be analyzed, or a general discussion conducted on a problem area, which can lead to the question, "How would you handle such a situation?" The warm-up period for spontaneous role playing often consists of identifying problems that the group would like to explore.

Enactment. In structured role playing, separate roles are distributed to the participants prior to conducting the activity. The written statements give role descriptions and identify role behaviors and points of difference. The trainer avoids intervening during the enactment, allowing the entire scene to proceed uninterrupted until the situation reaches a climax. In contrast, during the enactment of a spontaneous role play, the trainer intervenes frequently in an effort to highlight feelings and focus on individual responses.

Post-role-playing techniques. All role playing should be followed by a period of discussion in which the insights developed during the enactment are articulated by participants and observers. A discussion led by the trainer should focus on how the methods used in the role playing facilitated or hindered communication between the roles, not on the individuals taking the parts. Observers could be asked to report what they noticed, which may lead to a discussion about the problems of translating principles into actual communication skills. In spontaneous role playing the trainer asks each role player to react to the feelings, emotions, and tensions that developed during the enactment. The group is then asked for its reactions to the role play.

Role playing is an effective way for helping people understand the behavior of others. Much can also be learned from the other major type of simulation—games.

Games

A game is "any simulated contest (play) among adversaries (players) operating under constraints (rules) for an objective (winning)" (Gordon, 1972, p. 8). In human resource development serious games are used. They tend to simulate real-life problems and include a complex combination of cooperation, competition, winning, and losing. Some players or even teams of players may be more successful than are others, and in some cases, if the problem is solved, all players may win. In some instances winning is not the most crucial part of the game; how the participants use their resources to attain the maximum benefit may be more important than accomplishing the objective.

In training and development, games tend to follow two basic approaches: board games and role-playing games (Gordon, 1972). Board games are designed to be played on a gameboard on which the action occurs. Role-play games usually have written materials that include a scene and profiles of the players. In most cases all the players receive the same background information, but each one receives a unique role description that describes his or her specific role and relationship to other players, and the player's objectives. The information is provided to give players some basis for responding during the action. Rules are the only other information required. In role playing the rules are generally quite broad and define in what activities and decisions the player may be involved. Olivas and Newstrom (1981) conclude that "games can change attitudes, develop interpersonal skills, and achieve ready acceptance by the trainees. Most critical, simulations generally incorporate active participation and practice opportunities, thereby increasing the probability of learning and ease the transfer to the work environment" (p. 66).

Behavior Modeling

The third and final strategy for implementing a behavioral approach to human resource development is called *behavior modeling*. Zenger (1980) refers to behavior modeling as "the most exciting new technology in training" (p. 45). Research suggests that nearly all learning that results from direct experience can be acquired vicariously through observation of another person's behavior and the results for the person being observed (Bandura, 1969). Bandura suggests that a person can "acquire intricate response patterns merely by observing the performances of appropriate models" (p. 118).

Behavior modeling is based, according to Zenger (1980), on the idea that people learn by "(A) seing a good example, (B) being provided a cognitive framework to understand the important elements of the skill to be learned, then (C) practicing or rehearsing the skill, and finally (D) receiving positive feedback when one succeeds in doing it properly" (p. 45). Behavior modeling assumes that (1) specific skills are learned by practice and that (2) such activities as managing, leading, and problem solving involve a series of concrete behaviors that can be modeled, observed, practiced, reinforced, and integrated into the total behavioral repertory of a manager.

Behavior modeling is implemented best through the preparation of a series of videotapes that participants can view, identify with the situations, rehearse the modeled behavior under the coaching of a trainer, and transfer the skills back to their jobs (Rosenbaum, 1979). In a typical videotape modeling how a supervisor should handle a corrective interview, the model supervisor is to do the following:

1. Define the problem in terms of lack of improvement since the previous discussion.
2. Ask for, and actively listen to, the employee's reason for the continued behavior.
3. If disciplinary action is called for, indicate what action you must take and why.
4. Agree on specific actions to be taken to solve the problem.
5. Assure the employee of your interest in helping him/her to succeed and express your continued confidence in the employee.
6. Set a follow-up date.
7. Positively reinforce any behavior change in the desired direction. (Rosenbaum, 1979, p. 42)

After viewing the tape, supervisory trainees practice the modeled behaviors, receive immediate feedback, and work to use the new behaviors in their jobs.

The Experiential Approach

The third basic approach to modifying behavior is called _experiential and is based on the premise that people are most likely to believe their own experiences._ People change their behaviors, it is assumed, by examining their current beliefs in view of their reactions to situations in which they experience some significant emotional feeling. With an opportunity to reflect on what happened to them, they develop a personal explanation for their reactions and make a conscious effort to try alternative ways of behaving in another setting. There seems to be fairly widespread agreement that learning that develops from direct experience is significantly different from learning that results from more cognitive methods (Springer, 1981).

Experiential learning may occur both inside and outside the training area. People have experiences, create meaning from them, and try new ways of behaving. Outside the training area little discussion of the experience may take place, and the analysis may be unguided or misdirected. Experiences in the training area are structured so that trainees learn how to learn from their own experiences.

The major advantages of using an experiential learning approach can be expressed in five points (Bowen, Lewicki, & Hall, 1975):

1. Learning is more effective when it is active rather than passive.
2. Problem-centered learning is more enduring than is theory-based learning.
3. Two-way communication produces better learning than does one-way.
4. Participants learn more when they share control over and responsibility for the learning process.
5. Learning is more effective when thought and action are integrated.

STEPS IN EXPERIENTIAL LEARNING

Kolb, Rubin, and McIntyre (1974) describe an experiential learning model as consisting of a four-stage cycle: (1) An immediate, concrete experience is the basis for (2) observation and reflection; the observations are assimilated into an explanation consisting of (3) abstract concepts and generalizations which serve as guidelines for (4) testing the concepts and generalizations by behaving differently in new situations. In this view a person learns from participating in a concrete experience, reflecting on the experience, formulating generalizations from the reflections, and trying new behaviors that test the generalizations. Michalak and Yager (1979) formulated a six-stage experiential learning model that expands Kolb's theory and creates a systematic way of designing training. The six stages are (1) experience, (2) content input, (3) analysis, (4) generalizations, (5) practice, and (6) transfer. In this model each training unit begins with an experience, followed by the presentation of content information, with the experience being analyzed in terms of the information and principles presented, out of which the trainees formulate generalizations that may be tested as part of the practice stage, with the final stage being devoted to preparing the trainees to use their new knowledge and skills when they return to their jobs.

TRAINING METHODS CLASSIFIED BY STAGES

Four categories of training methods are suggested by the preceding experiential models: (1) supervising experiences, (2) presenting information, (3) facilitating analysis, and (4) directing practice.

Supervising Experiences

Experiential learning implies a degree of structuring of the experience so as to impose a point of view on the process. Thus the heart of the supervisory activity is conducting a *structured experience*. Middleman and Goldberg (1972) refer to structured experiences as closed systems deliberately constructed and set in motion by the facilitator. The structured experience has a boundary separating it from the discussion about the experience. The structured experience allows participants to discover information about themselves and what they know. In using a structured experience the facilitator directs an exercise in which participants do some activity. The activity could be role playing or making something; completing a questionnaire, rating form, or ranking form; or taking a test. I identified 36 different exercises for teaching concepts in organizational communication using structured experiences (Pace, 1977), all of which have been used in training sessions over the years.

Each structured experience should include a statement of the goals of the exercise, the materials necessary to conduct it, the physical setting and group size for which it is best suited, the process or step-by-step procedures and amount of time required to complete the exercise, and copies of worksheets, questionnaires, scales, or tests used in the exercise (Grove, 1976). Some structured experiences involve solving puzzles, analyzing problems, creating things and designs, engaging in brainstorming, and completing inventories.

To set the stage for analysis of the experience and to get the most out of the experiential process, participants should be encouraged to

1. Get involved in the exercise—participate with enthusiasm in the activities.
2. Consciously think about the relevance of the exercise to the theory, concepts, principles, and information presented for use in the analysis phase.
3. Think about and make notes about what happened during the exercise and what kinds of generalizations might be developed from the experience.

Presenting Information

Information can be presented in a variety of ways. Three basic categories of methods represent a convenient way of classifying them. Below is an outline of the most commonly used methods for presenting information:

Oral Methods

1. Presentational
   a. Lecture (one person)
   b. Dialogue (two persons)
   c. Colloquy (three to five persons)
2. Forum (presentation with audience participation)
   a. Interview (more formal two-person)
   b. Panel (more formal colloquy)
   c. Symposium (formal speeches from panel members)

Written Methods

1. Descriptive
   a. Essay—articles, books
   b. Programmed materials
   c. Incident
   d. Case history
2. Pictorial
   a. Diagrams
   b. Charts
   c. Pictures
   d. Slides
   e. Overhead transparencies

Audiovisual Methods

1. Mediated
   a. Sound film strips
   b. Videotapes
   c. Motion pictures
2. Simulated
   a. Demonstration
   b. Role plays
   c. Dramatizations/Vignettes
   d. On-the-job coaching

Facilitating Analysis

This phase in the experiential learning process is designed to assist the participants in discovering the meaning to them of the exercise and to formulate some generalizations and principles that can serve as guidelines for behaving differently in the future. Participants must be encouraged to develop generalizations from the activities in which they participate. Talking about experiences, films, diagrams, role playing, and reading immediately after they are exposed to them is often more important than are the experiences themselves. When experiences are related to information presented as part of the content input, we refer to the discussions as *information processing.*

Analysis and information processing are facilitated by creating an atmosphere of inquiry among participants. Inquiry is accomplished by stimulating participants to probe into the meaning of the exercise and to explore alternative interpretations of what happened. As a facilitator, pose questions, then wait and listen; since during long silences almost everyone is thinking, it is important for you to allow sufficient time for participants to think through what they wish to say. Work to get participants to offer suggestions and analyses of the experience. Assist them to phrase their ideas clearly, concisely, and completely. Strive to have every person contribute to the analysis and avoid allowing one member to monopolize the interaction. Keep the comments moving among all participants by frequently asking for more ideas. When discussion is slow, gently play the devil's advocate by introducing ideas that provide other ways of thinking about a situation. Throughout the analysis period, maintain and enhance the self-esteem of the participants by acknowledging any reactions, praising ideas, pointing out positive behaviors and their effects on others, and recording participant's ideas on a flip-chart.

Analysis can be facilitated by letting participants engage in small group discussions and by making reports.

Discussion formats. Analysis can be facilitated by using one or more of these formal group formats:

1. Buzz groups—Divide participants into groups of three and let them discuss the experience.
2. Phillips 66—Groups of six participants who discuss for six minutes.
3. Ring response—Start the discussion with a buzz group, then enlarge the discussion as others get involved.
4. Fishbowl—This consists of arranging the participants in a double circle—half inside and half outside; the inner group analyzes the experience while the outer group listens, then the groups change places.

Reporting formats. Analysis frequently continues as participants prepare for and listen to reports presented in front of the groups; on other occasions private reports in the form of notes or journal entries are effective ways to facilitate the analysis of experiences. Four reporting formats are

1. Individual summaries of reactions given to small groups.
2. Team representative reports.
3. Consultative or listening group reports.
4. Private journal reports or diary entries.

Following small-group analysis and reports, the trainer should assemble the entire group and facilitate a large-group analysis designed to formulate workable generalizations. Specific suggestions should be stated and printed on newsprint for group members to study, analyze, and modify. The next step in the training process is to have participants engage in the practice of specific skills that might be used to do their jobs.

Directing Practice

The basic idea of practice is to apply the skills learned to the job. Although the practice session occurs in the training setting, the principles for effective practice are essentially the same as on-the-job instruction. Figure 17.1 summarizes the four standard steps in directing the practice of on-the-job skills (Dooher & Marquis, 1956).

Prepare the trainee for practice. Let the trainee know that the skill can be learned with some reasonable effort and that you are interested in helping him or her learn a skill that will make work more efficient. Create motivation to learn the skill by relating the skill to the trainee's ability to do his or her work more easily and more effectively and to make a better living.

Set the pattern or sequence. Present the skill in some sequence. Explain and demonstrate the pattern or sequence for doing the skill one step at a time. Focus

FIGURE 17.1
Four Steps in Directing the Practice of a Skill

Steps	How do Do It
1. Prepare the trainee for practice.	A. Put the trainee at ease. B. Mention the name of the skill. C. Comment on the purpose of the skill. D. Relate the skill to the trainee's past experience.
2. Set the pattern or sequence of the skill in the trainee's mind.	A. Explain any materials needed to perform the skill. B. Demonstrate the skill, explaining each step slowly and clearly. C. Review the name, purpose, and steps in performing the skill.
3. Help the trainee perform the skill and begin to form a habit.	A. Listen and watch as the trainee performs the skill. B. Question the trainee on weak and key points. C. Have the trainee repeat the performance until the manual skills *and* the habits of thought have been acquired.
4. Check how well the trainee has acquired the skill.	A. Have the trainee perform the skill alone. B. Compare the performance against the standards of excellence. C. Review both areas of excellence and weakness for additional repetition.

on the main steps and key points. Avoid giving too much information at one time. Use simple, direct language. Encourage the trainee to be involved in the discussion. Demonstrate how the skill is to be performed. Highlight those behaviors that are essential to executing the skill well. Set a high standard. As the trainee watches you, the performance you give not only demonstrates how to do the skill but also represents how to do it well.

Begin to form a habit. Habits are formed by doing, so the trainee should actually perform the skill. In addition, through guided practice the trainee builds self-confidence and strengthens his or her willingness to try other skills. Start with simple behaviors and gradually work toward the more difficult ones. As the trainee practices, have him or her tell you how and why the skill is done that particular way. Correct errors and omissions as the trainee makes them. Rather than criticize the trainee, show him or her how the skill could be executed better; a correction becomes instruction and is usually accepted more eagerly. The best way to make corrections is to have the trainee make the adjustments. Thus a good procedure is to compliment the trainee on the practice effort and then ask the trainee if he or she can think of anything that could be done to make the performance better. If the trainee is unable to identify what needs to be corrected, then make the instructional suggestion. Avoid correcting too frequently. Exercise restraint in correcting during practice.

Check on how well the skill has been learned. Allow the trainee to perform the skill without your help. Encourage the trainee to ask questions about performing the skill. No matter how simple the question appears, respond with instructions that are serious and respectful. Check the trainee's performance as he or she does it alone but gradually taper off as his or her ability to perform the skill increases. Finally, if the trainee is doing well, tell him or her.

SUMMARY

In this chapter we have discussed the strategic role in human resource development. Strategies are methods, plans, and activities used to accomplish a specific goal. Four categories of strategies were identified: training, individual development, organization development, and technical resource development. Three underlying philosophies and theories for producing change were discussed: rational, behavioral, and experiential.

A rational approach assumes that what we believe determines how we behave. Rational emotive training and transactional analysis training were reviewed as two examples of a rational approach. A behavioral approach is rooted in the assumption that changes in human beings can be produced by focusing on observable behaviors rather than on ways of thinking. Three general behavior strategies were analyzed: structuring contingencies, simulations, and modeling. An experiential approach is based on the premise that people believe what they experience; hence experiential training is structured around having trainees learn from their experiences. Four categories of training methods associated with experiential training were discussed: supervising experiences, presenting information, facilitating analysis, and directing practice.

REFERENCES

BANDURA, ALBERT, *Principles of Behavior Modification.* New York: Holt, Rinehart & Winston, 1969.

BARTLETT, ALTON C., "Changing Behavior through Simulation: An Alternative Design to T-Group Training," *Training and Development Journal,* 21 (August 1967), 38–52.

BOIS, J. SAMUEL, *The Art of Awareness* (3rd ed.). Dubuque, Iowa: Wm. C. Brown, 1978.

COMBS, ARTHUR W., DONALD L. AVILA, and WILLIAM W. PURKEY, *Helping Relationships: Basic Concepts for the Helping Professions.* Boston: Allyn & Bacon, 1971.

CRAIGHEAD, W. EDWARD, ALAN E. KAZDIN, and MICHAEL J. MAHONEY, *Behavior Modification: Principles, Issues, and Applications.* Boston: Houghton Mifflin, 1976.

DOOHER, M. JOSEPH, and VIVIENNE MARQUIS, eds., *Effective Communication on the Job.* New York: American Management Associations, 1956.

ELLIS, ALBERT, and ROBERT A. HARPER, *A New Guide to Rational Living.* North Hollywood, Calif.: Wilshire Book Company, 1975.

GORDON, ALICE KAPLAN, *Games for Growth.* Chicago: Science Research Associates, Inc., 1972.

GROVE, THEODORE G., *Experiences in Interpersonal Communication.* Englewood Cliffs, N.J.: Prentice-Hall, 1976.

HALL, DOUGLAS T., DONALD D. BOWEN, ROY J. LEWICKI, and FRANCINE S. HALL, *Experiences in Management and Organizational Behavior.* Chicago: St. Clair Press, 1975.

JAMES, MURIEL, and DOROTHY JONGWARD, *Born to Win: Transactional Analysis with Gestalt Experiments.* Reading, Mass.: Addison-Wesley, 1971.

KOLB, DAVID A., IRWIN M. RUBIN, and JAMES M. MCINTYRE, *Organizational Psychology: A Book of Readings,* 2nd ed., pp. 27–42. Englewood Cliffs, N.J.: Prentice-Hall, 1974.

MICHALAK, DONALD F., and EDWIN G. YAGER, *Making the Training Process Work.* New York: Harper & Row, Pub., 1979.

MIDDLEMAN, RUTH R., and GALE GOLDBERG, "The Concept of Structure in Experiential Learning," *The 1972 Annual Handbook for Group Facilitators,* pp. 203–210. Iowa City, Iowa: University Associates, 1972.

MORRISON, JAMES H., and JOHN J. O'HEARNE, *Practical Transactional Analysis in Management.* Reading, Mass.: Addison-Wesley, 1977.

ODIORNE, GEORGE S., *Training by Objectives.* New York: Macmillan, 1970.

OLIVAS, LOUIS, and JOHN W. NEWSTROM, "Learning through the use of Simulation Games," *Training and Development Journal* (September 1981), pp. 63–66.

PACE, R. WAYNE, "An Experiential Approach to Teaching Organizational Communication," *The Journal of Business Communication,* 14 (Summer 1977), 37–47.

PACE, R. WAYNE, BRENT D. PETERSON, and M. DALLAS BURNETT, *Techniques for Effective Communication.* Reading, Mass.: Addison-Wesley, 1979.

ROSENBAUM, BERNARD L., "Common Misconceptions about Behavior Modeling and Supervisory Skill Training (SST)," *Training and Development Journal* (August 1979), pp. 40–44).

SCHEIN, EDGAR H., *Process Consultation: Its Role in Organization Development.* Reading, Mass.: Addison-Wesley, 1969.

SPRINGER, JUDY, "Brain/Mind and Human Resource Development," *Training and Development Journal* (August 1981), pp. 42–49.

WILLIAMS, ROBERT L., and JAMES D. LONG, *Toward a Self-Managed Life Style.* Boston: Houghton Mifflin, 1975.

WOHLKING, WALLACE, "Attitude Change, Behavior Change: The Role of the Training Department," *California Management Review,* 13 (Winter 1970), 45–50.

WOHLKING, WALLACE, and HANNAH WEINER, "Structured and Spontaneous Role-Playing," *Training and Development Journal* (June 1981), pp. 111–121.

ZENGER, JACK, "The Painful Turnabout in Training," *Training and Development Journal* (December 1980), pp. 36–49.

18

DESIGN, CONDUCT, AND EVALUATION OF STRATEGIES

Three basic approaches to training and development were identified and described in the preceding chapter. Figure 18.1 diagrams the relationships among rational, behavioral, and experiential philosophies and theories of training and development. In terms of the design, conduct, and evaluation of training and development strategies, as the figure suggests, the specific approach selected depends on the objectives to be accomplished. Thus underlying the design of each training and development program is the basic process of developing objectives.

USES OF OBJECTIVES

Two somewhat different philosophies govern the statement of objectives in training and development. The first philosophy argues that individual development is achieved most effectively when the skills and behaviors to be acquired are specified in advance. The statement of objectives to be reached describes what the person is to be like after the training and development experience. A well-stated objective successfully communicates to the trainees or participants what you want them to do; a poorly stated objective allows for more interpretations and fails to indicate directly the trainer's or developer's intentions (Mager, 1962). Barton (1973) argues, however, that stating objectives in advance is useful only when trainees are to acquire a "predetermined behavioral outcome" (p. vii).

Three conditions need to be met, however:

1. Trainee and trainer efforts need to be focused to develop specific behaviors in a minimum amount of time.
2. The results of training should be evaluated.
3. The behaviors to be mastered need to be precisely defined.

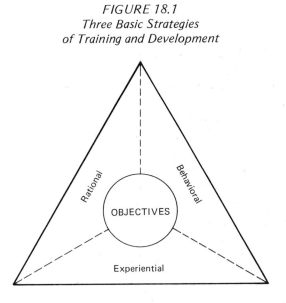

FIGURE 18.1
Three Basic Strategies
of Training and Development

Thus if it is not desirable to concentrate on the development of specific, well-defined behaviors that can be clearly assessed, then the statement of performance objectives in advance may not be particularly useful. Those who advocate a performance or behavior objective approach to development also argue that it is possible, more often than not, to specify the kind of behavior that should be demonstrated by the trainee at the end of the training period. If the objectives cannot be stated, they contend, it is impossible to determine whether the program is meeting the objectives.

The second philosophy suggests that specific behaviors are not particularly important, that specific competencies or behaviors often do not tell the difference between effective and ineffective employees, especially in complex and not well-defined situations. When the task consists of problems for which there may be many appropriate solutions, training in specific competencies may be more limiting than helpful. Barton (1973) explains that when the major concern is the process of having a new experience, or where trainees are attempting to discover the value or meaning of something, or where the situation consists of problems with few common characteristics, the statement of predetermined behavior objectives is less useful than is the design of trainee-centered activities. Combs (1965) has argued effectively that in education, the effective teachers use "themselves as instruments" (p. 9) to accomplish their goals. Some tasks are immensely personal and cannot be translated into behavior competencies.

Dyer (1978) suggests that managers need to develop abilities to "move into any situation and then learn how to observe, gather feedback, and learn what is happening" (p. 55). He contends that "complex organizational training exercises are needed to give managers experience in the total cycle from the gathering of data to implementation of action and evaluation of the consequences of the action" (pp. 55–56). Although some specific behaviors may apply in many situations, the implication is that many problems call for different actions from different managers and that the ability to recognize those differences may be more important than are specific behaviors; hence training with behavior objectives may be counterproductive.

As you may recognize, these two philosophies tend to express the theories of change represented by the *rational* and the *behavioral* strategies discussed in the preceding chapter. The former stresses discovering the meaning to the individual of experiences, and the latter stresses the acquisition of specific behaviors that are measurable and identifiable in advance. The effort to meld the rational and behavioral philosophies into a single, unified approach that integrates belief and action was referred to earlier as an *experiential approach.* Regardless of whether the activity is individual training and development, which emphasizes both technical and interpersonal skills acquisition, or organization development, which emphasizes intergroup and systems analysis and change, the ultimate concern is with what the trainee can do at the end of the training period. This suggests that the objectives of a training and development program ought to be stated in terms of performances. At the same time the development process should be structured so as to allow individuals to examine their beliefs and assumptions and develop personal meanings and explanations to undergird the specific behaviors and competencies.

TERMINAL AND INTERMEDIATE OBJECTIVES

In general, objectives are used to identify the performances expected of participants during and after a training session. *Intermediate objectives* indicate the specific performances that are expected of trainees when they successfully complete a particular segment of a training session. *Terminal objectives* refer to the performance that is expected of trainees when they complete the entire session and prepare to return to their jobs. If trainees successfully complete each section of a training course, they should be able to demonstrate a group of behaviors (one or more for each segment of the course). If the trainees are able to demonstrate all of the specific behaviors at the end of the complete course, together they should provide the trainees with some generalized skills that can be used and maintained in the organizational setting to which they return. Figure 18.2 shows the relationship of

FIGURE 18.2
Types of Performance Objectives
and Where They Are Demonstrated

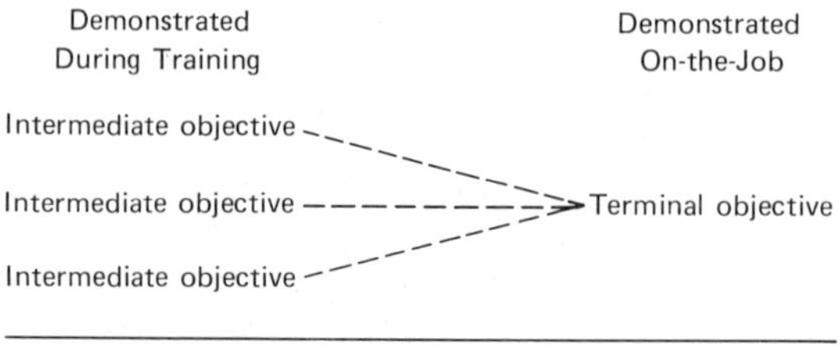

Demonstrated
During Training

Demonstrated
On-the-Job

Intermediate objective

Intermediate objective — — — — — — —> Terminal objective

Intermediate objective

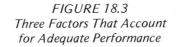

intermediate objectives to terminal objectives. The design of any training and development program begins with the statement of terminal objectives. Each terminal objective can be classified according to the content or deficiency that it is designed to alleviate.

CONTENT OF TERMINAL OBJECTIVES

In most cases three factors account for training deficiencies: (1) lack of information, (2) lack of psychomotor skills, or (3) lack of appropriate attitudes (which include beliefs, feelings, values, and preferences). Figure 18.3 shows how these three factors interrelate to affect performance. For an employee to perform at a minimally acceptable level, he or she must *understand* (have accurate and acceptable personal interpretations of the information), *appreciate* (have a favorable set of beliefs, feelings, values, and preferences), and have the *ability* (skill to physically and mentally execute the behaviors) to do the job.

Deficiencies in any or all of the three areas may lead to inadequate performance on the job. The statement of terminal objectives for any training program should be based upon the analysis completed and the concerns documented. If attitudinal concerns were identified, the training program should include terminal objectives designed to increase favorable attitudes; if informational concerns were identified, terminal objectives designed to increase understanding should be included; if inabilities to perform relevant psychomotor skills were identified, terminal objectives designed to improve psychomotor skills should be included.

FIGURE 18.3
Three Factors That Account
for Adequate Performance

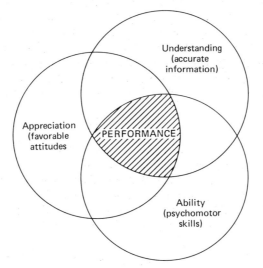

INTERMEDIATE OBJECTIVES

Training objectives of any type require that individuals change their behavior. Training deficiencies cannot be alleviated by changing the system or by managing people more carefully. Hence objectives to be accomplished during the training session are usually stated in specific behavior terms. Intermediate objectives should be related directly to one of the terminal objectives and refer to trainee behaviors. The statement of the intermediate objectives will tell both the trainer and the trainee exactly what the trainee should be able to do at the end of a given segment of the training session. Since intermediate objectives influence the selection of training methods most directly, we shall discuss how to state those kinds of objectives next.

STATING OBJECTIVES

An *intermediate objective* can be defined as the statement of a specific performance or set of behaviors that will be expected of the trainee upon completion of a specified training segment. Acceptable statements of intermediate objectives must meet the following criteria:

1. *They must make direct reference to some observable behavior.* The verb in the statement must refer to some action, or product of some action, that can be observed by a person.
Verbs that refer to observable behavior include the following:

define	diagram	rate
list	compare	choose
underline	categorize	revise
describe	distinguish	install
explain	compose	rearrange
identify	assemble	write
use	create	imitate
demonstrate	set up	role play
sketch	design	report
solve	fix	replace

2. *They must omit any reference to instructions, directions, and training activities.* The mastery of objectives by the trainees can be determined at any time, regardless of whether they are engaging in the training program. Learning activities should help trainees master the objectives, but engaging in the learning activities is not part of the measurement process. Such phrases as "after participating in . . .", "following an analysis of . . . ", and "observe a dyad interacting . . . " are either training activities, directions, or instructions and are inappropriate for performance objectives.

3. *They must include reliable and easily understood qualitative and quantitative ways of measuring the performance.* Performance objectives should indicate quanti-

tative and qualitative standards for determining whether trainees have achieved the objectives. A *quantitative* standard is expressed in terms of how many, how frequently, or with what percentage something occurs. A *qualitative* standard is expressed in terms of how well something is done or qualities of excellence.

4. *They must refer to the important conditions under which the performance is to occur.* Some examples of relevant and important conditions are, "with the aid of an organization chart," "in a ten-minute interview," "on a timed-test," "working in a group of five individuals," "when verbally presented by the trainer," and "by interacting for five minutes with another person." The main physical and psychological circumstances and pressures associated with the task to be accomplished should be indicated.

5. *They must specify the tools and supplies or reference materials available to the trainee; if no references are mentioned, the trainee is to perform the task from memory.* Statements such as "by looking at a picture," "given the use of a list," "by using only newsprint on a flip-chart and a felt pen," and "with the aid of one person and a standard set of tinker toys" refer to supplies, references, and assistance available for demonstrating the skills.

Sample Statement of Objectives

Following are some sample statements of objectives for training in communication skills. Each statement includes the phrase, "At the end of the training period, trainees will be able to . . . ," which is a reminder that the objective describes what the trainee is to do, *not* what the trainer does.

At the end of the training period:

1. When given a written communication incident, trainees will be able to underline examples of five elements of communication.
2. Using an official organization chart of the unit in which they work and working in teams of five or six individuals, each team will be able to trace and explain how three different types of messages are disseminated into the organization along upward, downward, and horizontal channels.
3. Trainees will be able to identify in writing at least one different scene from the film *The Eye of the Beholder,* which illustrates each of the following principles:
   a. Desires, goals, and purposes influence how and to what a person responds in any given situation.
   b. People describe what they believe an event, person, or object to be rather than what it really is.
4. Trainees will be able to recognize self-disclosure statements that occur during five minutes of interaction with an individual who has been instructed to explicitly communicate one bit of information from each of five different headings on a list of self-disclosure items. After five minutes participants will prepare a written list of the five bits of information and compare them with those intended to be communicated by the other person. Four of the five items should appear on the presenter's list.
5. Trainees will be able to interact with a presenter who is role playing an emotionally agitated employee for five minutes during which they use each

of the following techniques at least three times: reflection, paraphrase, open question, extending support. An observer should be able to identify each of the techniques by writing brief quotations of representative statements and/or describing behaviors exhibited by them in using each technique. During a ten-minute discussion period the presenter, the subject, and the observer should agree on the accuracy of the observer's identification on three out of four techniques.

6. Trainees will be able to demonstrate procedures for handling a complaint interview consistent with principles presented during the training session by interacting for ten minutes with a complainant in a role-playing interview. An observer should report that the procedures used are consistent with those described during the training session.

Objectives should be stated that indicate both terminal and intermediate performances desired of trainees. Clearly stated objectives should provide trainees with precise descriptions of the intentions of trainers. Well-stated objectives also provide specifications for the preparation of evaluation procedures and instruments. In fact, if objectives are carefully stated, actual evaluation procedures are suggested. Of course, objectives aid in focusing training methods in order to accomplish the goals established for the training session, to reduce irrelevancies, and to eliminate inadequacies.

PROCEDURES FOR DESIGNING AND DEVELOPING A TRAINING SESSION

Writing performance objectives—terminal and intermediate—may precede or follow determinations about program content. Most of the time, however, the content of the training and development program evolves out of the performance analysis.

Program Content

The content of any given training session is usually identified jointly by the training staff and the line managers from practical experience and theory. The result is typically a two-level outline of topics, much like that illustrated in Figure 18.4.

The program content should be determined by what the trainees must know to accomplish the objectives and perform their jobs up to standard. A typical outline for training in how to manage meetings more effectively is shown in Figure 18.5.

The content of training programs designed to strengthen the skills of supervisors and managers range widely but focus heavily upon interpersonal relations and communication forms. For example, a three-day training program designed to strengthen skills in managing employees who do not perform up to par might contain the content outlined in Figure 18.6.

Once a fairly detailed outline of the content has been written, the next step is to select a general strategy or approach, as discussed in the preceding chapter, that is most compatible with and relevant to the development of the skills identified.

FIGURE 18.4
Topics Used in Supervisory Training

Supervision

The supervisor's role and functions
   The basic functions of the supervisor
   The essentials of planning
   The requirements of good plans

Assigning work
   The role of organizational level in affecting work assignments
   The reasons why supervisors fail to assign work effectively
   Guidelines for making effective work assignments

Decision making
   Learning to make a decision
   Decision making and other supervisory functions
   Implementing the decision

Motivating employees
   The basics of motivation
   The overestimated role of money
   Current theories of motivation

Realities that shape managerial style
   The traditional leadership role
   Newer approaches to leadership
   The essence of effective leadership

Supervising for results
   Setting job objectives for employees
   Creating performance standards
   Scheduling
   Getting commitment

Managing supervisory time
   The pressures of time
   Guidelines for effective use of time
   Basic questions concerning time utilization

Training employees
   Instillation of good work habits
   Principles of effective training
   Follow-up with the learner

Communication: A Management Tool
   What makes effective communication
   What leads to good communication
   How to improve listening skills
   What body language can reveal

FIGURE 18.5
Topics for Training in Conducting Meetings

Conducting Meetings

Why meetings are important
  The role of effective meetings in increasing productivity
  The incredible costs of meetings

What goes wrong at meetings
  Confusion between process and content
  Hidden agendas, repetition, wheel-spinning

When to hold a meeting and when not to
  Hierarchical vs. horizontal meetings

How managers can increase group participation
  How to increase participation without losing control
  How to become a more effective participant

How to handle key meeting behaviors
  Facilitative methods and behaviors
  Things you can do to avoid problems
  Use of win/win decision methods

How to arrange meetings
  How to manage them
  How to build effective agendas
  How to set up a meeting room
  How to insure meeting follow-up

How to analyze your problem-solving style
  What is a model of human problem solving
  How to be a better problem solver

How to solve meeting problems
  How to reach consensus
  How to deal with difficult people
  How to remove organizational blocks
  How to get more people solving more problems
  How to use problem-solving training
  How to set up an internal problem-solving center

A rational approach has specific methods and training techniques associated with it, as do the behavioral and experiential approaches. You will probably adopt a basic approach to use as a starting point. As the details of the design begin to take form, you will no doubt look for specific methods in all general approaches that have the strongest set of exercises and activities for assisting your trainees to acquire the information, attitudes, and skills to be included in the session.

FIGURE 18.6
*Topics for Training in How to Manage
the Unsatisfactory Employee*

Unsatisfactory Employee

How to recognize unsatisfactory performance
  The marginal employee
  The unsatisfactory employee
  Definitions of poor employees

Causes of problem performance
  Managerial causes
  Organizational causes
  Individual problems
  Outside influences
  Abrasive employees

Laziness
  Reasons for apparent laziness
  Lack of motivation
  Unsatisfactory employee syndrome

Deciding who to salvage
  Moral and ethical considerations
  A matrix for making decisions

Managing the unsatisfactory employee
  Preventive approach
    Selection and screening
    Early detection of potential problems

  Therapeutic approach
    Coaching, counseling, training
    Getting commitment to improve

  Punitive approach
    Discipline
    Demotions, transfers, retirement

Problems with marginal employees
  Performance inadequacies
  Personal problems

How to handle people problems
  Age
  Sex
  Children

How to sever if you don't salvage
  How to handle fear of firing
  How to terminate

PRINCIPLES OF DESIGN

A training program consists of a set of objectives, some division of labor between staff and participants, a temporal sequence or time periods, and some identifiable training activities and experiences (Havelock & Havelock, 1973). The design of a training program is based on a few principles that guide decisions about objectives, labor, time, sequence, and appropriate activities.

Time Blocks

The amount of time to be devoted to any given training program is usually decided by a combination of organizational factors such as staff budgets available, number of employees who should be trained, physical facilities, costs, and workload. When those issues are settled, the length of the training program is usually determined by the specifications of different training methods. Frequently, however, a time block of three days is assigned to a particular training program. The task of the training staff is to design a program that will fit the amount of time available. Thus you start with a one-, three-, or five-day block of time and select the objectives, methods, and activities that can be handled during that period. Although some training programs run for as long as 80 hours, most training occurs in blocks of 8 to 40 hours.

Daily Schedule

When working with adult employees, the day often begins at 8:00 A.M. and ends at 5:00 P.M., although it can vary from 7:30 to 9:00 A.M. for starting times and from 3:30 to 6:00 P.M. for ending times. Most training programs should provide for segments long enough to conduct exercises and analyze them but short enough to keep participants from getting tired. In general the schedule for any given day should appear somewhat like that portrayed in Figure 18.7, ranging from 60- to 75-minute segments. As illustrated in the sample daily schedule, planning for detailed training events occurs within 75- and 60-minute blocks. Each period is usually planned so that it is self-contained and so that exercises, simulations, lecturettes, analysis, and practices will fit within the allotted time.

Each 75- and 60-minute block usually has one or more intermediate objectives associated with it. Each day or half-day culminates in the accomplishment of a terminal objective.

Training Sequence

A *training sequence* consists of those activities associated with the accomplishment of an intermediate objective. Training sequences combine to constitute a *training session,* and training sessions combine to constitute a *training program.* The basic building block of training programs is the training sequence.

The development of a training sequence is governed to a large extent by the basic approach chosen (rational, behavioral, experiential), which were illustrated in

252

FIGURE 18.7
Sample Daily Schedule

Daily Schedule

8:00 A.M. – 9:15 A.M.	Activities	(75 min.)
9:15 A.M. – 9:30 A.M.	Break	
9:30 A.M. –10:45 A.M.	Activities	(75 min.)
10:45 A.M. –11:00 A.M.	Break	
11:00 A.M. –12:00 A.M.	Activities	(60 min.)
12:00 noon– 1:00 P.M.	Lunch	
1:00 P.M. – 2:15 P.M.	Activities	(75 min.)
2:15 P.M. – 2:30 P.M.	Break	
2:30 P.M. – 3:45 P.M.	Activities	(75 min.)
3:45 P.M. – 4:00 P.M.	Break	
4:00 P.M. – 5:00 P.M.	Activities	(60 min.)

the preceding chapter. However, the design of a training sequence within any basic approach may be strengthened by adhering to four principles of activity alternation (Lynton & Pareek, 1967):

Principle 1: Alternate stimulation with reflection. Training sequences are something like great dramas; they provide tension but allow for relaxation. Continuous activity should not be regarded as the primary method. Trainees need time to reflect on the activity and to make sense out of what is happening.

Principle 2: Alternate personal involvement with safe distance. Training sequences need to be balanced between intense personal experiences and opportunities to offer detached, analytical, and conceptual comments. Continuous intensity may produce stress rather than learning, so alternate intensity with detachment.

Principle 3: Alternate talking about something with practicing it. Training sequences need to provide practice opportunities until improvement in the skill tapers off. Then time needs to be devoted to thinking and talking about those things that still present problems in order to prepare for the next practice session.

Principle 4: Alternate individual tasks with group processes. Training sequences ought to have a balance of individual events and group events, in which the group activities provide stimulation and the individual activities allow participants to push themselves along as individuals.

An Experiential Training Sequence

The experiential approach contains the elements of training that quite naturally provide for the alternation of stimulation and reflection, personal involvement and detachment, talking and practicing, and individual and group tasks. The model

FIGURE 18.8
Experiential Training Sequence

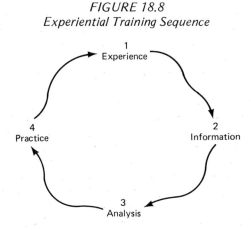

includes four distinct types of activities—experience, information, analysis, and practice—as shown in Figure 18.8. The order of activities in the training sequence should follow the order in the model. The process of ordering activities may be illustrated by arranging a half-day sequence. Figure 18.9 shows how the experiential activities combine to make a training sequence.

The training sequence develops in approximately the same order as the elements in the experiential model, moving from experience to information to

FIGURE 18.9
Sample Training Sequence
Illustrating the Application of Elements
in the Experiential Training Approach

8:00– 8:10	Clearing the Agenda Activity	Experience
8:10– 8:20	Ice-Breaker Activity	
8:20– 8:30	Lecturette	Information
8:30– 8:45	Large-Group Discussion	Analysis
8:45– 9:00	Self-Analysis Instrument	Experience
9:00– 9:05	Lecturette/Summary	Information
9:05– 9:15	Small-Group Discussion	Analysis
9:15– 9:30	Break/Informal Conversation	
9:30–10:00	Assertiveness Exercise	Experience
10:00–10:15	Lecturette	Information
10:15–10:45	Small-Group Discussion to Identify Relevant Skills	Analysis
10:45–11:00	Break/Informal Conversation	
11:00–12:00	Role-Play Skills	Practice

analysis; the sequence then returns to experience and moves to information and to analysis twice more before the culminating practice session. The number of preliminary rounds (from experience to information to analysis) that needs to be completed before a practice segment is introduced depends upon the complexity of the skills being developed and the amount of prerequisite information and analysis desirable for successful performance of the skills. The final stage in the design of a training session is the selection and refinement of exercises, instruments, discussion questions, and lecturettes so they fit the time periods and so they are consistent with the principles of alternation.

The completed design of a training session may consist of a large number of sequences, each involving several rounds of experience, information, analysis, and practice, plus detailed instructions for supervising experiences, presenting information, facilitating analysis, and directing practice. In addition a comprehensive daily training guide is usually prepared for use by the session leader in conducting the training. The entire package often extends to a hundred pages or more, since it contains copies of all materials to be used with exercises, including detailed instructions for conducting them, outlines of lecturettes, a list of equipment and material needs, evaluation forms, and the training room floor plan with indications for placement of equipment, tables, and chairs.

HOW TO CONDUCT A TRAINING SESSION

The conduct of a training session involves considerably more than standing in front of a group. Although the design of the session and the preparation of a leader's guide should provide most of the basic information and directions for supervising, presenting, facilitating, and directing activities, other details must also be taken care of. The list that follows is a summary of most of the major issues that need attention (Davis & McCallon, 1974).

1. *Dates* (month, week, days) for the session must be established and scheduled.
2. *Facilities* (meeting rooms) must be secured and scheduled.
3. *Equipment* (projectors, screens, flip-charts) must be located and scheduled or rented.
4. *Materials* (prereadings, handouts, instructions, instruments, puzzles, and other items involved in the activities) must be prepared, reproduced, sorted, stacked, and ordered for use.
5. *Aids* (pencils, felt pens, paper and notebooks, newsprint, overhead projections, pictures, and other aids) must be purchased, located, and boxed.
6. *Participants* (trainees) must be identified, recruited, and prepared to attend.
7. *Promotion* (advertising, notices, clearances) must be prepared and distributed with adequate information to make it simple for people to attend.
8. *Accommodations and travel* (sleeping rooms, ground and air transportation) often need to be arranged.
9. *Food and refreshments* (special luncheons, banquets, regular meals, refreshments for breaks) must be arranged, menus studied, and guarantees made.
10. *Meeting room setup* (arrangements of tables, chairs, screens, microphones, and easels) must be negotiated or handled by the training staff.

11.   *Staff and consultants* (those who will conduct and assist with the session and invited guests, including organization officials who may wish to or ought to extend greetings and openings, as well as award certificates of completion at the end) must be determined, contacted, and contracted with or invited.

12.   *Budget* (itemized list of funds available and disbursed and projected costs) sheets must be prepared to account for and explain expenditures. Items for which there is usually a chargeable cost include materials, staff, consultants, aids, facilities, accommodations, travel, meals, refreshments, promotion, and participant salaries.

After taking care of the many issues that must be considered in preparing for a training session, the actual training activity may seem like a very small part of the entire process.

Getting a Training Session Started

When all of the participants are assembled, materials are in place, and the physical surroundings have been checked for comfort and workability, you are ready to open the training session. Sometimes a formal welcome and greeting is in order, but in any case you will need to create a warm and cordial atmosphere. Frequently participants need to get acquainted with and accustomed to each other. Ice-breaker and get-acquainted exercises are very helpful at the beginning. The ground rules for participating in the session should be reviewed and participant expectations acknowledged. A review of the schedule and the topics and skills to be developed often help establish anticipation and increase motivation. Check the seating arrangements, ventilation, temperature, acoustics, and lighting as you proceed so that adjustments can be made before starting the first training segment. When the schedule is right, move into the first exercise. Materials should be nearby and a system set up to distribute them quickly to participants. Follow the plan, supervising experiences, presenting information, facilitating discussions, and directing practice sessions. At the end of each day have a dramatic motivational closing to leave trainees on an exciting high.

EVALUATION OF TRAINING

Few people working in human resource development deny the claim that the evaluation of training is not only the most important aspect of the entire process but also the most difficult. Smith (1980) argues convincingly that failures to evaluate the training process may be explained by three reasons: (1) *No one sees a need for evaluation.* The sessions and the support activities seem to be going along fairly well, so the actual need to evaluate does not seem particularly important. (2) *Evaluators do not know how to evaluate.* The major deficiencies lie in not knowing how to state evaluation objectives in precise and measurable terms or how to analyze the data once it has been gathered. Many trainers just do not know how to summarize data so that it can be interpreted and understood. (3) *The complexity of the trainer's job leads to other tasks having higher priority.* Training courses are often without adequate instructional guides, and frequent changes occur in course content. In addition there may be a long time lag between the training activity and the trainee's opportunity to apply the skills to improve job performance. Finally, the trainers and trainees may feel that they, rather than the training, are the subjects of evaluation, and they may not cooperate with evaluators.

Four problems result from these causes:

1. *No evaluation data are collected.*
2. *Evaluation data are unreliable and misleading.*
3. *Evaluation data fail to be presented in a timely fashion,* often too late to be used effectively.
4. *Evaluation data are incomplete,* frequently lacking information about potential causes.

Planning an Evaluation

As with other aspects of training, to be effective, evaluation must be planned. The first step in the process is to identify what should be known about training. The second step is to decide what should be measured. The third step is to identify ways of getting the data.

Answers to five questions seem critical in evaluating a training program:

1. Are the trainees satisfied?
2. Did the trainees experience information gain?
3. Did the trainees acquire the skills being developed?
4. Do the trainees use the skills on the job?
5. Does using the skills have a positive effect on the organization?

Finding answers to those questions constitutes the evaluation process. Table 18.1 summarizes what should be measured to answer each question and what kinds of data might produce relevant answers.

In order to evaluate satisfaction with the training experience, some measurement of trainee perceptions both during the training session and after the session when trainees return to the job is important. Satisfaction with program content, instructor styles, learning experiences, facilities, and related accommodations may all affect the quality of the training session. Information gain is usually measured directly by administering some type of test, either objective or subjective; however, much can be learned about what a person knows by listening to him or her explain ideas to others.

The evaluation of how well a trainee has developed the psychomotor skills needed to perform behaviors more effectively is a difficult task. Measures of performance are frequently based on observation and are quite subjective at times. How well a person performs a particular skill in practice sessions during training is often difficult to determine, and whether the skills are actually transferred and used on the job is generally not easy to determine either. Performance review reports, observations of work, and employee-reported problems may all give some indication of how well the trainee has acquired and uses the skills presented during the training session.

TABLE 18.1
Summary of Evaluation Issues

WHAT SHOULD BE INVESTIGATED	WHAT SHOULD BE MEASURED		WHAT SHOULD BE EXAMINED
	During the Session	*After the Session*	
Trainee satisfaction	Perceptions after training segments	Perceptions on the job	Oral and written comments and reactions to questionnaires
Trainee information gain	Knowledge of concepts	Explanations of concepts to others	Scores on objective tests, performance during exercises, observations of work
Trainee skills acquisition	Skills exhibited in practices	Skills used on the job	Performance review reports, observations of work, employee-reported problems
Effect of skills on the organization	Perceptions of others of value of changes to the organization	Actual value of changes to organization	Perceptions of supervisors, cost-effectiveness figures, problems reported by supervisors

Whether the behaviors developed in the training session will have a positive effect on the functioning of the organization is something that can only be predicted, especially when evaluated during the training session. Instructions to select the two or three most important job-related objectives and to evaluate how well they have been accomplished during the training may give an indication of the value of the objectives to the organization. As supervisors observe the work of employees, they may recognize problems or may notice trainees using behaviors that are of value to the organization. Naturally production figures and other objective indicators of performance that can be related to employee behaviors are usually excellent indicators of the effect of training on the organization.

SUMMARY

This chapter has discussed the design, conduct, and evaluation of strategies of training and development. Two philosophies of specifying objectives were summarized: (1) performance objectives can be stated and are essential for determining the effectiveness of training programs; (2) specific behaviors and competencies often do not tell the difference between effective and noneffective employees, and trainee-centered activities develop more flexible employees. It was suggested that an experiential approach to training combines the major benefits of both philosophies. Terminal objectives describe what trainees should be able to do back on the job, whereas intermediate objectives indicate what trainees should be able to do following specific training sequences. Appreciation and understanding of and the ability to perform behaviors were identified as factors that account for a person's performance. Objectives designed to produce favorable attitudes, provide accurate information, and develop psychomotor skills should be included in training programs.

Five characteristics of acceptable performance objectives were discussed. They include reference to observable behaviors, omission of directions and training activities, reliable and easily understood qualitative and quantitative ways of measuring the performance, inclusion of important conditions under which the performance is to occur, and inclusion of the tools, supplies, and references available to the trainee. Six sample statements of performance objectives were given.

The content of a training program is usually determined by what the trainees need to know and is portrayed in a two-level outline of topics. Three examples of program content were presented.

A training program was described as consisting of a set of objectives, a division of labor, blocks of time, and identifiable training activities. The sequence of training events was described in terms of a weekly and a daily time schedule. It was explained that training sessions are developed around 60- and 75-minute self-contained blocks.

A training sequence was defined as those activities associated with the accomplishment of an intermediate objective. Four principles for alternating training activities were discussed. The experiential training sequence was analyzed as an approach that naturally provides for the alternation of the key principles. A daily schedule for implementing the elements in experiential training was described. Twelve major issues in preparation for conducting a training session were listed. How to get a session started was discussed.

Three reasons why evaluation of training fails to be done and the four problems resulting therefrom were explained. Five questions critical to evaluating a training program were analyzed. Finally, trainee satisfaction, trainee information gain, trainee skills acquisition, and the effect on organization function of using the skills were identified as the key variables to be evaluated.

REFERENCES

BARTON, GRANT E., *Performance Objectives*. Provo, Utah: Brigham Young University Press, 1973.

COMBS, ARTHUR W., *The Professional Education of Teachers*. Boston: Allyn & Bacon, 1965.

DAVIS, LARRY NOLAN, and EARL McCALLON, *Planning, Conducting, and Evaluating Workshops*. Austin, Tex.: Learning Concepts, 1974.

DYER, WILLIAM G., "What Makes Sense in Management Training?" *Management Review*, 67 (June 1978), 50–56.

HAVELOCK, RONALD G., and MARY C. HAVELOCK, *Training for Change Agents*. Ann Arbor: The University of Michigan, 1973.

LYNTON, ROLF P., and UDAI PAREEK, *Training for Development*. Homewood, Ill.: Richard D. Irwin, 1967.

MAGER, ROBERT F., *Preparing Instructional Objectives*. Belmont, Calif.: Fearon, 1962.

SMITH, MARTIN E., "Evaluating Training Operations and Programs," *Training and Development Journal* (October 1980), pp. 70–78.

19

ADMINISTERING ORGANIZATIONAL COMMUNICATION

the administrative role
in human resource development

The success of any department, function, or program in a modern organization is, in large part, a result of the way in which it is administered. Human resource development, training and development, and personnel development departments are no exception.

COMMUNICATION AND ADMINISTRATIVE FUNCTIONS

Communication skills are so delicately interwoven with the skills of managing that a former president of the American Management Association wrote:

> More specifically, it [communication] is the way management gets its job done. There is little risk of over-simplification in saying that good managers are good communicators; poor managers are usually the opposite. (Dooher & Marquis, 1956, p. 5).

That may be why Mackenzie (1969) identified communicating as one of the three continuous functions, along with analyzing problems and making decisions, involved in the management process. As he so directly explains, those three functions, are "important at all times and in all aspects of the manager's job; therefore, they are shown to permeate his work process" (Exhibit I, pp. 81-86). Thus we feel comfortable discussing the administration of organizational communication and human resource development departments.

Because Mackenzie's diagram of the management-administrative process is particularly direct and cogent, we shall rely upon it for the basic structure of this chapter. In addition to the three continuous functions mentioned, he portrays five sequential functions—planning, organizing, staffing, directing, and controlling —that are implemented in sequence, with the manager moving from planning through controlling only to return to planning to make adjustments, thus starting the process over again. Each sequential function, such as staffing, has a distinct set of activities associated with it. Staffing, for example, involves selecting, orienting, training, and developing people. Mackenzie's model of the management process, as he indicates, "elevates staffing and communicating to the level of a function. Moreover, it establishes functions and activities as the two most important terms for describing the job of the manager" (p. 87).

DEFINITION OF ADMINISTRATION

Although the term *manager* is often used to refer to individuals who supervise the work of others and *management* is often defined as the process of getting things done through others, we have a preference for the terms *administrator* and *administration,* especially in the context of human resource development and organizational communication. Training, development, and communication represent fine blends of theory and practice involving both learning and managing. Shaw (1962) points out that "administration is the increasingly specialized activity which plans, organizes, and directs the resources of people and things to the support and enablement of teaching-learning situations . . . " (p. 46). An administrator is a person who is skilled in planning, organizing, staffing, directing, and controlling the human resource development and organizational communication program department. This chapter is about the administrative role.

The remainder of this chapter will discuss the primary activities that translate the sequential functions into action in a human resource training and development program. Figure 19.1 summarizes the sequential functions and primary activities associated with them. Rose (1964), in treating similar materials, comments that " it is difficult to clearly discuss a single function because in practice all functions are interwoven" (p. 51). Nevertheless, for simplicity, we shall cover the functions in sequence.

PLANNING: THE FIRST SEQUENTIAL FUNCTION

Planning is the process of predetermining a course of action. Otto and Glaser (1970) refer to this process in the context of *forecasting,* the first activity involved in planning, according to Mackenzie (1969). They explain that a training administrator's first task is to analyze the organization and the contribution the training and development department is making to the organization's mission, then the administrator must develop "a plan of action to direct the resources" in order to assist the organization in carrying out its mission (p. 21).

Forecasting

Forecasting consists of four basic steps.

1. *Look at the total organization and each of its parts to determine what the training and development department can contribute to the overall mission of the organization.*

FIGURE 19.1
Outline of the Main Sequential Functions and Their
Associated Primary Activities in Administering
a Human Resource Development Program

Sequential Functions	Activities
1. Planning	Forecasting
	Setting objectives
	Developing strategies
	Establishing program priorities
	Budgeting
	Setting procedures
	Developing policies
2. Organizing	Establishing organization structure
	Delineating relationships
	Creating position descriptions
	Establishing position qualifications
3. Staffing	Selecting
	Orienting
	Training
	Developing
4. Directing	Delegating
	Motivating
	Coordinating
	Managing differences
	Managing change
5. Controlling	Establishing reporting systems
	Developing performance standards
	Measuring results
	Taking corrective action
	Rewarding

This is accomplished by visiting with as many people and seeing as many different places as possible in the time allowed. Talk with staff and colleagues. Talk to your supervisor. Talk with other department heads. Talk with the chief executive officer as well as hourly workers. Read reports, booklets, and house organs to immerse yourself in the spirit and intent of the organization and to discover what has been done in the past.

2. *Evaluate the present formal and informal training and development activities to determine how successful they have been in helping employees perform their work.*

Make a list of the types of training and development activities that were available in the past. Indicate the purpose, number of people involved, number of hours or days devoted to each, training methods used, place where presented, the estimated cost per trainee, and effectiveness according to organization members.

3. *Identify present and potential organizational problems that the training and development department may help alleviate.*

This step may involve the development of a comprehensive analysis plan including task, needs, and performance appraisal analysis as discussed in Chapter 16, but it more often consists of identifying the areas in which detailed analyses will be conducted later. For example, orientation, technical job skills, supervision, middle and top management, sales, security, safety, and recruitment may be areas in which training can help performance.

Out of this analysis should come a set of long-range department objectives which indicate the major areas of emphasis, such as secretarial-clerical, presupervisory, first-level supervision, and middle manager training and development priorities.

4. *Assess the capabilities of the present training and development staff, equipment, and space to implement the goals and objectives identified with the money and time available.*

The resources with which an administrator has to work include staff, material and equipment, space, time, and money. In preparing a forecast, make realistic decisions about how well each of the resources can contribute to accomplishing the tentative goals. It may be necessary to request more resources or to limit the scope of the program.

Although the entire planning process could be considered simply a comprehensive forecast, as it has been presented to this point, a forecast gives an assessment of current circumstances and of future consequences if changes are not made. Planning involves six additional processes.

Six Additional Processes in Planning

Setting objectives. Setting objectives consists of describing the projected workload for the department including all major activities and programs. Objectives may include formal courses and workshops, counseling, on-the-job training, contracted programs, and informal personal development activities. The department's professional development activities, such as attendance at ASTD national conferences and expositions, should be included.

Developing strategies. Strategy development consists of deciding when and how to achieve activities organized according to functional areas, such as sales, clerical staff, and supervisors, or around problems.

Establishing program priorities. A superior plan always includes the assignment of priorities and the order in which the programs will be implemented. A time-line of steps involved in getting the courses and activities underway is always part of establishing priorities.

Budgeting. Budgeting is often referred to as "costing out the forecast." A *budget* is a financial plan for accomplishing the objectives. The most defensible way of developing a budget, according to Otto and Glaser (1970), is around programs. Instead of presenting top management with a budget, you offer them programs. If they agree with the plan, they will be more likely to allocate the budget. In that case the budget is the price to be paid for the programs. If the price is too high, you may have to hold some programs. Nevertheless, always tie budget to what the programs will accomplish.

According to Forbes (1980), costs that could be considered as part of the training investment include the following:

1. Production of materials such as videotapes, audiotapes, slides, illustrations, photographs, vugraphs, and binders.
2. Course design and development, including staff time, pilot seminars, evaluation, and special developer training sessions.
3. Capital investments, including depreciation.
4. Travel costs, including development travel and train-the-trainer seminars, delivery travel, participant and staff travel, and consultant and subject matter expert travel.
5. Meals, housing, car rental, and laundry costs for staff and participants during training sessions.
6. Conference room rental and related incidental costs such as refreshments and lunches.
7. Course resource costs, such as marketing guides and promotional literature.
8. Staff preparation time.
9. Delivery of course materials, including reproduction costs per package.
10. Extra copies of materials for file and distribution.
11. Equipment and materials shipping costs.
12. Corporate lost production in terms of average salary per day of training.
13. Delayed income costs.
14. Location costs comparing on-site versus off-site facilities.

To this list may be added clerical support salaries and professional development services for staff, such as membership in ASTD, journal subscriptions, professional travel, and professional development workshops and seminars.

Setting procedures. This consists of standardizing methods of carrying out plans.

Developing policies. Setting procedures and developing policies for making decisions on important and recurring issues often go hand-in-hand. They both represent processes that formalize procedures and decisions.

ORGANIZING: THE SECOND SEQUENTIAL FUNCTION

Once planning has been completed, the next step is to organize the resources to accomplish the plan. *Organizing consists of arranging and relating the resources for the effective accomplishment of objectives.* It involves four closely related activities.

Establishing organization structure. The main task of establishing the organizational structure is to prepare an organization chart. The chart portrays the positions in the organization as they relate to one another. The human resource training and development department has a structure of its own, usually with a director or administrator, assistants, and specialists. In large organizations the human resource training and development department may be divided into five or more subunits, including secretarial and clerical training, technical training, sales training, management training and development, and organization development. The organization chart for a human resource development department patterned after some major corporations includes positions similar to those shown in Figure 19.2.

Frequently, however, the human resource training and development department is staffed by one or two specialists who draw upon the technical expertise of other employees and use many outside sources, such as consultants and professional training companies, to provide most of the actual training and development activities. In most cases the human resource training and development department is located within personnel. In a medium-sized company the organization chart for the personnel area, including training and development, is similar to that in Figure 19.3.

Delineating relationships. Another important organizing activity is to describe or portray relationships among the positions and people. This is usually accomplished by drawing appropriate lines on the organization chart to show lines of communication.

FIGURE 19.2
Organization Chart of Major Human Resource Training
and Development Department

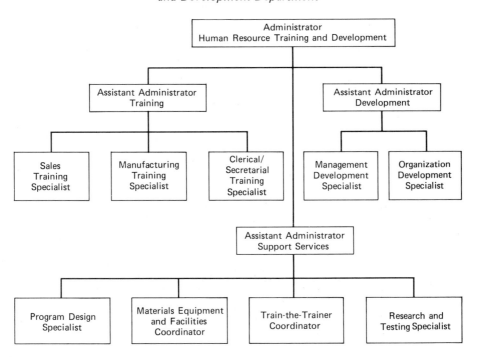

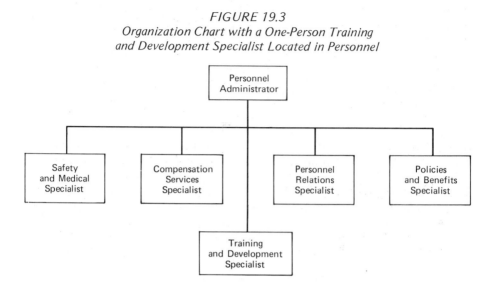

FIGURE 19.3
Organization Chart with a One-Person Training
and Development Specialist Located in Personnel

Creating position descriptions. In a formal organization the authority and duties are assigned to positions. Thus a major organizing activity is writing position descriptions. The position description of a training administrator usually consists of the following items: the position title, to whom the position reports, a list of duties or responsibilities, and a description of the limits of authority.

The training and development administrator is usually responsible for establishing and maintaining a program that enables employees of an organization to perform their current jobs at the most efficient level possible and to develop skills and abilities to prepare them to assume different positions in the organization or to move into jobs, positions, and careers that may not be as yet identified and defined. To accomplish these goals, the training and development administrator performs, at one time or another, most of the following duties:

1. Prepares a statement of training and development philosophy, policy, and procedures.
2. Prepares a statement of objectives for the department and disseminates them to the staff.
3. Prepares the department's budget and disburses funds to accomplish department objectives.
4. Supervises the work of staff members.
5. Reviews the performance of staff members and recommends salary increases and other personnel actions, such as developmental activities.
6. Prepares periodic reports to inform management about training needs, program effectiveness, and accomplishments.
7. Maintains a continuous analysis of organization training and development needs.
8. Advises top management on manpower requirements and changes in organization needs resulting from changes in the labor market.

9. Develops training programs for technical personnel, secretarial and clerical personnel, and for supervisors and managers.
10. Evaluates training courses available from commercial firms for relevance to the organization's training needs.
11. Arranges for training materials, equipment, and facilities.
12. Trains technical instructors to conduct in-house courses.
13. Assists line managers in conducting job skills and procedural training.
14. Edits written materials prepared by staff members.
15. Supervises and assists in the production of audiovisual and video materials.
16. Develops training manuals, course outlines, handouts, and exercises.
17. Collects performance data from supervisors for use in evaluating the effectiveness of training sessions.
18. Counsels employees on personal goals and job-related training.
19. Establishes prerequisites for entering courses and performance standards for satisfactory completion of courses.
20. Conducts training programs.
21. Promotes training and development opportunities throughout the organization.

Although there are probably numerous additional responsibilities, the preceding list gives a broad view of the activities of a training and development officer.

Establishing position qualifications. The preceding list, however, indicates little about the qualifications of individuals who might fill the position. Although the specific educational background desirable for careers in training and development may not be uniform across the country, it is clear that a bachelor's degree in organizational communication with a career emphasis in training and development provides excellent preparation.

STAFFING: THE THIRD SEQUENTIAL FUNCTION

Staffing consists of choosing the most competent people to fill positions in the organization. Phrasing a definition of competence is difficult, since the idea of what constitutes competence changes as a person matures in an organization. Rose (1964) estimates, for example, that first-level supervisors are required to use their technical abilities 50 percent of the time, whereas top-level managers use technical abilities only 15 percent of the time. On the other hand, first-level supervisors use conceptual abilities only 10 percent of the time, but top-level managers use conceptual abilities 60 percent of the time. Both levels use human relations abilities ranging from 40 percent of the time for first-level supervisors to 25 percent of the time for top-level managers.

Selecting. It seems apparent that entry-level employees ought to be chosen on the basis of their technical and human relations abilities first and their conceptual abilities last. As with other positions in an organization, human resource training and development positions also necessitate a development program. As employees mature in the organization and are selected for higher-level management positions, the kinds of abilities required change; employees must have a training and development program of their own to enhance conceptual abilities so they will be prepared to assume top-level positions.

Otto and Glaser (1970) explain that research with *the predictive index,* a self-report instrument using lists of adjectives, indicates that trainers are people "who have a strong interest in other people." They cooperate rather than compete with others and are usually unselfish and friendly. The best trainers are capable of following detailed instructions. They are patient and enjoy communicating with others and are generally service-oriented in their ambitions.

Orienting. Orienting is the task of familiarizing new employees with the organization, department, and job. An effective orientation provides the new employee with information about his or her workplace, colleagues, and the larger organization.

Training. Like any other employee, the human resource training and development specialist should have a program for professional and personal development. A career development plan takes into account what Charland (1981) calls the *career cycle.* He suggests that there are "three essential roles in every person's working life" (p. 88). These are listed as the *novice*—the young adult who is new to the responsibilities, roles, and skills of adulthood; the *expert*—the person who is more or less adept at some skill or job; and the *mentor*—the mature advisor and guide for others. Charland suggests that the roles may not be age-bound, that we may actually be alternating the roles throughout our lives, with each of us functioning as a novice in some areas, an expert in others, and a mentor in still others. Training is generally provided to help the novice become an expert.

Developing. The concept of development is closely related to that of training but is concerned more with preparing employees to make maximum use of their skills and abilities, to achieve satsifaction with their own goals, and to become top performers in the future. In human resource development Hutcheson and Chalofsky (1981) point out, "Work roles are often linked with specific program areas" (p. 13). That is, a career path might involve obtaining entry-level work skills by getting a bachelor's degree, for example, in organizational communication, working as a training specialist for a while, getting a master's degree in instructional science, working as a merchandising training manager, moving into career counseling for a while, then becoming director of corporate training and development. Although the career paths are almost limitless, what is important is taking an active role in planning and guiding your own career development rather than just waiting for chance to decide what you are going to be doing as an expert and mentor.

DIRECTING: THE FOURTH SEQUENTIAL FUNCTION

Directing is the effort to bring about some type of purposeful action focused on accomplishing the objectives. Directing involves, primarily, implementing the plans. There are five activities involved in directing.

Delegating. The main task of delegating is communicating to the employees the objectives, policies, and plans of the organization and the employees' duties and responsibilities. Precise ways in which employees will be held accountable for completing their duties should also be made clear. Simply, *delegating* means to assign duties, responsibilities, and authority to someone else. If the assignment is accepted, the supervisor has a delegate or representative. After delegation has occurred, the supervisor is primarily responsible for seeing that the delegate performs the task.

Motivating. Motivating represents the set of activities involved in persuading and inspiring employees to take the desired action, to carry out the assignments that have been delegated to them. Motivating usually involves two fundamental tasks: (1) ensuring that those being motivated know that they have a *goal* to achieve or a task to accomplish and (2) helping them *care* about the goal. A clear goal provides something toward which effort can be directed. Caring provides the emotional incentive to expend energy to accomplish the goal.

Coordinating. The act of coordination involves relating the efforts of various individuals in the most effective combinations in order to accomplish the goal. *Coordinating* is concerned with bringing the elements and aspects of a situation into some type of harmonious relationship with each other. The training and development administrator coordinates the workers, materials, and duties within his or her own unit with those of other units as well as those outside the organization. Coordinating in training and development may involve working with other supervisors to select the most appropriate programs, serving as liaison between trainers and top management, assisting staff members with daily training schedules, arranging for special demonstrations, providing information about sources of exercises, films, and other training methods, acting as a clearinghouse for new ideas, and participating in meetings.

Managing differences. The administration of any program, including training and development, requires the management of differences in ideas, preferences, and actions. The administrator should encourage independent thought, to minimize conformity and group thinking, while resolving conflict that interferes with the accomplishment of goals and objectives.

Managing change. Managing change involves stimulating employees to be creative in their work and innovative in achieving the goals of the program. In organizations in which stability exists, employees have learned how to deal with one another, how to do their work, and what to anticipate next. In sum, they are adjusted to the circumstances. When change occurs or is introduced, individuals are required to make new adjustments. Change is managed well when those adjustments are made with some degree of ease and the organization returns to a state of adjustment. Davis (1967) lists four responsibilities of administrators in managing change effectively: "(1) Make only useful, necessary change. Change by evolution, not revolution. (2) Recognize the possible effects of change and introduce it with adequate attention to human relations. (3) Share the benefits of change with employees. (4) Diagnose the problems remaining after a change occurs and treat them" (p. 403).

CONTROLLING: THE FIFTH SEQUENTIAL FUNCTION

Controlling involves five sets of activities that are all directed toward ensuring that progress is being made toward the accomplishment of program objectives according to the plan that was prepared initially.

Establishing reporting systems. The first task in carrying out the controlling function is to determine what types of data are critical or are needed, when, and how. This helps establish a reporting system. The training and development administrator keeps records of financial transactions, training activities and achievements, effectiveness of training facilitators and instructors, and demonstrations or indicators of the impact of training and development on the organization. Reports can take many different forms from informal descriptions to complex statistical summaries. An important consideration involves the issue of how much time, effort, and money can be used for the purpose of establishing and maintaining a reporting system. The administrator must make those important decisions about how frequently information is needed, what kinds of information to get, and from what sources to get it.

Developing performance standards. In order to determine whether the work has been done in an acceptable manner, it is necessary for the administrator to describe the conditions that will exist when the key duties are done in a satisfactory manner. As a general rule, standards for the satisfactory performance of duties should be stated in terms of quantity and quality so that both the administrator and the employee will know what is expected. The question to be answered is, "How can you tell when the performance results in a satisfactory job?"

Measuring results. One of the often difficult activities of an administrator is determining whether the work and progress being accomplished relates to the plans or whether there are serious deviations from the goals and standards. The major concern of the training and development department is proficiency in training and developing employees rather than operating machines or turning raw materials into objects. Although evaluation of the work of a training and development department may be less precise than evaluating a piece-rate worker, it may be more demanding. Thus a creative and continuing performance appraisal system is important.

Taking corrective action. Every administrator must be willing and able to make adjustments in the plans and changes in personnel in order to achieve the goals. Review and counseling are critical aspects of the administrator's job. The efficient conduct of counseling interviews after performance appraisal may be one of the most important communication events in taking corrective actions. On occasion, disciplinary interviews will also be held.

Rewarding. Rewards may take many forms, but a common classification is extrinsic or intrinsic. Money and better working conditions are examples of extrinsic reward since they are somewhat artificially related to an employee's behavior. Intrinsic reward, on the other hand, comes as a result of internal feelings, such as satisfaction resulting from completing a task, or the feeling of intellectual development coming from solving a problem. An effective administrator is sensitive to providing both types of rewards. Praise, financial gain, and certain types of discipline all serve as rewards and help ensure progress toward accomplishment of program objectives.

SUMMARY

This chapter has been devoted to analyzing the administrative role in human resource development and organizational communication. Mackenzie's (1969) model of the management-administrative process was used as the framework in which the human resource training and development administrative role was explained. Five sequential functions and 25 sets of activities were discussed. Planning, organizing, staffing, directing, and controlling represent the five sequential functions. The activities involved in fulfilling the functions were generally applied to the administration of a human resource training and development department.

REFERENCES

CHARLAND, WILLIAM A., JR., "Career Roles," *Western's World,* 12 (November–December 1981), 43–44, 88–89.

DAVIS, KEITH, *The Dynamics of Organizational Behavior.* New York: McGraw-Hill, 1967.

DOOHER, JOSEPH, and VIVIENNE MARQUIS, *Effective Communication on the Job.* New York: American Management Association, 1956.

FORBES, JERRY, "Sales Training and Field Sales: Cost Factors Which Impact Corporate Product ROI." Paper presented at Training 80, Sheraton Center, New York City, December 1980.

HUTCHESON, PEGGY, and NEAL CHALOFSKY, "Careers in Human Resource Development," *Training and Development Journal,* 35 (July 1981), 12–15.

MACKENZIE, R. ALEX, "The Management Process in 3-D," *Harvard Business Review* (November–December 1969), pp. 80–87.

OTTO, CALVIN P., and ROLLIN O. GLASER, *The Management of Training.* Reading, Mass.: Addison-Wesley, 1970.

ROSE, HOMER C., *The Development and Supervising of Training Programs.* American Technical Society, 1964.

SHAW, ARCHIBALD, "What Is Administration," *Educational Executives' Overview* (May 1962), p. 9.

NAME INDEX

SUBJECT
INDEX